*F*or many visitors, B&B accommodation is the best way to travel. Instead of large, anonymous hotels you stay in smaller, friendlier establishments – small hotels, guest houses and farmhouses, or in someone's own home. You also enjoy great value for money and high standards, as you'll see from this guide.

In this guide, the highest price is only £19 per person per night. And that's the top rate – most prices are even less expensive. In addition to good rates, you'll be pleasantly surprised by the standards of the accommodation. B&B has improved beyond recognition from the times when proprietors simply hung a sign outside the door and hoped for the best. B&B accommodation is comfortable – many rooms now have en-suite facilities – and welcoming. And you'll usually enjoy good home cooking into the bargain.

This is *the* official B&B guide for Wales. So you can be sure of standards, for the accommodation has been thoroughly checked out by us. The guide's contents also reflect our 'Quest for Quality' – the quality grading scheme for accommodation is fully explained within.

Customer care is another top priority. That's  why we have launched our 'Welcome Host' scheme – also fully explained within – to bring you the best in hospitality and service.

CONTENTS

Designed and published by the Wales Tourist Board, Brunel House, Cardiff CF2 1UY. Written by Roger Thomas Freelance Services. Printed by Mid Wales Litho Ltd. Colour reproduction by T.P.S. Studios Ltd. Typesetting by Ian Evans Associates. Maps by G. H. T. Studios. Distributed overseas by the British Tourist Authority. Copyright © 1994 Wales Tourist Board. ISBN 1 85013 057 4.

Llynnau Cregennen

YOUR GUIDE TO WALES

*I*n addition to its many other virtues, B&B accommodation gives you tremendous freedom. This go-anywhere flexibility suits Wales down to the ground, for it's a country waiting to be explored. This guide – which contains not only accommodation information – will put you fully in the picture. You'll find details of Wales's holiday areas and resorts, its countryside, events, traditional crafts and places to visit – in a nutshell, all the information you'll need to choose and book a holiday or short break.

New Quay harbour

Caernarfon Castle

THE BEST FOR BEAUTY

*W*ales's number-one attraction is its scenery. It contains no less than three national parks and five areas officially designated as being of 'Outstanding Natural Beauty'. Snowdonia, the Brecon Beacons and the Pembrokeshire Coast make up the trio of national parks. Its areas of outstanding beauty are the Gower Peninsula, Wye Valley, Isle of Anglesey, Llŷn Peninsula and Clwydian Range. And that's not taking into account the huge tracts of unspoilt countryside and coastline in unexplored Mid Wales.

2

Llangollen Steam Railway

THE BEST FOR ATTRACTIONS

*I*f that were not enough, this beautiful landscape is filled with fascinating places to visit. Wales is famous worldwide as a land of castles – over 100 are open to the public. Other historic sites, such as stone burial chambers, stretch back to the earliest times, while the recent past is recalled at mining museums and slate caverns.

Wales's range of attractions is kaleidoscopic. There are sea and mountain zoos, narrow-gauge railways, parks dedicated to wildlife, butterflies and the countryside, spectacular showcaves … even an energy-efficient 'village of the future'.

THE BEST FOR CRAFTS

*C*raft workshops are another big attraction throughout Wales. Stop off on your travels at a pottery, woollen mill, woodturner's, leatherworker's, candlemaker's, jeweller's or slate workshop. Look out also for the craft centres at Ruthin, Corris and Hay-on-Wye where a number of craftspeople work together.

Bryncir Woollen Mill

1994 will be an eventful time in Wales. There's something happening throughout the year – festivals with musical, medieval, Victorian and literary themes, sporting events, concerts, craft fairs, guided walks, exhibitions and agricultural shows. To give you a flavour of the times ahead, we've listed some events here, and also described a few major events in more detail. For full details, call in at a Tourist Information Centre when you arrive or contact the Wales Tourist Board for a free events leaflet.

SPRING TO AUTUMN
MID WALES FESTIVAL OF THE COUNTRYSIDE

A festival which brings together over 500 events taking place throughout beautiful Mid Wales – birdwatching, guided walks, arts and crafts, sheepdog trials, farm and garden visits. David Bellamy, a keen supporter, has called it 'the role model for sustainable tourism'.
Tel (0686) 625384

20 MAY - 5 JUNE
HAY FESTIVAL OF LITERATURE

Hay-on-Wye, the borderland 'town of books', provides an appropriate setting for this literary festival which has quickly established an international reputation. Attracts leading writers, poets and celebrities.
Tel (0497) 821299

5 - 10 JULY
LLANGOLLEN INTERNATIONAL MUSICAL EISTEDDFOD

A colourful, cosmopolitan gathering of singers and dancers from all over the world perform in the beautiful little town of Llangollen. A unique festival first held in 1947 to help heal the wounds of war by bringing the peoples of the world together.
Tel (0978) 860236

18 - 21 JULY
ROYAL WELSH AGRICULTURAL SHOW

Four days of fascination – and a show that attracts a wide audience to Builth Wells, not just from the farming

community but from all walks of life. One of Wales's premier events, held in the heart of the country, covering all aspects of agriculture – and a lot more besides.
Tel (0982) 553683

30 JULY - 6 AUGUST
ROYAL NATIONAL EISTEDDFOD

Wales's most important cultural gathering, dating back to 1176, and held at a different venue each year. A festival dedicated to Welsh, Britain's oldest living language, with competitions, choirs, concerts, stands and exhibitions. Translation facilities available. This year's event will be held near Neath, West Glamorgan.
Tel (0222) 763777

11 - 13 March
13th Folk Weekend
Llanwrtyd Wells, Powys

30 April - 2 May
The Great Llandudno
Extravaganza
Llandudno, Gwynedd

1 - 10 May
Holyhead Arts Festival
Holyhead, Anglesey, Gwynedd

7 - 21st May
Wrexham Maelor Arts Festival
Wrexham Maelor Borough, Clwyd

20 - 22 May
Llangollen International Jazz
Festival
Llangollen, Clwyd

28 May - 4 June
St David's Cathedral Festival
St David's, Pembrokeshire, Dyfed

29 May - 4 June
Newport International Festival of
Musical Theatre
Newport, Gwent

29 May - 4 June
Newport Spring Festival
Newport, Pembrokeshire, Dyfed

29 May - 5 June
Gŵyl Beaumaris Festival
Beaumaris, Anglesey, Gwynedd

30 May - 4 June
Eisteddfod Urdd Gobaith Cymru
Dolgellau, Gwynedd

11 June
Man versus Horse Marathon
(including mountain bikes)
Llanwrtyd Wells, Powys

11 - 18 June
World Harp Festival II
St David's Hall, Cardiff, South
Glamorgan

18 - 24 June
Three Peaks Yacht Race (Barmouth
to Fort William)
Barmouth, Gwynedd

18 - 27 June
Criccieth Festival of Music and
the Arts
Criccieth, Gwynedd

21 - 26 June
Lower Machen Festival
Machen, Gwent

25 June
RAF St Athan At Home Day and
Air Show
St Athan, nr Barry,
South Glamorgan

25 June - 3 July
Gregynog Festival
Nr. Newtown, Powys

1 - 2 July
Morris in the Forest (Morris
dancing, forest walks, etc)
Llanwrtyd Wells, Powys

1 - 3 July
Story Telling Festival
St Donat's Arts Centre, nr Llantwit
Major, South Glamorgan

8 - 9 July
Gŵyl Werin y Cnapan
Ffostrasol, Llandysul, Dyfed

14 - 23 July
Welsh Proms '94
St David's Hall, Cardiff, South
Glamorgan

18 - 31 July
Gower Festival
Gower, Swansea

21 July - 5 August
Dyffryn Festival of Music and
Drama
Dyffryn Gardens, St Nicholas,
nr Cardiff, South Glamorgan

23 - 30 July
Fishguard Music Festival
Fishguard, Dyfed

24 July - 31 July
Ian Rush International Soccer
Tournament
Aberystwyth, Dyfed

25 July - 31 July
Gŵyl Conwy Festival
Conwy, Gwynedd

31 July - 7 August
Llanwrtyd Wells Festival
Llanwrtyd Wells, Powys

11 - 12 August
United Counties Show,
Carmarthen, Dyfed

11 - 14 August
Mountain Bike Festival
Llanwrtyd Wells, Powys

21 - 28 August
Gŵyl Machynlleth Festival
Machynlleth, Powys

24 - 31 August
Vale of Glamorgan Festival
Various locations in the Vale of
Glamorgan

28 August - 3 September
Presteigne Festival of Music and
the Arts
Presteigne, Powys

29 August
World Bog-Snorkelling
Championship
Llanwrtyd Wells, Powys

1 - 5 September
World Lifesaving Championships
Empire Pool, Cardiff, South
Glamorgan

3 - 4 September
Newport Town & County Show
Newport, Gwent

17 September - 9 October
Cardiff Festival of Music
Cardiff, South Glamorgan.

20 - 23 September
Welsh International 4 Days of
Walks
Llanwrtyd Wells, Powys

23 September - 1 October
Tenby Arts Festival
Tenby, Pembrokeshire, Dyfed

20 - 23 October
Welsh International 4 Days of
Cycle Races
Llanwrtyd Wells, Powys

22 - 30 October
Llandudno International Festival
Llandudno, Gwynedd

22 - 23 and 29 - 30 October
Llangollen Canoeing Festival
Llangollen, Clwyd

14 - 20 November
Mid Wales Beer Festival
Llanwrtyd Wells, Powys

12 - 14 AUGUST
BRECON JAZZ

The streets of Brecon come alive with the sounds of summer jazz. A great three-day international festival with a wonderful atmosphere, which attracts the top names from the world of jazz. Over 80 concerts by

bands and solo artists held throughout the town, both indoors and in the open air, featuring jazz of all styles.
Tel (0874) 625557

20 - 28 AUGUST
LLANDRINDOD WELLS
VICTORIAN FESTIVAL

The Mid Wales spa town of Llandrindod Wells celebrates its Victorian past. The festival includes street theatre, walks, talks, drama, exhibitions and music – all with a Victorian flavour.
Tel (0597) 823441

*W*hen you travel through Wales you take a journey

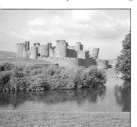

through time. You'll come across prehistoric and Roman remains, mighty medieval castles, manor houses and mansions, and memories of Britain's Industrial Revolution.

Caerphilly Castle

CROMLECHS AND CASTLES

Skeletal Pentre Ifan Cromlech in Pembrokeshire's Preseli Hills is one of many prehistoric monuments scattered throughout Wales. Thousands of years later, the Romans left camps, roadways, an extraordinary

amphitheatre and bath-house at Caerleon and unique gold mine at Pumsaint. But more than anything else, Wales is famous for its castles – mighty medieval monuments such as Caernarfon, Conwy and Caerphilly, as well

Carreg Samson Cromlech, Pembrokeshire Coast

as dramatic ruins like Carreg Cennen, Llandeilo and remote Castell-y-Bere hidden beneath Cader Idris.

HISTORIC HOUSES AND GARDENS

History also lives on at Llancaiach Fawr, a restored Tudor manor house in the Rhymney Valley which recreates the times of the Civil War. You can glimpse into grand country houses at National Trust properties such as Plas Newydd, Anglesey, Erddig near Wrexham

(an unusual 'upstairs, downstairs' house), and Powis Castle, Welshpool. Powis is also famed for its fabulous gardens, Britain's only formal gardens of the late 17th century to survive in their original form.

Plas Newydd, Llangollen

INDUSTRIAL HERITAGE

In Wales, you'll discover gripping monuments to the era of coal, slate, iron and steel. 'King Coal's' reign is remembered at places like the Big Pit Mining Museum, Blaenafon, and the Rhondda Heritage Park. North Wales's slate industry has a successful modern spin-off at the popular Llechwedd Slate Caverns, Blaenau Ffestiniog – and slate is also the theme at the town's Gloddfa Ganol Mountain Centre.

Llechwedd Slate caverns

WELCOME HOST

The Wales Tourist Board cares about the customer. That's why we have launched our Welcome Host scheme. Service and hospitality are as important as good accommodation and good food. Our Welcome Host programme, open to everyone from taxi drivers to hotel staff, places the emphasis on warm Welsh hospitality and first-class service.

Wales is renowned for its welcome. Recipients of the Welcome Host certificate or badge are part of a fine tradition – a tradition for friendliness embodied in the welcoming greeting of *croeso*.

A TASTE OF WALES

Good food is an essential part of any holiday. In Wales, you're in for a treat, for there's been an explosion of talent on the cooking scene. Throughout the country – in restaurants and hotels, inns and bistros – talented chefs are making the most of fresh, local produce to create tasty, innovative dishes as well as traditional favourites.

THE BEST RECIPE

Any good cook will tell you that you have to start with top-quality, fresh ingredients. Wales's larder is better supplied than most. It's full of produce such as succulent Welsh lamb, superb seafoods, delicious Pembrokeshire potatoes and wonderful cheeses. These ingredients are used to make not only old favourites such as *cawl* (a nourishing, hearty broth) and lamb served the traditional way. They also form the basis of modern, imaginative cuisine, often cooked with the lighter touch.

This is what the Taste of Wales-*Blas ar Gymru* scheme is all about. It seeks to promote the best in Welsh foods, traditional and contemporary. Look out for the distinctive membership sign on your travels.

*O*ne of Wales's big advantages is its ease of access. There are excellent road and rail links with most of Britain's main population areas – so you can forget about endless, expensive journeys, hold-ups and airport delays.

BY CAR

Travelling to South-West Wales? It's no problem when

you use the M4 and onward dual carriageway systems. The A55 North Wales coast 'Expressway' whisks traffic past the old bottlenecks, including Conwy. And Mid Wales is easily reached by the M54 which links with the M6/M5/M1.

Travelling by car is so easy

BY RAIL

InterCity, British Rail's flagship service, will speed you in style and comfort from London (Paddington) to Cardiff in less than 2 hours and to Swansea in under 3 hours (there are onward Regional Railways services to

South-West Wales). Fast InterCity trains also link London (Euston) with the North Wales coast, serving both Bangor and Holyhead.

Regional Railways' modern, air-conditioned trains provide a

BR's speedy InterCity service   direct link to Cardiff from the

South Coast, Exeter and Torbay, Birmingham, Manchester and Liverpool. North Wales is served by regular direct trains from Manchester. Aberystwyth and other Mid Wales resorts have direct services from Birmingham and Shrewsbury.

For further information, please contact British Rail-appointed travel agents or principal stations: Birmingham – Tel (021) 643 2711; Cardiff – Tel (0222) 228000; London (to North Wales) – Tel (071) 387 7070; London (to South Wales) – Tel (071) 262 6767; Manchester – Tel (061) 832 8353.

BY COACH

National Express provides a nationwide network of express coach services. Convenient services to Wales operate from London's Victoria Coach Station and from almost all other major towns and cities in England and Scotland. Good road links mean surprisingly quick journey times – at surprisingly low prices in comfortable, well-equipped coaches. Contact your

Come by coach

local travel agent or National Express office for details. National Express enquiries: Birmingham – Tel (021) 622 4373; Cardiff – Tel (0222) 344751; London – Tel (071) 730 0202; Swansea – Tel (0792) 470820.

Wales is an ideal car touring country

BY SEA

No less than five services operate across the Irish Sea:
Dublin to Holyhead and
Rosslare to Pembroke Dock
(both B&I); Dun Laoghaire to
Holyhead (which includes the
new high-speed Sealynx
catamaran) and Rosslare to
Fishguard (both Stena Sealink
Line); and Cork to Swansea
(Swansea-Cork Ferries)
which operates March to
September.

Fishguard harbour

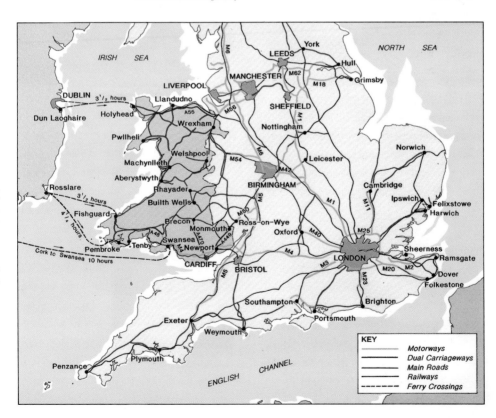

Llyn Brianne

When you arrive, you can enjoy the increasingly rare pleasures of the open road. Explore Wales by car on traffic-free routes, or hop on a bus. Train enthusiasts can travel around on scenic British Rail routes, or ride on a narrow-gauge 'Great Little Train'.

BY CAR

Apart from a few peak summer weekends, roads in Wales remain blissfully quiet. And many are highly

scenic – all you need is a copy of the 5 miles/inch Wales Tourist Map, available at Tourist Information Centres and bookshops.

Abergwesyn Pass

BY RAIL

Travelling around Wales by train is a delight. Take a scenic trip on the beautiful Heart of Wales line from Shrewsbury to Swansea, or on the Conwy Valley line

into the mountains from Llandudno Junction to Blaenau Ffestiniog. The views are also superb on the Cambrian Coast line, which runs along the mountain-backed shoreline from Pwllheli to Machynlleth and Aberystwyth. And ask

The Cambrian coast line, one of BR's most spectacular routes

about the money-saving unlimited-travel Rover fares, some of which include the use of bus services.

10

BY COACH

Within Wales you can travel cross-country by the Traws Cambria service which runs for over 200 miles on a daily schedule linking Bangor with Cardiff, calling in at

Coach touring, Mid Wales

places such as Caernarfon, Aberystwyth and Carmarthen.

Towns and resorts throughout Wales are, of course, connected by a whole range of local and regional services. Details from Tourist Information Centres and local bus stations.

Within North and Mid Wales you can combine coach and rail services through unlimited-travel Rover tickets (see 'By Rail' for details).

Talyllyn Narrow Gauge Railway

GREAT LITTLE TRAINS

You can't visit Wales without taking a ride on one of its famous narrow-gauge railways. Most are members of the Great Little Trains of Wales – contact them c/o The Station, Llanfair Caereinion, Powys SY21 0SF. Tel (0938) 810441.

11

*I*t's not surprising that bed and breakfasting in Wales is so popular. It's friendly. It's flexible. And it's great value for money. You'll not pay more than £19 per person per night for any B&B featured in this guide – and in most cases, the price is considerably less.

THE CONFIDENCE FACTOR

You can make your booking in confidence because the accommodation in this guide – from the remotest farmhouse to the largest hotel – has been thoroughly checked out by a personal visit from one of our inspectors.

Not only that, but we also clearly spell out the quality and standards for you. The Wales Tourist Board has led the way in the quest for quality by introducing a grading scheme for hotels, guest houses and farmhouses. And as well as giving establishments a quality grade, there's a 'Crown' classification to indicate facilities. The signs which appear next to the name of each establishment will tell you what you want to know.

HOTELS, GUEST HOUSES & FARMHOUSES

	Listed	1 Crown	2 Crowns	3 Crowns	4 Crowns	5 Crowns
Clean and comfortable accommodation	●	●	●	●	●	●
Adequate heating at no extra charge	●	●	●	●	●	●
No extra charge for baths or showers	●	●	●	●	●	●
Clean towels, fresh soap	●	●	●	●	●	●
Breakfast	●	●	●	●	●	●
A washbasin in your room or private bathroom	●	●	●	●	●	●
Comfortable lounge or sitting room		●	●	●	●	●
Beds no smaller than 6'3" x 3' (single) or 6'3" x 4'6" (double)		●	●	●	●	●
No nylon sheets		●	●	●	●	●
Cooked breakfast		●	●	●	●	●
Use of telephone		●	●	●	●	●
Tourist information		●	●	●	●	●
Help with your luggage			●	●	●	●
Private or en-suite bathrooms for at least 20% of the bedrooms			●	●	●	●
Colour TV in the lounge or your bedroom			●	●	●	●
Double beds with access and tables at both sides			●	●	●	●
Bedside lights			●	●	●	●
Early morning tea/coffee in your room, hot beverage in the evening			●	●	●	●
Early morning call			●	●	●	●
Private bathrooms for at least 50% of the bedrooms				●	●	●
Easy chairs, full length mirror, luggage rack, tea/coffee in your bedroom				●	●	●
Hairdryer, shoe cleaning equipment and ironing facilities available				●	●	●
A public telephone or one in your room				●	●	●
A hot evening meal				●	●	●
Private bathrooms for at least 90% of the bedrooms					●	●
Colour TV, radio and telephone in your bedroom					●	●
Room service – drinks and light snacks between 7am and 11pm					●	●
Lounge service of drinks and snacks to midnight					●	●
Evening meals, with wine, last orders 8.30pm or later					●	●
A quiet sitting area					●	●
Laundry services					●	●
Toiletries, message taking, newspapers on request					●	●
All bedrooms with bath, shower and WC en-suite						●
Direct dial telephone, writing table						●
Shoe cleaning and daily clothes pressing service						●
24-hour lounge service and room service with hot meals up to midnight						●
Restaurant open for breakfast, lunch and dinner with last orders 9pm or later						●
Full liquor licence						●
Night porter and porterage						●

READING THE SIGNS

In a nutshell, Crowns are your guide to the range of FACILITIES, SERVICES and EQUIPMENT (*not* quality) provided by hotels, guest houses and farmhouses. Please see the chart for a detailed explanation.

For your guide to QUALITY, you'll need to refer to the grades. They represent an overall appraisal of quality based on standards of furnishings, décor, comfort, service, food and so on.

De Luxe (A special accolade representing exceptional comfort and service)

Highly Commended (Excellent)

Commended (Very good)

Approved (Good)

WHAT TO BEAR IN MIND

Because Crowns are confined to facilities, a low Crown classification does not imply low standards – for example, a 1 Crown establishment of excellent quality might earn a Highly Commended grade.

In any case, most places in a lower Crown category will provide at least some of the facilities and services found at a higher level.

If no grade is shown, you can rest assured that the establishment has been inspected as part of the Crown classification scheme, and therefore provides – at the very least – comfortable accommodation.

LODGES

The new 'Lodge' category applies to purpose-built accommodation – along the lines of the American motel – aimed primarily at motorists. Located on main routes and key junctions, Lodges provide convenient overnight accommodation. Three categories apply – one, two and three 'Moons' – reflecting the RANGE OF FACILITIES available.

Please note that Lodges, like hotels, can also participate in the QUALITY grading scheme.

AWARD-WINNING GUEST HOUSES AND FARMHOUSES

If you're looking for something special, then pick a

guest house or farmhouse which has won a Wales Tourist Board Award. Award-winners – which can hold their own against many a hotel – boast superior standards of furnishings, facilities, comfort and surroundings.

ACCOMMODATING WHEELCHAIR USERS

The Wales Tourist Board actively encourages the provision of disabled facilities for visitors. Properties are visited on request to assess their suitability.

 Accessible to a wheelchair user travelling independently

 Accessible to a wheelchair user travelling with assistance

 Accessible to a wheelchair user able to walk a few paces and up a maximum of three steps

All relevant establishments are identified by the ♿ symbol and access grade.

PLEASE NOTE
All classifications and gradings were correct at the time of going to press. Inspections are on-going and improvements made by establishments may have resulted in a revised classification or grade since publication. Please check when booking.

BOOK DIRECT

Telephone or write to the place of your choice direct. It's as simple as that. If you phone, please check the prices and follow up the call with a letter of confirmation enclosing whatever deposit you've agreed with the proprietor.

CALL HOLIDAYS WALES

For full details of this free reservations service see page 117.

TICs FOR TRAVELLERS

If you're out and about in Wales and looking for a place to stay, then use the Bed Booking Service available through the network of Tourist Information Centres. This free service can arrange accommodation for you either locally or further afield. See the TIC list at the back of this brochure for more details.

PRICES

There's nothing more expensive in this guide than a per person price of £19 a night. And that's the top high-season price – you'll find that most rates quoted are even less.

Single rates are for *one* person in a single room. Double rates are for *two* people sharing a double or twin room.

All prices quoted include VAT at the current rate ($17^{1}/_{2}\%$). Prices and other specific holiday information

in this guide were supplied to the Wales Tourist Board during June – September 1993. So do check all prices and facilities before confirming your booking.

CHILDREN STAY FREE

Many hotels, guest houses and farmhouses offer free accommodation for children if sharing their parents' room (you only pay for their meals) – look out for the places with the ☎ symbol in this guide. Even if the symbol isn't displayed, it's worth asking about child reductions, for most operators will offer discounts for children.

Family holiday hotels, especially in major resorts, also cater for one-parent families.

DEPOSITS

Most operators will ask for a deposit when a reservation is being made. Some establishments may request payment in advance of arrival.

Nant Gwynant, Snowdonia

CANCELLATION AND INSURANCE

When you confirm a holiday booking, please bear in mind that you are entering a legally binding contract which entitles the proprietor to compensation if you fail to take up the accommodation. It's always wise to arrange holiday insurance to cover you for cancellation and other unforeseen eventualities. If you have to alter your travel plans, always advise the holiday operator or proprietor immediately.

LOOKING AFTER YOUR BEST INTERESTS

Whilst we are confident that your stay in Wales will be a success, there may be an occasion when your holiday accommodation does not meet expectations. In the unlikely event of this happening, please advise the owner or manager without delay, so that your grievances can be dealt with immediately. Proprietors welcome the chance to keep their guests happy. It is always very difficult for any problem to be resolved once the guest has left the accommodation.

KEY TO SYMBOLS

H	Hotel
GH	Guest House
FH	Farmhouse
L	Lodge
🛏	Total number of bedrooms
🛁	Number of en-suite bedrooms
AWARD	Recipient of the Wales Tourist Board Guest House and Farmhouse Award
P	Private car parking/garage facilities
🐕	Dogs/pets accepted by arrangement
⬛	Children under 12 accommodated free if sharing parents' room (meals charged extra)
♟	Liquor licence
⬛	Cots and high chairs provided – please check when booking
⬛	Central heating throughout
✂	Facilities provided for non-smokers
✂	Totally no-smoking establishment
☕	Tea/coffee making facilities in all bedrooms
🍽	Evening meals available by prior arrangement
TW	Taste of Wales member
⬛	Establishment is a working farm
♿	Accommodation is graded for access by visitors with disabilities
⇌	Railway Station

Please note: The symbols, together with the descriptive wording in the following advertisements, have been provided by the proprietors.

*I*t's easy to find your way around this guide. The rest of the book is filled with 'where to stay' information presented as follows. First, we divide the accommodation up into three main regions – North, Mid and South Wales – which are colour coded. Each region is then divided into smaller areas so that you can turn immediately to the specific part of Wales that interests you (see the map and index below).

Within each individual area, the resorts, towns and villages are listed alphabetically. Each place has a map reference enabling you to pinpoint it on the detailed gridded maps at the back of the book.

NORTH WALES

1 Isle of Anglesey
2 North Wales Coast Resorts
3 Llŷn – Snowdon's Peninsula
4 Snowdonia Mountains and Coastline
5 Clwyd Countryside and Heritage

MID WALES

6 Meirionnydd
7 Ceredigion
8 Montgomeryshire
9 Heart of Wales

SOUTH WALES

10 Pembrokeshire
11 The Coastline and Vales of Dyfed
12 Brecon and the Beacons
13 Swansea Bay, Mumbles and Gower
14 Cardiff and the South Wales Coast
15 Vale of Usk and Wye Valley
16 South Wales Valleys

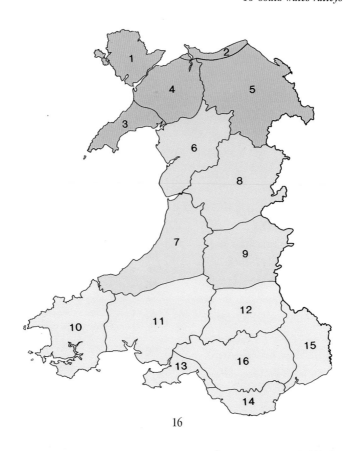

16

ERRATA

1. Page 15 - Key to Symbols

   Please use the following as your guide to the symbols used within the accommodation entries in this publication.

H	Hotel
GH	Guest House
FH	Farmhouse
L	Lodge
	Total number of bedrooms
	Number of en-suite bedrooms
AWARD	Recipient of the Wales Tourist Board Guest House and Farmhouse Award
P	Private car parking/garage facilities
	Dogs/pets accepted by arrangement
C	Children under 12 accommodated free if sharing parents' room (meals charged extra)
	Liquor licence
	Cots and high chairs provided – please check when booking
	Central heating throughout
	Facilities provided for non-smokers
	Totally no-smoking establishment
	Tea/coffee making facilities in all bedrooms
	Evening meals available by prior arrangement
TW	Taste of Wales member
	Establishment is a working farm
	Accommodation is graded for access by visitors with disabilities
	Railway Station

Please note: The symbols, together with the descriptive wording in the following advertisements, have been provided by the proprietors.

2. Page 14 - Children Stay Free

   Text should read:

   ...look out for the places with the [C] symbol in this guide.

*T*his region has it all – colourful and calm seashores, green hills and rugged highlands, big beaches and tiny coves. Families love the North Wales coast for its string

Much of the accommodation here is based along the coast – elegant Llandudno, in particular, has the largest selection of hotels and guest houses in Wales. Other

Erddig, nr Wrexham

of popular resorts, superb sands and up-to-the-minute attractions. Fans of the great outdoors head for the

Porth Dinllaen, Llŷn Peninsula

Snowdonia National Park, a spectacular upland area formed by the highest mountains in England and Wales. Those in search of the quieter style of seaside holiday make for the beautiful Isle of Anglesey, or the cliff-backed coves of the Llŷn Peninsula.

Dominant in the landscape is the Snowdonia National Park, a highland expanse of mountains, moors, lakes and wooded valleys. Further east, bordered by the lovely Vales of Conwy and Clwyd, are the lonely, heather-clad Hiraethog Moorlands. And rising above the lush Vale of Clwyd like silent guardians are the smooth, rounded hills of the Clwydian Range.

popular spots include Colwyn Bay, Rhyl and Prestatyn. Wooded Betws-y-Coed, medieval Ruthin and the mountain village of Beddgelert are amongst North Wales's many attractive inland destinations.

Wherever you choose to stay, coast or country, you'll

Snowdonia

find that everything's on your doorstep. You can spend the mornings in the mountains and the afternoons on

Portmeirion Italianate Village

Rhyl harbour

the beach, go walking in the hills or fishing off the pier. North Wales is a compact region. But don't underestimate the amount of things to see and do here. The region is bursting with attractions – everything from castles to slate caverns, sea and mountain zoos to butterfly and farm parks.

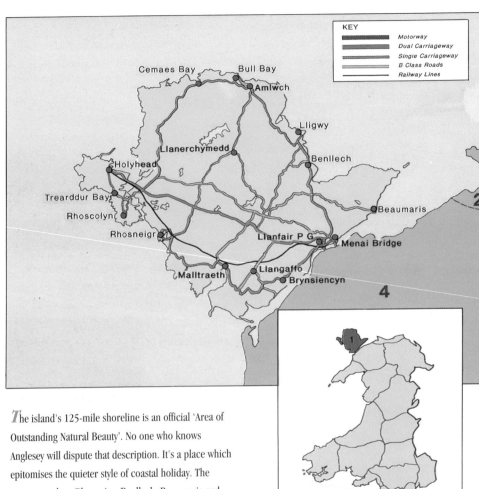

The island's 125-mile shoreline is an official 'Area of Outstanding Natural Beauty'. No one who knows Anglesey will dispute that description. It's a place which epitomises the quieter style of coastal holiday. The resorts, such as Rhosneigr, Benllech, Beaumaris and Moelfre, are small and subdued, the beaches are pristine, and the dunes and headlands are undisturbed save for the cry of seabirds.

Go to the cliffs of South Stack to see the island's coastline – and its prolific birdlife – at its most spectacular. At the opposite end of Anglesey, you'll find the spacious sands of Red Wharf Bay. Newborough is a strange area of forest, dune and sparkling sand. Cemaes Bay, the most northerly village in Wales, has the perfect sheltered harbour.

Anglesey's attractions and places to visit are as varied as its coastline. Call in at Llanfair PG (we're using the abbreviated version of the world's longest placename here!). And visit the National Trust's Plas Newydd, the award-winning Anglesey Sea Zoo, the Pili Palas Butterfly Farm and the island's many prehistoric sites.

BENLLECH
Map Ref: Ad2

Popular holiday village above a sweeping bay on Anglesey's east coast. 4 miles of good sands, safe bathing, sailing, bowls, walking. Nearby cliffs are rich in fossils. Visit the Rhuddlan Fawr Open Farm at nearby Brynteg.

BRYNSIENCYN
Map Ref: Ad4

Anglesey hamlet near shores of Menai Strait, looking across to Snowdonia. Bodowyr Burial Chamber, Plas Newydd stately home, Anglesey Bird World, Anglesey Model World, Fuel Farm Park, Bryntirion Open Farm, and award-winning Anglesey Sea Zoo all nearby.

CEMAES BAY
Map Ref: Ac1

Quaint, unspoilt village with stone quay, boating, fishing and swimming on rugged northern shores of Anglesey. Wylfa Nuclear Power Station open to the public.

HOLYHEAD
Map Ref: Aa2

Stands on Holy Island, linked by causeway to Anglesey. Port for Irish ferries. Roman remains and maritime museum in town. Sailing school. Sea angling, cliff and hill walking. Enjoy the sight of seabirds, coastal flora and the view from the cliffs to South Stack Lighthouse. RSPB centre located on cliffs. Penrhos Coastal Park on approach to the town. ⇌

Plas Newydd

LLANERCHYMEDD
Map Ref: Ac2

Central Anglesey village with easy access to island's beaches. Visit Din Llugwy, prehistoric remains of fortified village, the working windmill at Llanddeusant and the Llyn Alaw Visitor Centre.

LLANFAIR PG
Map Ref: Ad3

Famous for its 58-letter name of Llanfairpwllgwyngyllgogerychwyrndrobwll llantysiliogogogoch, which means 'St Mary's church by the white aspen near the violent whirlpool and St Tysilio's church by the red cave'. Fine craft centre with extensive choice of products. Plas Newydd stately home nearby. Marvellous views from the 90ft Marquess of Anglesey Column. Bryn Celli Ddu Burial Chamber. ⇌

LLANGAFFO
Map Ref: Ac4

On an Anglesey crossroads in the south-western corner of the island. Good bird-watching along Malltraeth Sands and Marsh, excellent, spacious beach at Newborough (drive through the forest), award-winning Anglesey Sea Zoo at Brynsiencyn.

RHOSNEIGR
Map Ref: Ab3

Attractive resort on a low-lying stretch of Anglesey's west coast, with pristine, spacious sandy beaches. Ideal place for the quieter style of seaside holiday. Good golf course. Outstanding prehistoric sites nearby, including Barclodiad y Gawres Burial Chamber. ⇌

TREARDDUR BAY
Map Ref: Aa2

Most attractive holiday spot set amongst low cliffs on Holy Island, near Holyhead. Ample accommodation, golden sands, golf, sailing, fishing, swimming.

H | The Golden Sands Hotel

Benllech Bay,
Isle of Anglesey,
Gwynedd LL74 8SP
Tel: (0248) 852384

"Golden Sands" aptly named due to its close proximity to the beach. Luxury en-suite rooms some with bath and shower and sea views; tea/coffee facilities. Dining room and conservatory bar overlooking beach. Olde Worlde bar with log fire downstairs. Sea food menu.

		SINGLE PER PERSON B&B		DOUBLE FOR 2 PERSONS B&B			12
							11
		MIN £ 17.00	MAX £ 19.00	MIN £ 36.00	MAX £ 38.00	OPEN 1-12	

H | Woburn Hill Hotel

High Street, Cemaes Bay,
Isle of Anglesey,
Gwynedd LL67 0HU
Tel: (0407) 711388/711190

Small friendly Hotel 5 minutes from beaches and old fishing harbour. Home cooked meals. En-suite rooms with colour television, centrally heated, beverage facilities, licensed bar and restaurant. Good selection of bar meals. Children welcome. Ideal for fishing and water sports, golf, riding, bird watching, walking, touring, relaxing, parking for cars and boats. Open all year around.

		SINGLE PER PERSON B&B		DOUBLE FOR 2 PERSONS B&B			5
							5
		MIN £ –	MAX £ –	MIN £ 30.00	MAX £ 36.00	OPEN 1-12	

GH | Roselea

26 Holborn Road,
Holyhead, Isle of Anglesey,
Gwynedd LL65 2AT
Tel: (0407) 764391

COMMENDED

Homely Guest House five minutes from ferry, station, beaches and golf course. Walking distance town centre. Good home cooking. Hot and cold, tea/coffee facilities and TV in bedrooms. Guest TV lounge. Open for late ferry. Also catering for new Sea Lynx ferry. Park, leisure centre nearby. Rooms furnished to high standard. Proprietor Mrs. S. Foxley.

		SINGLE PER PERSON B&B		DOUBLE FOR 2 PERSONS B&B			3
							–
		MIN £ 15.00	MAX £ 15.00	MIN £ 20.00	MAX £ 25.00	OPEN 1-12	

GH | Woodlands

Bangor Road, Benllech,
Isle of Anglesey,
Gwynedd LL74 8PU
Tel: (0248) 852735

HIGHLY COMMENDED

Situated alongside the A5025, Woodlands has six good sized bedrooms, all en-suite with TV and tea making facilities. Each room is decorated in a different style with antique furniture and decor. Guests are requested not to smoke in the bedrooms. There is a licensed bar and an excellent bar menu. Attractive gardens and a large car park for guests use.

		SINGLE PER PERSON B&B		DOUBLE FOR 2 PERSONS B&B			6
							6
		MIN £ 18.00	MAX £ 18.00	MIN £ 30.00	MAX £ 36.00	OPEN 1-12	

GH | Treddolphin Guest House

Beach Road, Penrhyn,
Cemaes Bay, Isle of Anglesey,
Gwynedd LL67 0ET
Tel: (0407) 710388

COMMENDED

Commanding a panoramic coastal view all bedrooms have H&C and shower. Visitors lounge, colour TV, centrally heated. Fire Certificate. Ample parking. Children welcome, half price when sharing parent's room. Free baby-sitting, free evening tea and biscuits. Near golf course and sports centre. For a welcoming service ring Roberta and Harold Williams.

		SINGLE PER PERSON B&B		DOUBLE FOR 2 PERSONS B&B			8
							–
		MIN £ 14.00	MAX £ 14.00	MIN £ 24.00	MAX £ 24.00	OPEN 1-12	

GH | Tan-y-Cytiau Country Guest House

South Stack Road,
Holyhead, Isle of Anglesey,
Gwynedd
Tel: (0407) 762763

HIGHLY COMMENDED

Country house peacefully situated in 3 acres of lovely gardens on slopes of Holyhead Mountain with magnificent views from all rooms. Adjacent to R.S.P.B. reserve. Ideal for walking and birdwatching. Self catering cottage in grounds, sleeps 7. Write or phone for brochure.

		SINGLE PER PERSON B&B		DOUBLE FOR 2 PERSONS B&B			7
							–
		MIN £ 19.00	MAX £ 19.00	MIN £ 33.00	MAX £ 35.00	OPEN 3-9	

FH | Tyddyn Goblet

Brynsiencyn,
Isle of Anglesey,
Gwynedd LL61 6TZ
Tel: (0248) 430296

AWARD

HIGHLY COMMENDED

Character Farmhouse set back 200 yards from A4080 road. Ground floor en-suite bedrooms with colour television and tea making facilities. Evening dinner optional. Attractive lounge and pleasant dining room with separate tables. Close to many of Anglesey's main attractions. Less than half an hour's drive from Snowdonia and the North Wales coast. Brochure Mrs. Williams.

		SINGLE PER PERSON B&B		DOUBLE FOR 2 PERSONS B&B			2
							2
		MIN £ 13.00	MAX £ 16.00	MIN £ 26.00	MAX £ 32.00	OPEN 1-12	

GH | Bryn Awel

Edmund Street,
Holyhead, Isle of Anglesey,
Gwynedd LL65 1SA
Tel: (0407) 762948

Centrally situated five minutes walk from car ferry, five minutes shops. TV lounge, central heating. Hot and cold water, tea making facilities all rooms. Sandy beaches nearby. Golf course one mile, day trips to Ireland. Beautiful coast line. Good home cooking, dining room separate tables. Children welcome. Pleasant family atmosphere, hospitality guaranteed.

		SINGLE PER PERSON B&B		DOUBLE FOR 2 PERSONS B&B			3
							–
		MIN £ 11.50	MAX £ 13.00	MIN £ 22.00	MAX £ 24.00	OPEN 1-12	

GH | Wavecrest

93 Newry Street,
Holyhead, Isle of Anglesey,
Gwynedd LL65 1HU
Tel: (0407) 763637

COMMENDED

Friendly comfortable family run Guest House in quiet location, yet only two minutes from Ferry, town centre and yards from beach. Ideal for break of journey en-route to Ireland. All rooms have H&C, tea making facilities, colour satellite TV, radio alarms and furnished to high standard. Large family en-suite room available. AA approved.

		SINGLE PER PERSON B&B		DOUBLE FOR 2 PERSONS B&B			4
							1
		MIN £ 12.00	MAX £ 15.00	MIN £ 24.00	MAX £ 30.00	OPEN 1-12	

FH | Drws-y-Coed

Llanerchymedd,
Isle of Anglesey,
Gwynedd LL71 8AD
Tel: (0248) 470473

AWARD / HIGHLY COMMENDED

With wonderful panoramic views of Snowdonia, this beautifully appointed farmhouse on a 550 acre working farm - beef, sheep, arable - is situated in peaceful wooded countryside in the centre of Anglesey. Comfortable en-suite bedrooms with all facilities. Central heating, log fire. Delicious cooking. Games room. Free pony rides, lovely walks, warm welcome assured from Mrs. Jane Bown.

		SINGLE PER PERSON B&B		DOUBLE FOR 2 PERSONS B&B			3
							3
		MIN £	MAX £	MIN £	MAX £	OPEN	
		19.00	19.00	34.00	38.00	1-12	

GH | Carreg Goch

Llanedwen, Llanfair PG,
Isle of Anglesey,
Gwynedd LL61 6EZ
Tel: (0248) 430315

Carreg Goch stands back from A4080 coast road and is 1 mile from National Trust property of Plas Newydd. The ground floor guest suite consists of double and twin bedrooms with shared bathroom/shower. Both rooms have french windows opening onto private patio. Glorious views of Snowdonia. Convenient for both beaches and mountains. Home cooking.

		SINGLE PER PERSON B&B		DOUBLE FOR 2 PERSONS B&B			2
							–
		MIN £	MAX £	MIN £	MAX £	OPEN	
		–	–	28.00	28.00	4-10	

GH | Moranedd Guest House

Trearddur Road, Trearddur Bay,
Isle of Anglesey,
Gwynedd LL65 2UE
Tel: (0407) 860324

Moranedd is a lovely house overlooking ¼ acre garden. Only five minutes stroll to the beach, shops, sailing and golf clubs. The bedrooms are large, with wash basins and tea-making facilities. Residents lounge with colour TV. AA/RAC listed.

		SINGLE PER PERSON B&B		DOUBLE FOR 2 PERSONS B&B			6
							–
		MIN £	MAX £	MIN £	MAX £	OPEN	
		13.00	15.00	26.00	30.00	1-12	

FH | Tre'rddol Farm

Llanerchymedd,
Isle of Anglesey,
Gwynedd LL71 7AR
Tel: (0248) 470278

AWARD / HIGHLY COMMENDED

Welcome to peace and paradise at this former historic 17th Century manor house. A 200 acre working farm, where guests comfort is a priority and food a speciality. Spacious en-suite rooms with TV, beverage facilities and heating, cosy lounge. Dinner optional. Free pony rides, centrally situated 6 miles from Llangefni off the B5109 to Holyhead Road. SAE for brochure.

		SINGLE PER PERSON B&B		DOUBLE FOR 2 PERSONS B&B			3
							3
		MIN £	MAX £	MIN £	MAX £	OPEN	
		19.00	–	36.00	38.00	1-11	

FH | Plas Farmhouse

Plas Llangaffo,
Isle of Anglesey,
Gwynedd LL60 5LR
Tel: (0248) 440452

L

Peaceful location situated near to Newborough Forest and Llandwyn Bay with its miles of golden sand. Dinner, bed and breakfast per person £130.00 per week. Children under 10 half price. Horse riding weekends. £99.00 per person including all meals from Friday night to Sunday Lunch. Learn to ride or improve your riding.

		SINGLE PER PERSON B&B		DOUBLE FOR 2 PERSONS B&B			5
		MIN £	MAX £	MIN £	MAX £	OPEN	
		13.00	14.00	26.00	26.00	1-12	

VISITOR'S GUIDES TO NORTH, MID AND SOUTH WALES

Don't visit Wales without these full-colour, information-packed guides.

Where to go and what to see.

Descriptions of towns, villages and resorts.

Hundreds of attractions and places to visit.

Detailed maps and plans.

Scenic drives, beaches, narrow-gauge railways, what to do on a rainy day.

£3.55 inc. p&p (see page 118)

GH | Sarn Faban Guest House

Penmynydd Road, Llanfair PG,
Isle of Anglesey,
Gwynedd LL61 5AZ
Tel: (0248) 712410

Situated one mile off Menai Bridge, central for all locations and beaches, Snowdonia and all amenities of North Wales. Central heating all rooms, including family rooms, TV lounge. Panoramic views in peaceful surroundings. Warm Welsh welcome with good home cooking. Brochure available.

		SINGLE PER PERSON B&B		DOUBLE FOR 2 PERSONS B&B			3
							2
		MIN £	MAX £	MIN £	MAX £	OPEN	
		15.00	15.00	28.00	28.00	1-12	

H | The Maelog Lake Hotel

Rhosneigr,
Isle of Anglesey,
Gwynedd LL64 5JP
Tel: (0407) 810204

Situated in the sand dunes just outside Rhosneigr, 150 yards from Broad beach with special rates for children. The Hotel overlooks the beautiful Llyn Maelog. With sea and course fishing. Horse riding, surfing, walks all to hand. Quiet room and TV lounge. Bar meals available with vegetarian dishes. All rooms have beverage trays. Open all year.

		SINGLE PER PERSON B&B		DOUBLE FOR 2 PERSONS B&B			13
							4
		MIN £	MAX £	MIN £	MAX £	OPEN	
		15.00	17.50	30.00	35.00	1-12	

Trearddur Bay

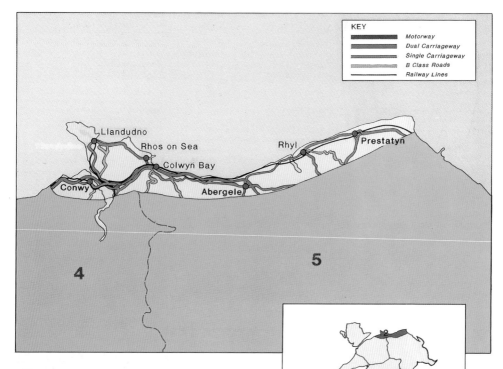

KEY
Motorway
Dual Carriageway
Single Carriageway
B Class Roads
Railway Lines

Llandudno
Rhos on Sea
Colwyn Bay
Conwy
Abergele
Rhyl
Prestatyn

4

5

*T*his popular stretch of coastline has all the ingredients for entertainment-packed or relaxing seaside holidays. Llandudno, the dignified 'Queen' of the Welsh resorts, preserves a period charm now rarely found at the seaside. Its wide promenade, pier, wealth of Victorian architecture and magnificent setting between two headlands give it a unique personality. But don't think that the resort is stuck in the 19th century – its many attractions include a cabin lift, copper mines and ski slope.

On the other hand, we could say that neighbouring Conwy is essentially a 13th-century town (especially since it is now by-passed by through traffic). Dominated by its mighty castle and ring of ancient walls, Conwy is undoubtedly one of Britain's best-preserved medieval towns.

The sands, which begin at Llandudno, stretch all the way to Prestatyn. Colwyn Bay and Rhyl are perennially popular family resorts. Overlooking Colwyn Bay's superb beach is the famous Welsh Mountain Zoo. Rhyl's colourful seafront is bursting with attractions – its Sun Centre and lofty Skytower to name but two. And there's a similar family appeal at Prestatyn, where attractions include the Nova Centre.

ABERGELE
Map Ref: Bd4

Convenient centre, located between Colwyn Bay and Rhyl, for exploring the popular coastal resorts. Wooded walks nearby, 18-hole golf course, livestock market. Miles of sand at nearby Pensarn. ⇌

COLWYN BAY
Map Ref: Bc4

Attractive bustling seaside resort. Promenade amusements. Good touring centre for Snowdonia. Leisure centre, Eirias Park, Dinosaur World, famous Mountain Zoo with Chimpanzee World. Puppet theatre. Golf, tennis, riding and other sports. Wide range of hotels and guest houses. Quieter Rhos on Sea at Western end of bay. ⇌

CONWY
Map Ref: Bb4

Historic town with mighty castle and complete ring of medieval town walls. Dramatic estuary setting. Many ancient buildings including Aberconwy House and Plas Mawr. Telford Suspension Bridge, popular fish quay, spectacular wall walks. Golf, pony trekking, Butterfly House, aquarium, pleasure cruises. Tiny 'smallest house' on quay. Touring centre for Snowdonia with good range of accommodation. ⇌

Conwy Castle

LLANDUDNO
Map Ref: Bb3

Premier coastal resort of North Wales with everything the holidaymaker needs. Two beaches, spacious promenade, Victorian pier, excellent shops, wide selection of hotels and guest houses. Donkey rides, Punch and Judy, ski slope, Alice in Wonderland exhibition, art gallery, old copper mines open to the public. Visit the Great Orme headland above the resort and ride by cabinlift or tramway. Conference centre. Many daily coach excursions. ⇌

Llandudno

PRESTATYN
Map Ref: Be3

Family seaside resort in Clwyd, with good-value accommodation. Entertainment galore at superb Nova Centre including heated swimming pools and aquashute. Sailing, swimming on long, sandy coastline. Close to pastoral Vale of Clwyd and Clwydian Range. ⇌

RHOS ON SEA
Map Ref: Bb3

Attractive seaside village linking Llandudno and Colwyn Bay with promenade, beach, golf, water-skiing, puppet theatre. Colwyn Bay Mountain Zoo nearby.

GH	The Haven Guest House

Towyn Road,
Belgrano, Abergele,
Clwyd LL22 9AB
Tel: (0745) 823534

Cliff and Barbara Pilley welcome you to the Haven, a friendly Guest House with single double and family rooms, having central heating, hot and cold water. Shaver points, tea and coffee making facilities, all ingredients supplied. Lounge with colour TV, dining room has separate tables. Access to rooms and lounge at all reasonable times.

		SINGLE PER PERSON B&B		DOUBLE FOR 2 PERSONS B&B		🛏 4
		MIN £	MAX £	MIN £	MAX £	OPEN
		13.00	13.00	24.00	24.00	1-12

GH	Crossroads

Coed Pella Road,
Colwyn Bay,
Clwyd LL29 7AT
Tel: (0492) 530736

Family run, established Victorian Guest House, with considerable charm and relaxing atmosphere. Although in the town centre, there are scenic views of the mountains and woods from rooms. All bedrooms have colour television and hot drinks facilities. Solarium. Open all year except Christmas. Warm welcome guaranteed. Colwyn Bay is the touring centre of North Wales. All attractions and locations are within easy reach. AA QQ.

		SINGLE PER PERSON B&B		DOUBLE FOR 2 PERSONS B&B		🛏 5
		MIN £	MAX £	MIN £	MAX £	OPEN
		12.00	14.00	24.00	28.00	1-12

GH	Glan Heulog

Llanrwst Road,
Conwy,
Gwynedd LL32 8LT
Tel: (0492) 593845

Spacious Victorian house, close to the castle and historic walled town of Conwy. A friendly guest house with traditional home cooking. Ideal for touring Snowdonia and North Wales coast, Bodnant Garden, etc. Ask about our winter breaks and romantic weekends.

		SINGLE PER PERSON B&B		DOUBLE FOR 2 PERSONS B&B		🛏 7
		MIN £	MAX £	MIN £	MAX £	🛁 4
		13.00	15.00	26.00	30.00	OPEN 1-12

H	Edelweiss Hotel

Off Lawson Road,
Colwyn Bay,
Clwyd LL29 8HD
Tel: (0492) 532314
Fax: (0492) 534707
COMMENDED

Impressive 19th Century country house set in its own wooded grounds. Large car park, children and pets welcome. All 25 bedrooms have CTV with movie channel, radio alarm, direct dial telephone, kettle, private bath or shower and W.C. Central situation, easy access to all amenities. Wide choice on all menus. Taste of Wales member renowned for fine food.

		SINGLE PER PERSON B&B		DOUBLE FOR 2 PERSONS B&B		🛏 25
		MIN £	MAX £	MIN £	MAX £	🛁 25
		18.00	–	36.00	–	OPEN 1-12

GH	Bryn Derwen

Woodlands,
Conwy,
Gwynedd LL32 8LT
Tel: (0492) 596134

Spacious Victorian home with lovely garden max 10 min walk from historic walled town of Conwy. A warm welcome from a hostess with excellent knowledge of North Wales, the perfect place to stay while seeing it all and learning the history and legends. AA listed.

		SINGLE PER PERSON B&B		DOUBLE FOR 2 PERSONS B&B		🛏 4
		MIN £	MAX £	MIN £	MAX £	🛁 1
		12.50	16.00	25.00	36.00	OPEN 3-12

GH	Pen-y-Bryn Tearooms

Lancaster Square,
Conwy,
Gwynedd LL32 8DE
Tel: (0492) 596445
HIGHLY COMMENDED

Guests are once again invited to sample Pen-y-Bryn's own brand of hospitality and comfort, on offer above their unique 16th Century tearooms. (Egon Ronay recommended). All bedrooms have central heating, colour TV's hairdryer and beverage facilities. Two rooms have private shower and toilet. Non smoking throughout. Private car parking available nearby.

		SINGLE PER PERSON B&B		DOUBLE FOR 2 PERSONS B&B		🛏 3
		MIN £	MAX £	MIN £	MAX £	🛁 2
		20.00	–	30.00	38.00	OPEN 1-12

H	Grosvenor Hotel

106-8 Abergele Road,
Colwyn Bay,
Clwyd LL29 7PS
Tel: (0492) 531586

Centrally situated close to the leisure centre and park, only a short walk to the beach. Children welcome at reduced rates when sharing with two adults. Baby listening service. Licensed bar, games room, large car park. All rooms have TV, radio/intercom, tea and coffee facilities, H&C. Evening meals available.

		SINGLE PER PERSON B&B		DOUBLE FOR 2 PERSONS B&B		🛏 18
		MIN £	MAX £	MIN £	MAX £	🛁 2
		16.90	17.90	33.80	35.80	OPEN 1-12

GH	Church House

Llanbedr-y-Cennin,
Conwy Valley,
Gwynedd LL32 8JB
Tel: (0492) 660521
HIGHLY COMMENDED

Lovely 16th Century listed building with oak beams and inglenook fireplaces. It has central heating, TV, H&C, tea trays in its two double bedrooms. Situated in a small village complete with 16th Century Inn in the Snowdonia foothills, just off the B5106 between Conwy and Betws-y-Coed. Ideal for Bodnant Garden, sightseeing, walking etc.

		SINGLE PER PERSON B&B		DOUBLE FOR 2 PERSONS B&B		🛏 2
		MIN £	MAX £	MIN £	MAX £	🛁
		–	19.00	–	32.00	OPEN 1-12

FH	Henllys Farm

Llechwedd,
Conwy,
Gwynedd LL32 8DJ
Tel: (0492) 593269
AWARD
HIGHLY COMMENDED

In the heart of beautiful countryside ideally placed for touring Snowdonia, North Wales coast, Bodnant Garden and Anglesey. 1½ miles from Conwy. 1 double, 1 family bedrooms both with ensuite tea/coffee making facilities, TV lounge. Good home cooking from fresh local produce own lamb. A warm Welsh welcome awaits you from Mrs. Ceinwen Roberts.

		SINGLE PER PERSON B&B		DOUBLE FOR 2 PERSONS B&B		🛏 2
		MIN £	MAX £	MIN £	MAX £	🛁 2
		18.00	19.00	30.00	36.00	OPEN 2-11

H | Ashby Hotel

31 Church Walks,
Llandudno,
Gwynedd LL30 2HL
Tel: (0492) 875608

HIGHLY COMMENDED

Attractive Victorian detached house now a comfortable family run licensed hotel. Located between both shores in quiet tree lined road close to Great Orme and amenities. Excellent home cooked food, varied menu. Spacious rooms with en-suite facilities, colour TV, beverage makers. All bedrooms no smoking. Centrally heated. A warm welcome awaits you at the Ashby.

P ⚓ ✂ 🛏 🍴		SINGLE PER PERSON B&B		DOUBLE FOR 2 PERSONS B&B		🛏 7 🛁 7
		MIN £ –	MAX £ –	MIN £ 33.00	MAX £ 38.00	OPEN 1-12

H | Carmel Private Hotel

17 Craig-y-Don Parade,
Promenade, Llandudno,
Gwynedd LL30 1BG
Tel: (0492) 877643

COMMENDED

Situated in a prime position on the main promenade, Carmel welcomes you to a family run Hotel with excellent home cooking. Twin ground floor en-suite bedroom. All other rooms on 2 floors only. Some rooms en-suite, colour TV, tea/coffee making facilities in all bedrooms. Separate dining room tables, close to conference centre and Arcadia Theatre.

P ⚓ ✂ 🛏 🍴		SINGLE PER PERSON B&B		DOUBLE FOR 2 PERSONS B&B		🛏 10 🛁 5
		MIN £ 13.50	MAX £ 18.50	MIN £ 27.00	MAX £ 33.00	OPEN 4-10

H | Lynton

80 Church Walks,
Llandudno,
Gwynedd LL30 2HD
Tel: (0492) 875057

HIGHLY COMMENDED

A small homely Hotel fifty yards from the pier. Close to shops, skiing and all amenities. All rooms are decorated to a high standard with en-suite bathroom, colour TV, tea/coffee tray and telephone. Highly recommended home cooking with choice of menu, vegetarian and special diets catered for. Four poster room available. Car park.

P 🐕 C 🛏 🍴		SINGLE PER PERSON B&B		DOUBLE FOR 2 PERSONS B&B		🛏 11 🛁 11
		MIN £ 18.00	MAX £ 19.00	MIN £ 36.00	MAX £ 38.00	OPEN 1-12

H | Brannock Hotel

36 St. David's Road,
Llandudno,
Gwynedd LL30 2UH
Tel: (0492) 877483

COMMENDED

Situated between both shores, close to shops, railway station, etc. Car parking, central heating, separate tables. Open all year (except Christmas). Colour TV and tea/coffee making facilities in all rooms, some en-suite. Varied home cooking with choice of menu. Access to rooms at all times. Senior citizens discount. Special winter breaks. AA/RAC listed. Telephone for brochure.

P 🛏 🍴 🐕		SINGLE PER PERSON B&B		DOUBLE FOR 2 PERSONS B&B		🛏 7 🛁 4
		MIN £ 14.00	MAX £ 17.00	MIN £ 28.00	MAX £ 34.00	OPEN 1-12

H | Cliffbury Hotel

34 St David's Road,
Llandudno,
Gwynedd LL30 2UH
Tel: (0492) 877224

HIGHLY COMMENDED

Non smoking quietly situated in garden area. En-suite available. Colour TV, tea/coffee facilities. Car parking, family rooms available. Good food with special diets catered for. Close to beaches, shops and entertainments. Open all year with central heating in winter. Access to rooms all day. Perfect for touring, walking, climbing or visiting castles in area.

P 🛏 🐕 🍴 🍷		SINGLE PER PERSON B&B		DOUBLE FOR 2 PERSONS B&B		🛏 8 🛁 4
		MIN £ 14.50	MAX £ 17.00	MIN £ 29.00	MAX £ 34.00	OPEN 1-12

H | Tan Lan Hotel

Great Orme's Road,
West Shore, Llandudno,
Gwynedd LL30 2AR
Tel: (0492) 860221

HIGHLY COMMENDED

Elegant family hotel offering real value for money. Situated on level ground on quieter West Shore near gardens. Ideal for touring Snowdonia. All rooms ground or first floor with en-suite, colour TV, hospitality tray, central heating. Traditional cooking with choice. Lovely lounges and bar lounge. Private car park. High recommended. May we welcome you?

P 🐕 🍷 ✂ 🛏 🍴		SINGLE PER PERSON B&B		DOUBLE FOR 2 PERSONS B&B		🛏 18 🛁 18
		MIN £ 19.00	MAX £ 19.00	MIN £ 38.00	MAX £ 38.00	OPEN 3-11

H | Brigstock Hotel

1 St David's Place,
Llandudno,
Gwynedd LL30 2UG
Tel: (0492) 876416

HIGHLY COMMENDED

*Select non smoking Hotel. Gardens area, en-suite rooms available twin or double. Colour television, beverage facilities, central heating. Licensed bar, pay phone, key access. Car park, good home cooking, choice of menu. Separate dining tables. Close to all amenities. Friendly atmosphere. Enjoy a non-smoking environment. AA/RAC ***

P 🛏 🍷 🍴		SINGLE PER PERSON B&B		DOUBLE FOR 2 PERSONS B&B		🛏 10 🛁 6
		MIN £ 17.00	MAX £ 19.00	MIN £ 34.00	MAX £ 38.00	OPEN 1-11

H | Karden House Hotel

16 Charlton Street,
Llandudno,
Gwynedd LL30 2AA
Tel: (0492) 879347

COMMENDED

Conveniently situated close to beach, shops, station. Vera and Des Steward provide friendly, caring service. Fresh home cooking, (vegetarian/allergy diets available). Tea/coffee, central heating all rooms, en-suite available. Licensed bar, separate lounge. Open Christmas, reductions O.A.P's/children. Ideally situated for visiting scenic beauty spots and activities on great Orme, skiing, toboggan run, cable car.

🛏 🍷 🍴		SINGLE PER PERSON B&B		DOUBLE FOR 2 PERSONS B&B		🛏 10 🛁 1
		MIN £ 12.00	MAX £ 13.50	MIN £ 24.00	MAX £ 27.00	OPEN 1-12

H | Westdale Hotel

37 Abbey Road,
Llandudno,
Gwynedd LL30 2EH
Tel: (0492) 877996

HIGHLY COMMENDED

Westdale is a comfortable Hotel with a good friendly atmosphere. Situated on the level in a quiet road facing Haulfre gardens, within easy walking distance of shops and beaches. Large ground and first floor bedrooms with bathrooms en-suite. Centrally heated throughout, choice of menu. Licensed bar, car park, dinner optional. SAE for details.

P 🛏 🍷 🐕		SINGLE PER PERSON B&B		DOUBLE FOR 2 PERSONS B&B		🛏 12 🛁 3
		MIN £ 14.50	MAX £ 15.50	MIN £ 29.00	MAX £ 36.00	OPEN 3-10

H | Westbourne Private Hotel

8 Arvon Avenue,
Llandudno,
Gwynedd LL30 2DY
Tel: (0492) 877450

COMMENDED

Licensed, very central Hotel situated in pleasant tree lined Avenue on flat ground close to all amenities. First class food and friendly quick service. All bedrooms contain colour TV and tea making facilities and full central heating. Most bedrooms en-suite including one on ground floor. For colour brochure ring Doris or write with SAE for full details and booking form.

		SINGLE PER PERSON B&B		DOUBLE FOR 2 PERSONS B&B			🛏 12
		MIN £	MAX £	MIN £	MAX £		🛁 7
		15.50	17.50	31.00	35.00		OPEN 4-10

GH | Winston Guest House

5 Church Walks,
Llandudno,
Gwynedd LL30 2HD
Tel: (0492) 876144

COMMENDED

Family run for the past 22 years. 80 yards from the pier. Close to ski slope and shopping centre. Colour TV in all bedrooms, tea coffee facilities provided each day. Full central heating. Evening meal provided, choice of menu. Different diets catered for. Comfortable lounge with colour television. No restrictions. AA listed.

		SINGLE PER PERSON B&B		DOUBLE FOR 2 PERSONS B&B			🛏 7
		MIN £	MAX £	MIN £	MAX £		🛁 7
		16.00	17.50	30.00	33.00		OPEN 1-12

GH | Sunnyside

146 Dinerth Road,
Rhos-on-Sea, Colwyn Bay,
Clwyd LL28 4YF
Tel: (0492) 554048

[L]

A warm Welsh welcome awaits you at our home situated in the town of Rhos-on-Sea. Adjacent to Colwyn Bay and Llandudno offering ample shopping facilities. Miles of excellent coastline and easy driving distance to the Mountains of Snowdonia. Lovely country views from our home with a good home cooked breakfast to start off your day and excellent value accommodation.

		SINGLE PER PERSON B&B		DOUBLE FOR 2 PERSONS B&B			🛏 2
		MIN £	MAX £	MIN £	MAX £		🛁 -
		-	-	-	25.00		OPEN 1-12

GH | Bryn Tawel

19 St David's Road,
Llandudno,
Gwynedd LL30 2UL
Tel: (0492) 877979

[L]

COMMENDED

Mr. & Mrs. D. Holdsworth invite you to their small but friendly guest house situated in Llandudno's most pleasant road. This family run guest house offers a warm and friendly atmosphere coupled with personal service and excellent food. Centrally located to both shores and shops.

		SINGLE PER PERSON B&B		DOUBLE FOR 2 PERSONS B&B			🛏 7
		MIN £	MAX £	MIN £	MAX £		🛁 -
		13.00	-	26.00	-		OPEN 1-11

GH | Roughsedge House

26/28 Marine Road,
Prestatyn,
Clwyd LL19 7HD
Tel: (0745) 887359

COMMENDED

Family run establishment, close to beaches, Pontins Presthaven Sands, Nova complex, golf, bowls and Offa's Dyke. Pleasant rooms, some en-suite, all with colour TV, tea/coffee facilities and clock radios. Home cooking, choice of menu, special diets, residential licence. Centrally heated, open lounge fire. Handy to rail and bus services and town centre. Children welcome, Credit cards accepted. AA

		SINGLE PER PERSON B&B		DOUBLE FOR 2 PERSONS B&B			🛏 10
		MIN £	MAX £	MIN £	MAX £		🛁 3
		13.00	18.00	26.00	36.00		OPEN 1-12

Alice in Wonderland Visitor Centre, Llandudno

GH | Cranberry House (Non-smoking)

12 Abbey Road,
Llandudno,
Gwynedd LL30 2EA
Tel: (0492) 879760

HIGHLY COMMENDED

Cranberry House is a small, elegant Victorian House. Hosts Mr. & Mrs. Aldridge offer a very high standard of comfort and service and have taken tremendous trouble to furnish and decorate their home in a manner which complements its period of origins. Delicious home cooked meals with emphasis on fresh produce. Within easy reach of all amenities. Private car parking. AA QQQ

		SINGLE PER PERSON B&B		DOUBLE FOR 2 PERSONS B&B			🛏 5
		MIN £	MAX £	MIN £	MAX £		🛁 5
		-	-	32.00	38.00		OPEN 3-10

GH | The Cedar Tree

27 Whitehall Road,
Rhos-on-Sea, Colwyn Bay,
Clwyd LL28 4HW
Tel: (0492) 545867

Comfortable friendly guest house 300 yards promenade, convenient Snowdonia, Llandudno, Conwy, Caernarfon, Bodnant Garden. Rail and coach stations 1 mile. Private parking. All bedrooms en-suite, centrally heated, tea/coffee facilities. Family rooms. Special rates children sharing parent's room. Separate tables. Attractive lounge with colour television. Fire Certificate. Weekly terms available. Non smoking.

		SINGLE PER PERSON B&B		DOUBLE FOR 2 PERSONS B&B			🛏 7
		MIN £	MAX £	MIN £	MAX £		🛁 7
		15.00	17.00	30.00	34.00		OPEN 1-12

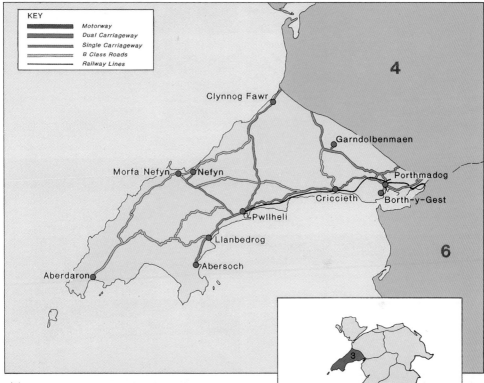

*T*he Llŷn Peninsula juts out into the sea from the mountains of Snowdonia. Its coastline is mostly dramatic, sometimes breathtakingly so – it's therefore no surprise to discover that Llŷn's shores have been declared an 'Area of Outstanding Natural Beauty'.

Llŷn's narrow finger of land points towards Ireland. And it's to the west that Llŷn sets its sights, for the peninsula retains a traditional, almost Celtic atmosphere. You sense it when exploring the wildly beautiful coastline, or when gazing across patchwork fields studded with old farmsteads.

It's a place where the culture is in tune with the landscape. Llŷn clings firmly to its Welsh ways, but it also has a long tradition of welcoming visitors. Criccieth, for example, is a charming little

castle-crowned resort which has been popular since Victorian times. Further along the south coast there's Pwllheli, another well-established resort close to the exciting new Starcoast World leisure complex. Abersoch, further south again, is a popular sailing centre, Aberdaron stands at the spectacular 'Land's End' of North Wales, and Nefyn, on the north coast, boasts an excellent choice of sandy beaches.

27

ABERSOCH
Map Ref: Ac5

Dinghy sailing and windsurfing centre with safe, sandy beaches. Superb coastal scenery with easy walks. Pony trekking, golf, fishing and sea trips. Llanengan's historic church nearby.

CLYNNOG FAWR
Map Ref: Ac5

'The Cathedral of Llŷn' is the name given to the church in this large village on the coastal plain. Ideal for quiet seaside holidays. Centre for walking and touring the peninsula. Museum of Welsh Country Life nearby.

CRICCIETH
Map Ref: Ad7

Ideal family resort with safe beach and seafront hotels. Romantic ruined castle on headland overlooking sea. Salmon and trout in nearby rivers and lakes. Festival of Music and the Arts in June. Village of Llanystumdwy with Lloyd George Museum nearby. ⇌

PORTHMADOG
Map Ref: Ae7

Harbour town and shopping centre named after William Madocks, who built mile-long Cob embankment. Steam narrow-gauge Ffestiniog Railway runs to Blaenau Ffestiniog, with its slate caverns. Also Welsh Highland Railway. Pottery, maritime museum, car museum. Portmeirion Italianate village and good beaches nearby. ⇌

PWLLHELI
Map Ref: Ac7

Small resort big in appeal to sailors; 200 craft are moored in its Outer Harbour. Promenade with excellent spacious beach, shopping, golf, leisure centre. River and sea fishing. Exciting Starcoast World, a major attraction, nearby. ⇌

Starcoast World, Pwllheli

Criccieth Castle

GH Llysfor Guest House

Abersoch,
nr. Pwllheli,
Gwynedd LL53 7AL
Tel: (0758) 712248

COMMENDED

A well established family run guest house our aim is to please and make your stay enjoyable. H&C, shaver points, tea/coffee facilities all bedrooms. Some en-suite. Comfortable dining room, separate lounge with TV, licensed. One minute to beach overlooking harbour, private parking, own grounds. Fire Certificate. Reduced rates for children. Enquiries Mrs. F. Hiorns.

	SINGLE PER PERSON B&B		DOUBLE FOR 2 PERSONS B&B			8
	MIN £ 13.50	MAX £ 17.50	MIN £ 27.00	MAX £ 35.00	OPEN 3-10	2

H Glyn y Coed Hotel

Porthmadog Road,
Criccieth,
Gwynedd LL52 0HL
Tel: (0766) 522870

HIGHLY COMMENDED

Lovely Victorian house overlooking sea, mountains, castle. Cosy bar, highly recommended home cooking, catering for most diets. En-suite bedrooms, with colour TV and tea-making facilities. One ground floor bedroom in annexe. Parking in grounds. Children and pets welcome. All centrally heated. AA/RAC. Credit cards. SAE brochure with pleasure.

	SINGLE PER PERSON B&B		DOUBLE FOR 2 PERSONS B&B			10
	MIN £ 19.00	MAX £ –	MIN £ 38.00	MAX £ –	OPEN 1-12	10

GH Craig-y-Mor Guest House

West Parade,
Criccieth,
Gwynedd LL52 0EN
Tel: (0766) 522830

HIGHLY COMMENDED

Having decided on North Wales, now contact us. Top value. We are on the West front of Criccieth. Ideally situated for touring Snowdonia, Meirionnydd and Llŷn Peninsula. Home cooked food served (including vegetarian). Comfortable single to family sized bedrooms with en-suite facilities, radio, television and full central heating. Children very welcome by B & A Williamson.

	SINGLE PER PERSON B&B		DOUBLE FOR 2 PERSONS B&B			7
	MIN £ 17.00	MAX £ 19.00	MIN £ 34.00	MAX £ 38.00	OPEN 3-10	7

GH Ty Draw Guest House

Lôn Sarn Bach,
Abersoch,
Gwynedd LL53 7EL
Tel: (0758) 712647

HIGHLY COMMENDED

Ty Draw guest house set in large gardens overlooking Cardigan Bay, and well known for its relaxed and happy atmosphere. 5 minutes easy stroll to village and beach. Excellent maps/guides provided for walks and all activities, plus our own "Good Food" guide for the area. Drying room available. Large, secure car and boat park. Self catering available. AA Recommended.

	SINGLE PER PERSON B&B		DOUBLE FOR 2 PERSONS B&B			7
	MIN £ 14.00	MAX £ 18.00	MIN £ 28.00	MAX £ 36.00	OPEN 4-9	–

H Min-y-Gaer Hotel

Porthmadog Road,
Criccieth,
Gwynedd LL52 0HP
Tel: (0766) 522151
Fax: (0766) 522151

COMMENDED

A pleasant licensed hotel, conveniently situated near the beach with delightful views of Criccieth Castle and the Cardigan Bay coastline. 10 comfortable rooms (9 en-suite) are all centrally heated with colour TV and tea/coffee making facilities. An ideal base for touring Snowdonia. Reduced rates for children. Car parking on premises. AA/RAC listed.

	SINGLE PER PERSON B&B		DOUBLE FOR 2 PERSONS B&B			10
	MIN £ 16.50	MAX £ 19.00	MIN £ 33.00	MAX £ 38.00	OPEN 3-10	9

PETS WELCOME

You'll see from the symbols that many places to stay welcome dogs and pets. Although some sections of beach may have restrictions, there are always adjacent areas - the promenade, for example, or quieter stretches of sands - where dogs can be exercised on and sometimes off leads. Please ask at a Tourist Information Centre for advice.

GH Plas Caer Pwsan

Clynnog Fawr,
nr. Caernarfon,
Gwynedd LL54 5PF
Tel: (0286) 660529

COMMENDED

Edwardian country house in historic village set in an acre of wooded garden overlooking Caernarfon Bay. Ideal for walking and touring in Llŷn Peninsula and Snowdonia National Park. Excellent home cooking. Comfortable lounge with log fire and TV. Central heating. Bathroom with shower; two separate toilets. All bedrooms with sea views H&C, tea making facilities. Private parking.

	SINGLE PER PERSON B&B		DOUBLE FOR 2 PERSONS B&B			3
	MIN £ –	MAX £ –	MIN £ 27.00	MAX £ –	OPEN 5-9	

Porthmadog harbour

FH	Bryn Efail Uchaf Farm

Garndolbenmaen,
Gwynedd LL51 9LQ
Tel: (076 675) 232

Traditional stonebuilt farmhouse on working beef and sheep farm. En-suite family room, twin bedroom, vanity units, shaver point, tea making facilities, lounge, colour TV. Enjoy a taste of farm life in comfortable surroundings and relaxed atmosphere. An excellent base for exploring the Llŷn Peninsula or Snowdonia. Criccieth only 5 miles, Porthmadog 6 miles, Caernarfon 12 miles.

		SINGLE PER PERSON B&B		DOUBLE FOR 2 PERSONS B&B			2
							1
		MIN £ 12.50	MAX £ 14.00	MIN £ 25.00	MAX £ 30.00	OPEN 4-10	

GH	Skellerns

35 Madoc Street,
Porthmadog,
Gwynedd LL49 9BU
Tel: (0766) 512843

[L]

'Friendly welcome for all. Good home cooking, heating in all rooms. Colour TV in all bedrooms, tea/coffee making facilities. Keys supplied. Special rates for children. Shops, buses, trains, cinema nearby. Ideally situated for visiting Portmeirion Italianate Village, the mountains of Snowdonia, the Ffestiniog Railway. Sandy beaches nearby. Open all year. Proprietor Mrs. R. Skellern.

		SINGLE PER PERSON B&B		DOUBLE FOR 2 PERSONS B&B			3
							-
		MIN £ 12.00	MAX £ 13.00	MIN £ 24.00	MAX £ 26.00	OPEN 1-12	

FH	Yoke House Farm

Pwllheli,
Gwynedd LL53 5TY
Tel: (0758) 612621

A beautiful wooded drive welcomes you to this Georgian farmhouse on a 310 acre working farm, where guests are invited to watch the milking, calf feeding etc. Tastefully furnished. One double, one family and one twin room, all with wash basins, shaver points and hospitality tray. Exciting nature trail organised for guests.

P		SINGLE PER PERSON B&B		DOUBLE FOR 2 PERSONS B&B			3
							-
		MIN £ 15.50	MAX £ 16.50	MIN £ 32.00	MAX £ 33.00	OPEN 4-10	

GH	The Oakleys Guest House

The Harbour,
Porthmadog,
Gwynedd LL49 9AS
Tel: (0766) 512482

[L]

Situated on the harbour in Porthmadog. An excellent base for visiting Snowdonia, Portmeirion and the beaches of Llŷn Peninsula, taking in Pwllheli, Abersoch and Criccieth. Fishing sea trout, salmon, golf course nearby. Spacious free car park. Comfortable lounge, informal holiday atmosphere. 2 bedrooms with showers, one bedroom en-suite. Electric blankets. Contact Mr. & Mrs. H.A. Biddle.

P	SINGLE PER PERSON B&B		DOUBLE FOR 2 PERSONS B&B			8
						1
	MIN £ 14.00	MAX £ 15.00	MIN £ 28.00	MAX £ 30.00	OPEN 3-10	

JOURNEY THROUGH WALES

Magnificently produced book, the ideal gift or memento.

High quality photographs with accompanying text take you on a tour of Wales.

Classic views of Wales's scenic mountains and coastline.

A complete pictorial record - everything from castles to craft workshops, picturesque villages to narrow-gauge railways.

£4.80 inc. p&p (see page 118)

Portmeirion Italianate Village

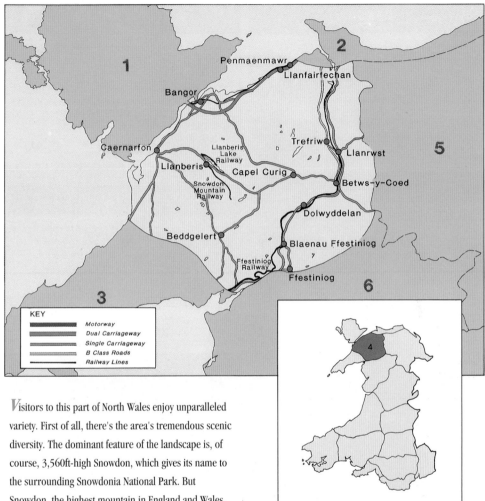

Visitors to this part of North Wales enjoy unparalleled variety. First of all, there's the area's tremendous scenic diversity. The dominant feature of the landscape is, of course, 3,560ft-high Snowdon, which gives its name to the surrounding Snowdonia National Park. But Snowdon, the highest mountain in England and Wales, is only a handful of miles from the Menai Strait and Conwy Bay. It's no exaggeration to say that you can be standing on Snowdon's summit in the morning, and in the afternoon enjoy a view of the Menai Strait from Bangor's beautifully renovated Victorian pier.

There's also a huge choice of places to visit. The list – a long one – includes Caernarfon Castle, the National Trust's Penrhyn Castle, Llanberis's narrow-gauge railways and museums, Beddgelert's Sygun Copper Mine, and two popular attractions at Blaenau Ffestiniog, the Llechwedd Slate Caverns and the Gloddfa Ganol Mountain Centre.

Variety is again the keynote when deciding where to stay. Choose the mountain resorts of Betws-y-Coed, Llanberis or Beddgelert. Or stay along the coast at Penmaenmawr, Llanfairfechan, Bangor or Caernarfon.

31

BANGOR
Map Ref: Ae3

Compact cathedral city of character overlooking the Menai Strait; gateway to Anglesey and Snowdonia's Ogwen Valley, with university college and 6th-century cathedral. Attractions include Theatr Gwynedd, Penrhyn Castle, museum and art gallery and an exquisitely renovated pier. Heated swimming pool, yachting and fishing. ⇝

BEDDGELERT
Map Ref: J8 Ae6

Village romantically set amid glorious mountain scenery, with Nant Gwynant Valley to the east and rocky Aberglaslyn Pass to the south. Snowdonia's grandeur all around; Wordsworth made a famous dawn ascent of Mount Snowdon from here. Marvellous walks; links with legendary dog named Gelert. Visit Sygun Copper Mine and Cae Du Farm Park, two nearby attractions.

BETWS-Y-COED
Map Ref: Bb6

Wooded village and popular mountain resort in picturesque setting where three rivers meet. Good hotels and guest houses, close to best mountain area of Snowdonia. Tumbling rivers and waterfalls emerge from a tangle of treetops. Trout fishing, craft shops, golf course, railway and motor museums, Snowdonia National Park Visitor Centre. Nature trails very popular with hikers. Swallow Falls a 'must'. ⇝

BLAENAU FFESTINIOG
Map Ref: Ba7

One-time centre of the Welsh slate industry, now a tourist town with two cavernous slate quarries - Llechwedd and Gloddfa Ganol - open to visitors. Narrow-gauge Ffestiniog Railway runs from Porthmadog. Nearby Stwlan Dam, part of hydro-electric scheme, reached through marvellous mountain scenery. Visitor centre explains how electricity is generated. ⇝

CAERNARFON
Map Ref: Ad4

Dominated by magnificent 13th-century castle, most famous of Wales's medieval fortresses. Many museums in castle, maritime museum in town. Caernarfon Air World at Dinas Dinlle, Segontium Roman Fort and Museum on hill above town. Popular sailing centre, old harbour, market square, Lloyd George statue. Holiday centre at gateway to Snowdonia. Parc Glynllifon nearby.

CAPEL CURIG
Map Ref: Ba6

Village ringed by Snowdonia's highest mountains, with accommodation and craft shops. Great favourite with climbers. Good walking and fishing.

Llynnau Mymbyr

FFESTINIOG
Map Ref: Dc1

Stands on a high bluff looking towards the sea. Neighbour of Blaenau Ffestiniog, with its slate caverns and narrow-gauge Ffestiniog Railway. The Cynfa Waterfalls spring from moorland above the town.

GARNDOLBENMAEN
Map Ref: Ad6

Small hillside village high above the sea, 4 miles from Criccieth. Nearby woollen mill to visit and excellent walking. Good base for touring Llŷn Peninsula and Snowdonia.

LLANBERIS
Map Ref: Ae4

Popular centre for walkers and climbers, least difficult (5 miles) walk to Snowdon summit starts here. For easy ride up take Snowdon Mountain Railway. Many things to see and do in this lively mountain town – Llanberis Lake Railway, slate industry museum, Power of Wales interpretive centre with unforgettable trip into the awesome tunnels of the Dinorwig Hydro-Electric Scheme, activity-packed Padarn Country Park, ancient Dolbadarn Castle, Bryn Brâs Castle at nearby Llanrug.

LLANFAIRFECHAN
Map Ref: Ba4

Quiet resort with good accommodation. Hill walking, pony trekking, mountain scenery, fishing. Safe swimming. Fine views across bay to Puffin Island and Anglesey. Golf course. Aber Waterfalls in hills near town. ⇌

LLANRWST
Map Ref: Bb6

Attractive town where the crystal-clear River Conwy runs through lush meadows; chief shopping centre of Upper Conwy Valley. Handsome bridge designed by Inigo Jones in 1636. Gwydir Park has bowling, putting and childrens playground. Good range of accommodation. Charming Gwydir Uchaf Chapel and scenic Llyn Gerionydd in woodlands above town. Gwydir Castle open to the public. Bodnant Garden 8 miles away. ⇌

PENMAENMAWR
Map Ref: Ba4

Small coast resort, now by-passed, below mighty headland which posed immense challenges to road and rail engineers. Sailing, water-skiing, safe swimming, golf. On edge of Snowdonia National Park. Medieval Conwy nearby. ⇌

TREFRIW
Map Ref: Bb5

Woollen mill village on west side of Conwy Valley, with Trefriw Wells Spa. Lakes at Llyn Geirionydd and Llyn Crafnant, both local beauty spots. Good walking country.

Llanberis Lake Railway

H	Bangor Pavilion Hotel & Restaurant

Junc. A5/A55, Llys Gwynt,
Llandegai, Bangor,
Gwynedd LL57 4BG
Tel: (0248) 370345
Fax: (0248) 355959
Reservations: freephone (0800) 515836

HIGHLY COMMENDED

34 bedroomed modern Hotel, situated in countryside with views of Snowdonia. Bedrooms have private bathroom, remote control colour TV with Sky, alarm clock, trouser press, hospitality tray, hairdryer. Delightful restaurant and bar. Ideal base for touring the North Wales resorts, Anglesey and Snowdonia. 23 miles from Holyhead.

P C	🍴	SINGLE PER PERSON B&B		DOUBLE FOR 2 PERSONS B&B		🛏 34
		MIN £	MAX £	MIN £	MAX £	🛁 34
✂	🍽		38.00		38.00	OPEN 1-12

FH	Goetre Isaf Farmhouse

Caernarfon Road,
Bangor, Gwynedd LL57 4DB
Tel: (0248) 364541
Fax: (0248) 364541

👑

Superb country situation with magnificent views. Although isolated Goetre Isaf is only 2m(3km) from Bangor mainline station. Ideal touring centre for the mountains of Snowdonia, Isle of Anglesey and the beaches of the Llŷn Peninsula. Imaginative farmhouse cooking. Special diets accommodated. Vegetarians welcome. All bedrooms with dial-phone facilities. Stabling by arrangement.

P	🐕	SINGLE PER PERSON B&B		DOUBLE FOR 2 PERSONS B&B		🛏 3
🛏	🍽	MIN £	MAX £	MIN £	MAX £	🛁 2
✂ 🐾		15.00		26.00		OPEN 1-12
TW						

GH	Plas Colwyn Guest House

Beddgelert,
Gwynedd LL55 4UY
Tel: (0766 86) 458
Fax: (0766 86) 514

👑 👑

Explore Snowdonia's beauty, then enjoy a warm welcome. Delicious, fresh, home cooked meals served in our intimate licensed restaurant, special diets and vegetarians welcome. All rooms with refreshment facilities. Guest's own lounge with log fire. Private parking and non smoking throughout. Families, walkers and pets welcome. Northern section organiser for Cambrian Way Walkers Association.

P C	🍴	SINGLE PER PERSON B&B		DOUBLE FOR 2 PERSONS B&B		🛏 6
		MIN £	MAX £	MIN £	MAX £	🛁 3
🐾	🍽	14.00	14.00	28.00	36.00	OPEN 1-12

GH	Yr-Elen

Llandegai,
Bangor,
Gwynedd LL57 4LD
Tel: (0248) 364591

👑

Set in beautiful countryside within walking distance of the historic National Trust property Penrhyn Castle. Views of Snowdonia and sea. Perfectly situated for visiting Anglesey, Gwynedd, Irish-sea crossing. Ground floor rooms with TV, teasmade, wash basins, adjacent bathroom for sole use of guests. Off road parking. A5122 convenient from A5/A55. Guest comments "exceptional value" "superior" "homely B & B".

P	🍴	SINGLE PER PERSON B&B		DOUBLE FOR 2 PERSONS B&B		🛏 2
🛏		MIN £	MAX £	MIN £	MAX £	🛁 –
🐾		–	25.00	30.00		OPEN 3-11

GH	Ael y Bryn

Caernarfon Road,
Beddgelert,
Gwynedd LL55 4UY
Tel: (0766 86) 310

👑

A detached house with beautiful views across the River Colwyn and Moel Hebog Mountain. All rooms have vanity units, with shaver points and tea/coffee making facilities. Packed lunches and good home cooked evening meals available. Vegetarians welcome. Ample free parking. A well situated family run house, ideal for holidays in the Snowdonia National Park.

P	🍴	SINGLE PER PERSON B&B		DOUBLE FOR 2 PERSONS B&B		🛏 3
🛏	🍽	MIN £	MAX £	MIN £	MAX £	🛁 –
✂		–	28.00	32.00		OPEN 1-12

H	Swallow Falls Hotel

Betws-y-Coed,
Gwynedd LL24 0DW
Tel: (0690) 710796
Fax: (0690) 710796

👑 👑

COMMENDED

Situated just outside the picturesque village of Betws-y-Coed in the beautiful Snowdonia National Park nestling between the mountains and the sea. The Hotel has 12 en-suite bedrooms with two licensed bars offering delicious home cooked food. Ideal base for walking and climbing! Don't miss our unique Welsh fudge pantry, see demonstrations and enjoy free tasting.

P	🐕	SINGLE PER PERSON B&B		DOUBLE FOR 2 PERSONS B&B		🛏 12
🛏	🍴	MIN £	MAX £	MIN £	MAX £	🛁 12
✂	🍽		30.00		35.00	OPEN 1-12
🐾						

GH	Rainbow Court

Pentir,
nr. Bangor,
Gwynedd LL57 4UY
Tel: (0248) 353099

👑 👑

Rainbow Court is situated in a quiet village with easy access to A5/55, golf, horse riding, water sports, mountain walking, beaches and many interesting attractions. Superb accommodation in a totally non smoking establishment. With a highly commended restaurant serving imaginative traditional and vegetarian cuisine, plus a selection of dreamy mouth watering gateaux.

P	🍴	SINGLE PER PERSON B&B		DOUBLE FOR 2 PERSONS B&B		🛏 2
🛏	✂	MIN £	MAX £	MIN £	MAX £	🛁 2
🐾	🍽	19.00	19.00	25.00	34.00	OPEN 1-12

GH	Colwyn

Beddgelert,
Gwynedd LL55
Tel: (0766 86) 276

👑 👑

Small riverside cottage guest house built about 1700. Warm, friendly and informal. Low beams and original open stone fireplace. En-suite bedrooms with fresh white linen. In the centre of an unspoilt and picturesque village at the foot of Snowdon, surrounded by wooded mountains, lakes and streams. Small inns, cafes and shops in village. Walkers (muddy boots) and wet dogs welcome. Midweek discount low season. B&B £16.00-£19.00. Booking is advisable. Also cottage sleeps two - £125.00-£195.00.

P	🐕	SINGLE PER PERSON B&B		DOUBLE FOR 2 PERSONS B&B		🛏 4
🛏	🍽	MIN £	MAX £	MIN £	MAX £	🛁 4
		16.00	19.00	–	–	OPEN 1-12

GH	Awelon

Plas Isa,
Llanrwst,
Gwynedd LL26 0EE
Tel: (0492) 640047

👑

Small guest house 150 yards from A470, situated on the outskirts of Llanrwst, 4 miles north of Betws-y-Coed. Quality bedrooms with H&C, teamakers, colour TV's and new beds. Private parking. Central for walking and touring Snowdonia. Clean friendly accommodation with a Welsh family. Providing substantial breakfasts and optional dinners. Guest lounge. Shower in bathroom. Pets welcome. SAE brochure.

P	🍴	SINGLE PER PERSON B&B		DOUBLE FOR 2 PERSONS B&B		🛏 3
🐾	🍽	MIN £	MAX £	MIN £	MAX £	🛁 –
		15.00	15.00	25.00	27.00	OPEN 3-11

GH | Bron Celyn Guest House

Llanrwst Road,
Betws-y-Coed,
Gwynedd LL24 0HD
Tel: (0690) 710333

HIGHLY COMMENDED

Enjoy traditional comfort and good food in a relaxed atmosphere. Situated within Snowdonia National Park overlooking picturesque Village of Betws-y-Coed. We provide the ideal base for walking, touring, exploring this interesting area. All rooms have colour TV and beverage trays. Most rooms en-suite. Hearty breakfasts, packed lunches, snacks, evening meals. Special diets by arrangement.

P 🏠 🛏		SINGLE PER PERSON B&B		DOUBLE FOR 2 PERSONS B&B		🛏 5
✂ 🍽 🪑		MIN £	MAX £	MIN £	MAX £	🛁 3
		16.00	17.00	35.00	38.00	OPEN 1-12

GH | Bryn Llewelyn

Holyhead Road,
Betws-y-Coed,
Gwynedd LL24 0BN
Tel: (0690) 710601

COMMENDED

Welcome to Betws-y-Coed. Bryn Llewelyn is an attractive stone house near the centre of this beautiful Snowdonia Village. Restaurants, shops, riverside and forest walks close to our doorstep. Within easy reach of mountains, castles, slate mines, beaches et. Comfortable rooms with central heating, tea/coffee, television on request. Guests' lounge. Ample car park. AA/RAC.

P 🏠 🛏		SINGLE PER PERSON B&B		DOUBLE FOR 2 PERSONS B&B		🛏 7
✂ 🪑		MIN £	MAX £	MIN £	MAX £	🛁 2
		13.00	15.50	26.00	35.00	OPEN 1-12

GH | The Ferns Guest House

Holyhead Road,
Betws-y-Coed,
Gwynedd LL24 0AN
Tel: (0690) 710587

HIGHLY COMMENDED

Keith and Teresa Roobottom welcome you to their delightful Victorian non-smoking guest house in the heart of Snowdonia. There are eight bedrooms each tastefully furnished. Each one has Colour TV, beverage tray, central heating and en-suite facilities. A delightful breakfast room where a varied menu awaits you. Car park a great asset in this popular village. AA QQQ. Recommended. RAC acclaimed.

P 🪑		SINGLE PER PERSON B&B		DOUBLE FOR 2 PERSONS B&B		🛏 8
🍴 🍽		MIN £	MAX £	MIN £	MAX £	🛁 7
♀		14.00	16.00	32.00	36.00	OPEN 1-12

GH | Bryn Afon

Pentre Felin,
Betws-y-Coed,
Gwynedd LL24 0BB
Tel: (0690) 710403

A beautiful Victorian stone house on the bank of the Llugwy River. Perfect area for walking, climbing, golf, fishing activities or relaxing days taking in the scenery. Comfortable rooms all with beverage tray, TV, centrally heated, some en-suite. All diets catered for. Own car park. Welcoming hosts Marion and Bill.

P 🪑		SINGLE PER PERSON B&B		DOUBLE FOR 2 PERSONS B&B		🛏 7
🛏 🪑		MIN £	MAX £	MIN £	MAX £	🛁 2
✂ 🍽		14.00	19.00	28.00	38.00	OPEN 1-12

GH | Coed-y-Fron

Vicarage Road,
Betws-y-Coed,
Gwynedd LL24 0AD
Tel: (0690) 710365

A lovely Victorian building in middle of village in quiet elevated position. Superb outlook over Betws-y-Coed which is the premier touring centre for Snowdonia. Dining room, lounge, 7 bedrooms, 3 en-suite, plus 2 extra bathrooms all H&C, central heating, tea and coffee, colour TV, parking, Fire Certificate held. Warm welcome awaits you.

P 🏠		SINGLE PER PERSON B&B		DOUBLE FOR 2 PERSONS B&B		🛏 7
🪑 🪑		MIN £	MAX £	MIN £	MAX £	🛁 3
		14.00	16.00	30.00	34.00	OPEN 1-12

GH | Fron Heulog Country House

Betws-y-Coed,
Gwynedd LL24 0BL
Tel: (0690) 710736

HIGHLY COMMENDED

"The Country House in the Village!" Friendly welcome from Jean and Peter Whittingham to their elegant Victorian stone built house in peaceful wooded riverside scenery. Snowdonia's ideal centre - tour, walk, relax. Excellent modernised accommodation - comfort; warmth; style. Bedrooms available with full en-suite bathrooms. "More home than Hotel". Croeso! Welcome!

P 🍽		SINGLE PER PERSON B&B		DOUBLE FOR 2 PERSONS B&B		🛏 4
🪑 🍽		MIN £	MAX £	MIN £	MAX £	🛁 4
🪑		14.00	19.00	24.00	38.00	OPEN 1-12

GH | Bryn Bella Guest House

Llanrwst Road,
Betws-y-Coed,
Gwynedd LL24 0HD
Tel: (0690) 710627

HIGHLY COMMENDED

Small Victorian guest house noted for its caring and friendly atmosphere. Situated in a quiet elevated position overlooking Betws-y-Coed. All rooms tastefully decorated, some en-suite. Beverage facilities and colour TV. Guest lounge and patio from which to enjoy spectacular views. Superb breakfast. Special vegetarian diets catered for. Pay phone. Ample private parking. Special weekly rates.

P		SINGLE PER PERSON B&B		DOUBLE FOR 2 PERSONS B&B		🛏 5
✂ 🪑		MIN £	MAX £	MIN £	MAX £	🛁 3
		14.00	14.00	30.00	36.00	OPEN 1-12

GH | Eirianfa Guest House

15-16 Castle Road,,
Dolwyddelan,
Gwynedd LL25 0NX
Tel: (06906) 360

APPROVED

Homely guest house in Snowdonia Park between Betws-y-Coed and Bleanau Ffestiniog. Relaxing guest lounge. Double or twin-bedded rooms. All en-suite, remote-controlled satellite colour television, tea making facilities. Excellent home cooked meals, laundry/drying services. Central for touring Snowdonia, coastal resorts, slate mines etc. Ideal for trekking, hiking, climbing, fishing. Reductions: short breaks, weekly stay. Brochure awaiting.

🛏 🪑		SINGLE PER PERSON B&B		DOUBLE FOR 2 PERSONS B&B		🛏 3
✂ 🍽		MIN £	MAX £	MIN £	MAX £	🛁 3
🪑		-	-	24.00	28.00	OPEN 1-12

GH | Glan Llugwy Guest House

Holyhead Road,
Betws-y-Coed,
Gwynedd LL24 0BN
Tel: (0690) 710592

COMMENDED

Small friendly guest house overlooking River Llugwy and Gwydr Forest. Beautiful walking country all round. Central for Snowdonia and coast. All rooms central heating, H&C, tea/coffee making facilities. Colour TV, guest's lounge. Private parking. Fire certificate held. Family, double, twin and single rooms available. Showers. A warm welcome awaits you. Good fishing locally.

P 🏠		SINGLE PER PERSON B&B		DOUBLE FOR 2 PERSONS B&B		🛏 5
🪑		MIN £	MAX £	MIN £	MAX £	🛁 -
		13.50	15.00	23.00	26.00	OPEN 1-12

GH | Mount Pleasant

Betws-y-Coed,
Gwynedd LL24 0BN
Tel: (0690) 710502

[L]

Pleasant comfortable guest house, situated in the scenic village of Betws-y-Coed. Pretty centrally heated rooms with H&C, colour televisions, tea/coffee facilities. Woodland views vegetarians/vegans catered for. Children welcome. An ideal place to start and end your day. Phone to make your booking or call in on your travels for a friendly welcome.

P	♻	SINGLE PER PERSON B&B		DOUBLE FOR 2 PERSONS B&B		🛏	4
🛏	🐾						–
✂	🏠	MIN £	MAX £	MIN £	MAX £	OPEN	
		13.00	–	26.00	34.00	1-12	

FH | Maes Gwyn Farmhouse

Pentrefoelas,
Betws-y-Coed,
Gwynedd LL24 0LR
Tel: (0690) 770668

[L]
HIGHLY COMMENDED

17th Century farmhouse with oak beams and panelling coal/log fire. One double and one family room. Both with Hot and cold with tea/coffee facilities. Good touring centre for North Wales which includes famous Betws-y-Coed, pony trekking, woollen mills, slate mines, water falls, 40 minutes drive to Snowdonia. Also seaside towns of Llandudno, Rhyl, Colwyn Bay.

P	🐾	SINGLE PER PERSON B&B		DOUBLE FOR 2 PERSONS B&B		🛏	2
							–
		MIN £	MAX £	MIN £	MAX £	OPEN	
		12.50	13.50	25.00	27.00	4-11	

GH | Afallon

Manod Road,
Blaenau Ffestiniog,
Gwynedd LL41 4AE
Tel: (0766) 830468

👑
HIGHLY COMMENDED

Situated in Snowdonia National Park. Family run guest house, good food, clean homely accommodation. Wash basins, shaver point, colour TV, tea/coffee facilities. Central heating all rooms. Separate shower, bathroom, toilet. Slate mines, narrow gauge Railway, Castles, beaches, within easy reach. Dinner by arrangement. Children reduced rates. Dogs by arrangement. A Welsh welcome awaits all our guests. Mrs Griffiths.

P	🐾	SINGLE PER PERSON B&B		DOUBLE FOR 2 PERSONS B&B		🛏	3
C	🏠						–
✂	🍴	MIN £	MAX £	MIN £	MAX £	OPEN	
♨		12.00	14.00	24.00	–	1-12	

GH | Ty'n-y-Celyn House

Llanrwst Road, Betws-y-Coed,
Gwynedd LL24 0HD
Tel: (0690) 710202
Fax: (0690) 710800

👑 👑
HIGHLY COMMENDED

Ty'n-y-Celyn House is situated in a quiet position in Snowdonia National Park and overlooking the picturesque village. It is superbly and tastefully re-furnished for comfort and relaxation. there are beautiful views of the Llugwy Valley, surrounding mountains and the Conwy and Llugwy rivers. Robust breakfast and warm welcome awaiting from Maureen and Clive Muskus.

P	🐾	SINGLE PER PERSON B&B		DOUBLE FOR 2 PERSONS B&B		🛏	8
🛏	🍷						8
✂	🏠	MIN £	MAX £	MIN £	MAX £	OPEN	
♨	🍴	–	–	38.00	–	1-12	

FH | Ty Coch Farm & Trekking Centre

Penmachno,
Betws-y-Coed,
Gwynedd LL25 0HJ
Tel: (0690) 760248

👑 👑
APPROVED

Set in lovely valley in hills two miles from village, six miles from Betws-y-Coed. Good centre for touring, walking, fishing, Snowdon narrow gauge railways, woollen mills, waterfalls, trekking available but optional. Short drive to beaches. Many recommendations and return visits. Guests made very welcome. Good food with very comfortable accommodation. Full Fire Certificate.

P	🐾	SINGLE PER PERSON B&B		DOUBLE FOR 2 PERSONS B&B		🛏	4
✂	🏠						4
♨	🍴	MIN £	MAX £	MIN £	MAX £	OPEN	
TW		–	–	28.00	30.00	1-12	

GH | Gwynfryn

Gellilydan,
Blaenau Ffestiniog,
Gwynedd LL41 4EA
Tel: (0766685) 225

👑

Friendly welcome assured. Quiet situation between Ffestiniog and Porthmadog. Detached house of character off A470, village of Gellilydan. Slate mines, Ffestiniog railway, castles, walks, beaches within easy reach. Many recommendations and return visits. One double, one family/twin bedroom with wash basins, shaver points, tea/coffee facilities. Central heating, TV lounge. Good food. Homely Welsh welcome. Children welcome.

P	🏠	SINGLE PER PERSON B&B		DOUBLE FOR 2 PERSONS B&B		🛏	2
♨	🍴	MIN £	MAX £	MIN £	MAX £	OPEN	–
		12.00	13.00	24.00	26.00	1-11	

GH | Tan-y-Cyrau

Betws-y-Coed,
Gwynedd LL24 0BL
Tel: (0690) 710653

👑
HIGHLY COMMENDED

Peace and quiet and glorious views are what to expect at Tan-y-Cyrau. An elevated unique alpine style house situated on a private forestry road, only 5 minutes from village. Superb walks from House. Delightful rooms. Two have own wc. All have colour TV, heating, washbasins, tea/coffee facilities, lovely secluded gardens. Non smokers only. Good parking.

P	🏠	SINGLE PER PERSON B&B		DOUBLE FOR 2 PERSONS B&B		🛏	3
♨	🍴	MIN £	MAX £	MIN £	MAX £	OPEN	–
		14.00	15.00	25.00	32.00	1-12	

FH | Tyddyn Gethin Farm

Penmachno,
Betws-y-Coed,
Gwynedd LL24 0PS
Tel: (0690) 760392

👑 👑

Tyddyn Gethin farm is 200 yards off B406, 3 ½ miles from Betws-y-Coed and ½ mile from Penmachno, lovely views from farmhouse. Clean and comfortable, good home cooking. Ideal for touring, very central. Dining room, separate tables, 2 sitting rooms, colour TV in one room. Bathroom with shower, hot and cold in bedrooms, shaver points, shower room. Ample parking. Always a warm welcome here.

		SINGLE PER PERSON B&B		DOUBLE FOR 2 PERSONS B&B		🛏	3
		MIN £	MAX £	MIN £	MAX £	OPEN	–
		12.50	14.00	24.00	28.00	1-12	

H | Gorffwysfa Private Hotel

St David's Road,
Caernarfon,
Gwynedd LL55 1BH
Tel: (0286) 672647

👑 👑

A warm welcome awaits at our Victorian licensed hotel. Situated in a quiet area, yet close to all amenities. All rooms are en-suite with radio, colour TV, drinks facilities. Comfortable spacious accommodation throughout. Traditional breakfast and dinner menus. Ideal touring base to explore Snowdonia, Anglesey and the coast. Families welcome. Private parking. Send for brochure.

P	🐾	SINGLE PER PERSON B&B		DOUBLE FOR 2 PERSONS B&B		🛏	6
🛏	🍷						6
✂	🏠	MIN £	MAX £	MIN £	MAX £	OPEN	
♨	🍴	18.00	–	30.00	34.00	1-12	

H | Menai Bank Hotel

North Road, Caernarfon,
Gwynedd LL55 1BD
Tel: (0286) 673297
Fax: (0286) 673297

HIGHLY COMMENDED

*Family owned period Hotel with original features. Extensive sea views. Close castle and Snowdonia. Tastefully decorated bedrooms. Tea makers, colour televisions, clock radios, ground floor bedroom. Attractive restaurant, varied menu, bar, residents lounge with sea views, pool table. Hotel car park. Flower gardens, Access, Visa, Amex. Short breaks. En-suite supplement. AA/RAC **. Brochure.*

	SINGLE PER PERSON B&B		DOUBLE FOR 2 PERSONS B&B		15
					10
	MIN £ 19.00	MAX £ 19.00	MIN £ 28.00	MAX £ 35.00	OPEN 1-11

GH | Bryn Helyg Guest House

24 Segontium Terrace,
Caernarfon,
Gwynedd LL55 2PH
Tel: (0286) 676549

Small quality guest house near shops and mountains, views overlooking river, harbour and castle. Colour TV, Tea making facilities. Comfortable furnishings. Spacious rooms. Non smoking. Five miles from Snowdon.

	SINGLE PER PERSON B&B		DOUBLE FOR 2 PERSONS B&B		3
					-
	MIN £ 15.00	MAX £ 15.00	MIN £ 26.00	MAX £ 30.00	OPEN 1-12

GH | Tyn Llwyn Cottage

Llanllyfni,
Caernarfon,
Gwynedd LL54 6RP
Tel: (0286) 881526

Situated on a quiet country road. Half a mile off the A487 Caernarfon to Porthmadog Road. Beautiful Welsh stone cottage with exposed beams and attractive garden. Ideal for walking, bird watching, castles, beach. We have two en-suite bedrooms, one ground floor and one bedroom with your own private bathroom. All with TV, tea/coffee made when requested.

	SINGLE PER PERSON B&B		DOUBLE FOR 2 PERSONS B&B		3
					2
	MIN £ -	MAX £ -	MIN £ 34.00	MAX £ 36.00	OPEN 3-10

H | Menai View Hotel

North Road, Caernarfon,
Gwynedd LL55 1BD
Tel: (0286) 674602

COMMENDED

A warm welcome awaits you at this AA/RAC Victorian licensed town house. Overlooking beautiful Menai Strait. All rooms central heating, colour TV, tea/coffee facilities, many rooms have sea views, some en-suite. Ground floor en-suite bedroom. Many original features, lounge bar has extensive sea views. Close to castle, town centre. Excellent central base for castles, mountains, lakes and railways of Snowdonia, beaches on the Llŷn and Isle of Anglesey. Many attractions open all year.

	SINGLE PER PERSON B&B		DOUBLE FOR 2 PERSONS B&B		8
					4
	MIN £ 15.00	MAX £ -	MIN £ 25.00	MAX £ -	OPEN 1-12

GH | Caer Siddi

Llanddeiniolen,
Caernarfon,
Gwynedd LL55 3AD
Tel: (0248) 670462

AWARD | HIGHLY COMMENDED

Former Georgian vicarage. Peaceful rural setting surrounded by trees, glorious views to Snowdon, Caernarfon Bay and the rivals. Ideally situated for Gwynedd attractions, 4 miles to Caernarfon. Fully modernised warm spacious accommodation. TV lounge. Children price reductions. Farmhouse breakfast, 3 course evening meals, home baking, tea/coffee making facilities. Fire Certificate. Private parking area. Private walled garden.

	SINGLE PER PERSON B&B		DOUBLE FOR 2 PERSONS B&B		2
					-
	MIN £ 14.00	MAX £ -	MIN £ 28.00	MAX £ -	OPEN 1-12

GH | The White House

Llanfaglan,
Caernarfon,
Gwynedd LL54 5RA
Tel: (0286) 673003

HIGHLY COMMENDED

A large quietly situated country house in own grounds, magnificent views to sea and mountains. All rooms have either bathrooms en-suite or private facilities, colour TV, tea/coffee makers. Two bedrooms ground floor. Guests welcome to use lounge, outdoor pool and gardens. Ideally situated for ornithologists, walkers, windsurfing, golf and Welsh castles.

	SINGLE PER PERSON B&B		DOUBLE FOR 2 PERSONS B&B		5
					3
	MIN £ 16.50	MAX £ 18.50	MIN £ 33.00	MAX £ 37.00	OPEN 1-11

H | Prince of Wales Hotel

Bangor Street,
Caernarfon,
Gwynedd LL55 1AR
Tel: (0286) 673367

21 comfortable bedrooms, many en-suite. All with television and hospitality tray. Pensioner reductions available. Renowned restaurant featuring traditional home cooking. Vegetarians catered for. Two friendly bars. Live entertainment every Sunday. Ideally located near Caernarfon's famous castle. Good base for touring Snowdonia, only 7 miles to Snowdon, 40 minutes driving to Holyhead and Irish ferries.

	SINGLE PER PERSON B&B		DOUBLE FOR 2 PERSONS B&B		21
					13
	MIN £ 17.50	MAX £ -	MIN £ 35.00	MAX £ -	OPEN 1-12

GH | Gwynant

Stryd Ganol, Saron,
Bethel, nr. Caernarfon,
Gwynedd LL55 1YP
Tel: (0248) 670029

Gwynant in the village of Bethel is beautifully placed as a base from which to enjoy a holiday in Snowdonia, Anglesey and North Wales. Comfortable accommodation, 2 bedrooms with bathroom en-suite. Adequate parking facilities. Walking, climbing, sailing, canoeing, fishing, bird watching, castles, museums, craft centres, horse riding, all within reasonable travelling distance.

	SINGLE PER PERSON B&B		DOUBLE FOR 2 PERSONS B&B		4
					2
	MIN £ 15.00	MAX £ 19.00	MIN £ 30.00	MAX £ 38.00	OPEN 1-12

FH | Pengwern Farm

Saron, Llanwnda,
Caernarfon,
Gwynedd LL54 5UH
Tel: (0286) 830717

 AWARD | DE LUXE

Charming spacious farm house of character set in 130 acres of land. Beautifully situated between mountains and sea. Well appointed bedrooms all with en-suite or private facilities. The land runs down to Foryd Bay and is noted for its bird life. Situated 3 miles from Dinas Dinlle beach. Jane Rowlands has a cookery diploma and provides all the excellent meals. Excellent access.

	SINGLE PER PERSON B&B		DOUBLE FOR 2 PERSONS B&B		3
					3
	MIN £ 19.00	MAX £ 19.00	MIN £ 30.00	MAX £ 38.00	OPEN 2-11

GH	Bryn Glo

Capel Curig,
Betws-y-Coed,
Gwynedd LL24 0DT
Tel: (06904) 215/312

Warm welcome in family run refurbished Welsh cottage. Situated in Snowdonia National Park on A5 Holyhead Road. Ideal for walking, climbing, canoeing, cycling, sketching, photography, etc. Fresh home cooked meals, Welsh teas, packed lunches, vegetarian and special diets catered for.

P ▥ ▤ ⚲ 🍴 TW	SINGLE PER PERSON B&B		DOUBLE FOR 2 PERSONS B&B		🛏 3 🛁 2
	MIN £ 15.00	MAX £ 17.00	MIN £ 27.00	MAX £ 30.00	OPEN 1-12

GH	Tŷ Clwb

The Square,
Ffestiniog,
Gwynedd LL41 4LS
Tel: (0766 76) 2658

HIGHLY COMMENDED

Set amidst mountains, wooded valleys and close to the coast, Tŷ Clwb offers quality accommodation in a peaceful village. A tastefully modernised 18th century stone guest house, all bedrooms are en-suite with mountain views. Large, comfortable lounge with TV and south facing balcony overlooking beautiful countryside. A warm welcome and high standards guaranteed.

⚲ ▥ ⚲	SINGLE PER PERSON B&B		DOUBLE FOR 2 PERSONS B&B		🛏 3 🛁 3
	MIN £ –	MAX £ –	MIN £ 28.00	MAX £ 36.00	OPEN 1-12

H	Glyn Afon Hotel

High Street, Llanberis,
Gwynedd LL55 4HA
Tel: (0286) 872528
Fax: (0286) 872528

8 bedroomed family run Hotel centrally situated Llanberis village, 10 minutes Mount Snowdon and its railway. Twin, double, family accommodation, some en-suite. All with television, tea/coffee facilities. Central heating. Residents lounge. Parking. Table d'hôte, à la carte menu. Convenient Holyhead Ferry. Central for touring all North Wales attractions.

P ⚲ ⚲ ▥	SINGLE PER PERSON B&B		DOUBLE FOR 2 PERSONS B&B		🛏 8 🛁 2
	MIN £ 14.00	MAX £ 16.00	MIN £ 26.00	MAX £ 34.00	OPEN 1-12

GH	Llugwy Guest House

Capel Curig,
Betws-y-Coed,
Gwynedd LL24 0ES
Tel: (06904) 218

COMMENDED

Established over 100 years. Located in centre of village five miles from Snowdon. Ideal for walking, climbing, fishing, boating, beaches, small trains, castles, ski slope. Two public lounges, one with TV. Beamed dining room, central heating, tea/coffee making facilities in bedrooms, superb mountain views. Small parties specially catered for. Drying room available.

P ⚲ ⚲ 🍴	SINGLE PER PERSON B&B		DOUBLE FOR 2 PERSONS B&B		🛏 6 🛁 –
	MIN £ 15.50	MAX £ 16.50	MIN £ 27.00	MAX £ 30.00	OPEN 1-12

H	Alpine Lodge Hotel

1 High Street, Llanberis,
Caernarfon,
Gwynedd LL55 4EN
Tel: (0286) 870294

COMMENDED

Situated at the quieter Caernarfon end of Llanberis, overlooking the lake and mountains. All the rooms have full size private bathrooms, colour televisions and tea and coffee making facilities. Alpine Lodge Hotel offers a wide choice of main courses for breakfast. A large private car park and an informal friendly welcome.

P ⚲ ▥	SINGLE PER PERSON B&B		DOUBLE FOR 2 PERSONS B&B		🛏 6 🛁 6
	MIN £ –	MAX £ –	MIN £ 35.00	MAX £ –	OPEN 1-12

H	Gwynedd Hotel

High Street,
Llanberis, Snowdonia,
Gwynedd LL55 4SU
Tel: (0286) 870203
Fax: (0286) 870203

Set at the foot of Snowdon and opposite Lake Padarn with its magnificent surroundings. The Gwynedd is an ideal base for touring and walking. There are eleven fully equipped en-suite guest rooms. the lounge bar provides a relaxing setting to enjoy a drink or bar meals. Alternatively the elegant restaurant provides a comprehensive à la carte menu.

▥ ⚲ ▥ TW 🍴	SINGLE PER PERSON B&B		DOUBLE FOR 2 PERSONS B&B		🛏 11 🛁 10
	MIN £ 16.00	MAX £ 19.00	MIN £ 32.00	MAX £ 38.00	OPEN 1-12

AWARD-WINNING GUEST HOUSES AND FARMHOUSES

AWARD

Look out for the Wales Tourist Board Award on the pages of this brochure. Award-winners offer extra-special standards of comfort, furnishings and surroundings. They're as good as many a hotel. And proprietors will have completed college training in tourism.

H	Dolafon Hotel

High Street,
Llanberis,
Gwynedd LL55 4SU
Tel: (0286) 870993

COMMENDED

A pleasant family hotel in its own grounds. Near foot route to Snowdon. Seven en-suite, two family rooms with colour TV and tea/coffee all rooms. Comfortable lounge, residents bar. Rambling, climbing groups welcome. An ideal base for touring or exploring our lakes and local amenities including lakeside and mountain railways.

P ⚲ ⚲ 🍴	SINGLE PER PERSON B&B		DOUBLE FOR 2 PERSONS B&B		🛏 9 🛁 7
	MIN £ 14.50	MAX £ 18.00	MIN £ 29.00	MAX £ 36.00	OPEN 1-12

GH	Cerrig Drudion

Nant Peris,
Caernarfon,
Gwynedd LL55 4UN
Tel: (0286) 871327

Situated in the centre of Snowdonia, at the foot of Llanberis Pass. An ideal base for hill walking and central for touring North Wales. Cerrig Drudion is an old farmhouse standing in a quiet location off the main road, in its own grounds. Among farmland and lovely mountain views. 5 minutes drive from Llanberis.

P ▥	SINGLE PER PERSON B&B		DOUBLE FOR 2 PERSONS B&B		🛏 3 🛁 –
	MIN £ 14.50	MAX £ 14.50	MIN £ 29.00	MAX £ 29.00	OPEN 1-12

GH — Crochendy

2 Mur Mawr,
Llanberis,
Gwynedd LL55 4SU
Tel: (0286) 870700

Small guest house with excellent facilities in secluded setting within Snowdonia National Park. Delightful garden overlooking Padarn Lake and Llanberis village. Easy access to many places of interest and recreational activities. Personal service by proprietors Jane and Peter Richards. Food is homecooked where possible. Diets taken care of, also vegetarian. A friendly welcome to all.

SINGLE PER PERSON B&B		DOUBLE FOR 2 PERSONS B&B			3
MIN £	MAX £	MIN £	MAX £	OPEN	1
–	–	26.00	36.00	2-11	

GH — Bron Eirian

Town Hill,
Llanrwst,
Gwynedd LL26 0NF
Tel: (0492) 641741

HIGHLY COMMENDED

An attractive Victorian country house in a peaceful elevated position overlooking the Conwy Valley and Snowdonia Mountains. Bron Eirian offers warm comfy rooms, all en-suite. Tastefully furnished having tea making facilities and TV's. Hearty breakfast. Dinner on request. Convenient to Bodnant Garden, Betws-y-Coed, Gwydyr Forest and coast. Station nearby. Be assured of a warm welcome.

SINGLE PER PERSON B&B		DOUBLE FOR 2 PERSONS B&B			3
MIN £	MAX £	MIN £	MAX £	OPEN	3
19.00	–	32.00	36.00	1-12	

H — Princes Arms Hotel

Trefriw,
Gwynedd LL27 0JP
Tel: (0492) 640592
Fax: (0492) 640592

Quiet location with easy access to all of Snowdonia's attractions. En-suite rooms with private lounge. Beautiful views, full facilities including TV, beverages, telephone, drying room, central heating. Enviable reputation for restaurant and bar meals. Real ales, pack lunches, attentive friendly service. Special break packages available. A rather nice place to find.

SINGLE PER PERSON B&B		DOUBLE FOR 2 PERSONS B&B			9
MIN £	MAX £	MIN £	MAX £	OPEN	6
17.50	19.00	35.00	38.00	1-12	

GH — Plas Heulog

Llanfairfechan,
Gwynedd LL33 0HA
Tel: (0248) 680019
Central Res: 061 224 2855

A cosy and welcoming country house nestling in the wooded foothills of Snowdonia, with breathtaking views across the Menai Strait to Anglesey. It is set in its own beautiful grounds and accommodation is in main house or adjacent chalets with en-suite facilities. Outdoor enthusiasts welcome. Guided walks available. Boot/drying room.

SINGLE PER PERSON B&B		DOUBLE FOR 2 PERSONS B&B			23
MIN £	MAX £	MIN £	MAX £	OPEN	10
10.00	–	20.00	–	1-12	

GH — The White Cottage

Maenan (A470),
Llanrwst,
Gwynedd LL26 0UL
Tel: (0492) 640346

Situated in the beautiful Conwy Valley, 2 miles north of Llanrwst. All rooms have open views, H&C and central heating. Comfortable lounge with colour TV. Bathroom with shower (toilet separate). Relax in lovely garden or stroll in woodland dells. Two good hotels close by for evening meals. Bodnant Garden and many local attractions within easy reach.

SINGLE PER PERSON B&B		DOUBLE FOR 2 PERSONS B&B			3
MIN £	MAX £	MIN £	MAX £	OPEN	–
14.00	15.00	24.00	26.00	3-11	

GH — Crafnant Guest House

Trefriw,
Gwynedd LL27 0JH
Tel: (0492) 640809

COMMENDED

This 100 year old farmhouse, now refurbished as guest house, nestles in the pretty village of Trefriw beneath some of the most beautiful lakes and scenery of Snowdonia. Some en-suite facilities. Walkers welcome with reduced rates for children, groups and winter breaks. Choose from our varied menu for a perfect end to your day.

SINGLE PER PERSON B&B		DOUBLE FOR 2 PERSONS B&B			6
MIN £	MAX £	MIN £	MAX £	OPEN	–
15.00	17.50	26.00	32.00	1-12	

GH — The Towers

Promenade,
Llanfairfechan,
Gwynedd LL33 0DA
Tel: (0248) 680012

Magnificent old manor house situated on sea front below northern slopes of Snowdonia. Superb views across Menai Strait to Anglesey. Standing in its own lawned grounds with large car park. All major beauty spots of Snowdonia close at hand. Ideal centre for touring. All rooms have private facilities and drink makers available. Mountaineering available.

SINGLE PER PERSON B&B		DOUBLE FOR 2 PERSONS B&B			3
MIN £	MAX £	MIN £	MAX £	OPEN	3
16.00	19.00	32.00	38.00	1-12	

GH — Cynlas

Fernbrook Road,
Penmaenmawr,
Gwynedd LL34 6ED
Tel: (0492) 623491

AWAITING GRADING

"Welcome to Cynlas" comfortable accommodation. Home cooking. Free tea/coffee facilities all rooms. One twin, one family and one double en-suite. Sealmountain views. We are noted for cleanliness, good food and friendliness. Enclosed parking. A perfect base for all North Wales walking, golf. 3 miles safe & sandy beach. Situated edge of Snowdonia National Park. Pleasant gardens. Horse riding nearby. Children welcome.

SINGLE PER PERSON B&B		DOUBLE FOR 2 PERSONS B&B			3
MIN £	MAX £	MIN £	MAX £	OPEN	1
15.00	15.00	30.00	30.00	4-9	

GH — Llys Caradog Guest House

Trefriw,
Gwynedd LL27 0RQ
Tel: (0492) 640919

A friendly welcome awaits you in our large Welsh stone guest house and tea room. Central heating, Aga cooking, TV lounge. Tea making, H&C in all rooms. Showers. Children welcome. Many beautiful walks to nearby lakes and mountains. Coast within easy reach. Brochure available. Contact Alan and Ann Jones.

SINGLE PER PERSON B&B		DOUBLE FOR 2 PERSONS B&B			4
MIN £	MAX £	MIN £	MAX £	OPEN	–
12.00	15.00	24.00	30.00	1-12	

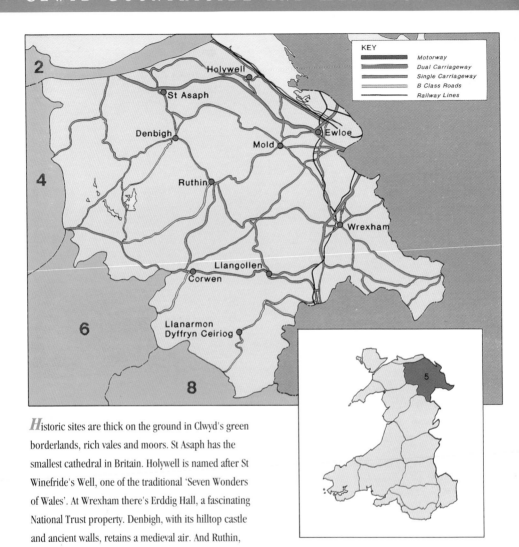

KEY

	Motorway
	Dual Carriageway
	Single Carriageway
	B Class Roads
	Railway Lines

*H*istoric sites are thick on the ground in Clwyd's green borderlands, rich vales and moors. St Asaph has the smallest cathedral in Britain. Holywell is named after St Winefride's Well, one of the traditional 'Seven Wonders of Wales'. At Wrexham there's Erddig Hall, a fascinating National Trust property. Denbigh, with its hilltop castle and ancient walls, retains a medieval air. And Ruthin, where Tudor and Georgian influences rub shoulder, is an architectural gem.

That's by no means all. Opulent Bodelwyddan Castle houses works from the National Portrait Gallery. The Clywedog Valley Heritage Park at Wrexham preserves sites of rural and industrial heritage. And Llangollen, home of the celebrated International Musical Eisteddfod, is overlooked by Castell Dinas Brân.

Part of the Offa's Dyke Footpath runs north from Llangollen to the rounded summits of the Clwydian Range, an 'Area of Outstanding Natural Beauty'. This range commands marvellous views across much of Clwyd – below into the rich farming country of the verdant Vale of Clwyd, westwards to the lakes, moors and forests of the Hiraethog Moorlands, and southwards to the Berwyn Mountains.

CORWEN
Map Ref: Be7

Pleasant market town in Vale of Edeyrnion. Livestock market held regularly. Fishing in River Dee, swimming pool, good walks. Well-located touring centre for Snowdonia and border country.

DENBIGH
Map Ref: Be5

Castled town in Vale of Clwyd with much historic interest. Friary and museum. Pony trekking, riding, fishing, golf, tennis and bowls. Indoor heated swimming pool. Centrally located for enjoying the rolling hills of Clwyd, a rich farming area full of small, attractive villages.

HOLYWELL
Map Ref: Cb4

Place of pilgrimage for centuries, the 'Lourdes of Wales' with St Winefride's Holy Well. Remains of Basingwerk Abbey (1131) nearby. Leisure centre with swimming pools. Greenfield Valley Heritage Park.

LLANGOLLEN
Map Ref: Ec1

Romantic town on River Dee, famous for its International Musical Eisteddfod; singers and dancers from all over the world come here every July. The town's many attractions include a canal museum, pottery, weavers, ECTARC European Centre for Traditional and Regional Cultures, and a standard-gauge steam railway. Plas Newydd (home of 'Ladies of Llangollen' fame) is nearby. Valle Crucis Abbey is 2 miles away in a superb setting and ruined Castell Dinas Brân overlooks the town. Browse throught the town's little shops; stand on its 14th-century stone bridge; cruise along the canal. Golf course and wonderful walking in surrounding countryside.

MOLD
Map Ref: Cb5

County town of Clwyd, on edge of Clwydian Range. Theatr Clwyd offers wide range of entertainment. Visit Daniel Owen Centre memorial to 'the Dickens of Wales'. Golf course. Loggerheads Country Park in wooded setting to the south-west.

RUTHIN
Map Ref: Ca6

Attractive and historic market town noted for its fine architecture; curfew is still rung nightly! Many captivating old buildings. Medieval banquets in Ruthin Castle. Ancient St Peter's Church has beautiful gates and carved panels. Good range of small shops; craft centre with workshops. Ideal base for Vale of Clwyd.

ST ASAPH
Map Ref: Be4

City with the smallest cathedral in Britain, scene of the annual North Wales Music Festival. Prehistoric Cefn Caves nearby. Pleasantly sited on River Elwy in verdant Vale of Clwyd. Three important historic sites on doorstep - medieval Rhuddlan Castle, Bodelwyddan Castle (with noted art collection) and Bodrhyddan Hall.

WREXHAM
Map Ref: Cc6

Busy industrial and commercial town, gateway to North Wales. St Giles's Church has graceful tower and altar piece given by Elihu Yale of Yale University fame (his tomb is in the churchyard). Visit Erddig Hall, an unusual country house on outskirts and the Clywedog Valley Heritage Park. Good shopping and excellent little heritage centre. Industrial museum at neighbouring Bersham. Art gallery, swimming pool, golf. ⇌

H | Corwen Court Private Hotel

London Road,
Corwen,
Clwyd LL21 0DP
Tel: (0490) 412854

Situated on the A5. Converted old police station and courthouse. Six prisoners' cells now single bedrooms, H&C in each, three only sharing a bathroom. Double bedrooms have bathroom en-suite. Comfortable lounge. Colour TV. Dining room with separate tables where magistrates once presided. Centrally heated. Fire Certificate. AA listed. Convenient base for touring North Wales.

	SINGLE PER PERSON B&B		DOUBLE FOR 2 PERSONS B&B		🛏 10
					4
	MIN £	MAX £	MIN £	MAX £	OPEN
	13.00	14.00	26.00	28.00	3-11

FH | College Farm

Peniel, Denbigh,
Clwyd LL16 4TT
Tel: (0745) 70276

HIGHLY COMMENDED

College Farm is situated in a peaceful and unspoilt area of Clwyd yet only 3 miles from Denbigh, just off the B4501 and 16 miles from the coast. Home cooked food served using own produce when available. Tastefully decorated with tea/coffee in bedrooms. A warm welcome is assured by the bilingual Parry Family. 'Croeso'.

	SINGLE PER PERSON B&B		DOUBLE FOR 2 PERSONS B&B		🛏 2
	MIN £	MAX £	MIN £	MAX £	OPEN
	15.00	16.00	28.00	30.00	3-10

GH | Dinbren House

Dinbren Road,
Llangollen,
Clwyd LL20 8TF
Tel: (0978) 860593

Lovely country house in 2½ acre gardens. Beautiful views yet easy walking distance to Llangollen. Large comfortable "Laura Ashley" bedrooms all with tea/coffee, television and wash basins. Guests own bathroom and shower room. Family room available. Short Drive Chester and Snowdonia. Ample parking in grounds.

	SINGLE PER PERSON B&B		DOUBLE FOR 2 PERSONS B&B		🛏 3
	MIN £	MAX £	MIN £	MAX £	OPEN
	15.00	16.00	30.00	32.00	1-12

GH | Tyn-Llidiart

Carrog Road,
Corwen,
Clwyd LL21 9RS
Tel: (0490 41) 2729

HIGHLY COMMENDED

Welcome to Tyn-Llidiart a country house set in the Dee Valley by the River Dee overlooking the Berwyn Mountains. Rooms are en-suite with colour TV, tea/coffee making facilities, clock radio. Also provided hairdryers/shampoos. Guests comfort are our main concern. We are a central base for the coast and countryside. Many sports facilities close by.

	SINGLE PER PERSON B&B		DOUBLE FOR 2 PERSONS B&B		🛏 2
					2
	MIN £	MAX £	MIN £	MAX £	OPEN
	15.00	15.00	30.00	30.00	1-12

GH | The Hall

Lygan-y-Wern,
Pentre Halkyn, Holywell,
Clwyd CH8 8BD
Tel: (0352) 780215
Fax: (0352) 780187

HIGHLY COMMENDED

Conveniently situated near A55, 15 miles Chester, 70 miles Holyhead. Open all year. Self contained centrally heated cottage in reconstructed 18th Century cottages - comprising 5 bedrooms (one en-suite) plus 2 bathrooms, dining room and sitting room. Lovely grounds. Children welcome. Good local pubs and hotels for evening meal. No smoking in bedrooms. We accept credit cards.

	SINGLE PER PERSON B&B		DOUBLE FOR 2 PERSONS B&B		🛏 5
					1
	MIN £	MAX £	MIN £	MAX £	OPEN
	14.00	16.00	–	38.00	1-12

GH | Glanafon Guest House

Abbey Road,
Llangollen,
Clwyd LL20 8SS
Tel: (0978) 860725

L

Friendly family run Victorian guest house overlooking River Dee and Canal tow path. Spacious comfortable twin, double and family bedrooms, with H&C, TV, tea/coffee, guests own lounge. Lovely views. Private parking. Children welcome with reduced rates. Ideally situated for fishing, canoeing, walking, touring. View of steam railway from twin room. 8 minute walk town centre.

	SINGLE PER PERSON B&B		DOUBLE FOR 2 PERSONS B&B		🛏 2
	MIN £	MAX £	MIN £	MAX £	OPEN
	14.00	15.00	28.00	30.00	1-12

GH | Cayo Guest House

74 Vale Street,
Denbigh,
Clwyd LL16 3BW
Tel: (0745) 812686

Long established centrally situated guest house. Guests have access at all times. Family rooms available, most rooms en-suite. Well behaved dogs welcome. Good food using local produce, special menus on request. Centrally heated. TV lounge. Ideal for touring North Wales. Excellent area for golf, gliding, angling, walking, riding holidays can be arranged.

	SINGLE PER PERSON B&B		DOUBLE FOR 2 PERSONS B&B		🛏 5
					4
	MIN £	MAX £	MIN £	MAX £	OPEN
	14.00	16.00	28.00	32.00	1-12

FH | Greenhill Farm

Bryn Delyn,
Holywell,
Clwyd CH8 7QF
Tel: (0352) 713270

Welcome to our 15th Century timber framed farmhouse overlooking the Dee estuary. Modernised to include 1 family room (en-suite), twin and double bedrooms all with tea making facilities. We have a comfortable oak beamed lounge and panelled dining room. Also a games/utility room with washing facilities and snooker table. Children are made especially welcome.

	SINGLE PER PERSON B&B		DOUBLE FOR 2 PERSONS B&B		🛏 3
					1
	MIN £	MAX £	MIN £	MAX £	OPEN
	15.00	–	30.00	–	3-10

GH | The Grange

Grange Road,
Llangollen,
Clwyd LL20 8AP
Tel: (0978) 860366

HIGHLY COMMENDED

An attractive country house of character situated in town, within a tranquil and secluded 2 acre garden. Spacious and comfortable twin, double and family bedrooms, all en-suite with tea/coffee facilities and central heating. Child reductions and cot available. Interesting beamed lounge with colour TV. Parking in grounds.

	SINGLE PER PERSON B&B		DOUBLE FOR 2 PERSONS B&B		🛏 3
					3
	MIN £	MAX £	MIN £	MAX £	OPEN
	–	–	32.00	35.00	1-12

GH | Hendy Isa

nr. Horseshoe Pass,
Llangollen,
Clwyd LL20 8DE
Tel: (0978) 861232

Attractive country house in picturesque historic valley 1½ miles from town. Abundant wildlife with friendly shire horses in adjoining fields. Our rooms are spacious and tastefully furnished with modern facilities including fire alarms. Ideal base for visiting historic sites, touring, walking, steam railway or canal trips. Many attractions. Wholesome breakfasts. Evening meals available within walking distance.

	SINGLE PER PERSON B&B		DOUBLE FOR 2 PERSONS B&B		🛏 4
	MIN £	MAX £	MIN £	MAX £	🛁 4
	–	–	30.00	38.00	OPEN 1-12

FH | Dee Farm

Rhewl,
Llangollen,
Clwyd LL20 7YT — COMMENDED
Tel: (0978) 861598
Fax: (0978) 861187

This long white farm house is so named because the River Dee lies just below it's garden with superb views. Furnished to a high standard, twin bedrooms either en-suite or with private bathroom, central heating, tea and coffee. Good walking country. Golf, fishing and many interesting historic places to visit nearby.

	SINGLE PER PERSON B&B		DOUBLE FOR 2 PERSONS B&B		🛏 2
	MIN £	MAX £	MIN £	MAX £	🛁 2
	–	–	30.00	34.00	OPEN 2-11

FH | Hill Farm

Llong,
Mold,
Clwyd CH7 4JP
Tel: (0244) 550415

Georgian house on 300 acre dairy farm, between Mold and Chester. Convenient for Snowdonia coast, Chester and National Trust properties. Golf, riding, fishing nearby. Large bedrooms, centrally heated, wash basins, tea/coffee. Guests sitting room with open fires, beams, antiques. Many eating places nearby. Traditional farmhouse breakfast with choice. AA listed. No smoking in bedrooms.

	SINGLE PER PERSON B&B		DOUBLE FOR 2 PERSONS B&B		🛏 3
	MIN £	MAX £	MIN £	MAX £	
	16.00	18.00	28.00	30.00	OPEN 1-12

GH | The Old Vicarage Guest House

Bryn Howel Lane,
Llangollen,
Clwyd LL20 7YR
Tel: (0978) 823018

Attractive 17th Century country house set in private grounds offering spacious quality accommodation. The former Vicarage is located besides the River Dee at the head of the Vale of Llangollen, amidst outstanding natural beauty. Bar and restaurant meals, the picturesque Canal Marina and Telfords' Aquaduct are all just a short walk away. Brochure available.

	SINGLE PER PERSON B&B		DOUBLE FOR 2 PERSONS B&B		🛏 6
	MIN £	MAX £	MIN £	MAX £	🛁 3
	–	–	26.00	34.00	OPEN 1-12

FH | Tyn Celyn Farmhouse

Tyndwr,
Llangollen,
Clwyd LL20 8AR
Tel: (0978) 861117

Oak beamed farmhouse with beautiful views, situated in scenic position on the outskirts of Llangollen. All bedrooms have en-suite bathrooms, tea/coffee making facilities and colour television. One ground floor bedroom available, family bedroom available, cot available. Ideally situated for walking, fishing, canoeing, horse riding and touring Chester, Snowdonia and North Wales. Ample Secure Parking.

	SINGLE PER PERSON B&B		DOUBLE FOR 2 PERSONS B&B		🛏 3
	MIN £	MAX £	MIN £	MAX £	🛁 3
	–	–	32.00	35.00	OPEN 1-12

FH | Maes Garmon Farm

off Gwernaffield Road,
Gwernaffield, Mold,
Clwyd CH7 5DB — HIGHLY COMMENDED
Tel: (0352) 759887

Converted stable adjoining 17th Century farmhouse. A welcome of tea and homemade scones. Wealth of beams, rich furnishing in oak and pine. Guests own lounge and dining room. Bedrooms - two double, one twin all with vanity units and showers. Luxuriously appointed throughout. Beautiful three acre gardens, summer-house, pond and stream. Convenient for Chester and Snowdonia.

	SINGLE PER PERSON B&B		DOUBLE FOR 2 PERSONS B&B		🛏 3
	MIN £	MAX £	MIN £	MAX £	🛁 3
	17.00	19.00	–	30.00	OPEN 1-12

GH | Whitegate

Grange Road,
Llangollen,
Clwyd LL20 8AP
Tel: (0978) 860960
Fax: (0978) 860960

The perfect base from which to explore Llangollen and North Wales. Whitegate is an attractive Edwardian family house set on the edge of Llangollen adjacent to Plas Newydd, renowned as the home of the "Ladies of Llangollen". Ample parking. Children welcome. Guest sitting room. Beautiful walking country. Two interesting National Trust properties nearby.

	SINGLE PER PERSON B&B		DOUBLE FOR 2 PERSONS B&B		🛏 3
	MIN £	MAX £	MIN £	MAX £	🛁 –
	–	–	30.00	–	OPEN 1-12

GH | Castilla

Cilcain Road,
Pantymwyn, Mold,
Clwyd CH7 5EH — HIGHLY COMMENDED
Tel: (0352) 741585

Friendly family run home in pleasant rural village location, well situated for touring. Three miles from the bustling market town of Mold, and thirty minutes drive from historic Chester. Close to Loggerheads Country Park, Clwydian Hills and Offa's Dyke path. Spacious bedroom and separate guests lounge with colour TV. Breakfasts of quality, quantity and variety.

	SINGLE PER PERSON B&B		DOUBLE FOR 2 PERSONS B&B		🛏 1
	MIN £	MAX £	MIN £	MAX £	🛁 1
	15.00	17.00	25.00	28.00	OPEN 1-11

GH | Argoed Guest House

off Mwrog Street, Llanfwrog,
Ruthin, Clwyd LL15 1LG
Tel: (0824) 703407 — COMMENDED
Fax: (0824) 703407

An attractive timbered house with full central heating. Standing in private grounds with parking facilities. En-suite, twin bedded room and double rooms available. Visitors lounge. TV, tea/coffee making facilities all rooms. Showers and baths. Beautiful garden with own stream. Superb views of Clwydian Hills. Convenient for Medieval Banquets at Ruthin Castle. Member Award Winning B&B (G.B) Organisation.

	SINGLE PER PERSON B&B		DOUBLE FOR 2 PERSONS B&B		🛏 3
	MIN £	MAX £	MIN £	MAX £	🛁 1
	17.50	–	30.00	35.00	OPEN 1-12

GH | Berllan Bach

Fforddlas,
Llandyrnog
Clwyd LL16 4LR
Tel: (0824) 790732 or (0374) 128494

A lovely barn conversion 200 years old. Sits at foot of Clwydian Range, within easy reach of Ruthin, Chester, Snowdonia and the coast. Each bedroom has been individually designed with french windows opening onto patio areas. En-suites, colour TV's, tea/coffee making facilities. Olde Worlde lounge with Inglenook fireplace. Conservatory. Children and dogs warmly welcomed.

P	🐕	SINGLE PER PERSON B&B		DOUBLE FOR 2 PERSONS B&B		🛏 3
🏠	🍴					🛁 3
🔥	🍽	MIN £	MAX £ 35.00	MIN £	MAX £ 38.00	OPEN 1-12

GH | The Old Rectory

Clocaenog,
Ruthin,
Clwyd LL15 2AT
Tel: (0824) 750740

Comfortable Georgian rectory set in a quiet village in a valley below Clocaenog Forest, one mile off B5105, Ruthin four miles. Centrally heated throughout. All bedrooms with wash basins or en-suite. Lounge, colour TV. Ideal centre for Snowdonia, Llangollen, North Wales and Chester. Craft studio/workshop adjoins premises where colourful canalware is created.

P	☕	SINGLE PER PERSON B&B		DOUBLE FOR 2 PERSONS B&B		🛏 3
C	🍴					🛁 1
🏠	🍽	MIN £ 15.00	MAX £ 18.00	MIN £ 30.00	MAX £ 36.00	OPEN 1-12

GH | Plas Penucha

Caerwys,
Mold,
Clwyd CH7 5BH
Tel: (0352) 720210

HIGHLY COMMENDED

Welcome to this 16th Century farmhouse altered over succeeding generations but retaining history and serenity in comfortable surroundings. Extensive gardens overlooking Clwydian Hills. Spacious lounge with extensive library. Four well equipped bedrooms (two en-suite). Full central heating, log fires. 2 miles A55 expressway. Ideal touring centre for North Wales. Brochure from Nest Price.

P	☕	SINGLE PER PERSON B&B		DOUBLE FOR 2 PERSONS B&B		🛏 4
C	🍴					🛁 2
🔥	🍽	MIN £ 16.50	MAX £ 16.50	MIN £ 33.00	MAX £ 33.00	OPEN 1-12

GH | Eyarth Station

Llanfair DC, Ruthin,
Clwyd LL15 2EE
Tel: (0824) 703643
Fax: (0824) 707464

  AWARD
HIGHLY COMMENDED

Former railway station, now a superbly converted country house. Six bedrooms, all en-suite with shower. TV lounge, swimming pool, car park, magnificent views. Located in beautiful countryside, only 3 minutes drive to Ruthin castle, town and medieval banquet. Centre for Chester, Snowdonia, Llangollen, Bala, coast. Home cooking. Credit cards accepted. Listen to our local Welsh choir. BTA commended, AA merit awards.

P	🐕	SINGLE PER PERSON B&B		DOUBLE FOR 2 PERSONS B&B		🛏 6
🏠	🍴					🛁 6
🔥	🍽	MIN £ –	MAX £ 19.00	MIN £ –	MAX £ 38.00	OPEN 1-12

FH | Pentre Bach

Llandyrnog,
nr. Ruthin,
Clwyd LL16 4LA
Tel: (0824) 790725

Situated between the market towns of Ruthin and Denbigh. Pentre Bach, built in 1745 as a farmhouse, today provides an ideal base, for a peaceful break, but just a short drive to the coast, Snowdonia and the historic city of Chester. Comfortable guest bedrooms with all facilities.

P	🍴	SINGLE PER PERSON B&B		DOUBLE FOR 2 PERSONS B&B		🛏 2
🔥	🍴					🛁 2
		MIN £ 17.50	MAX £ 19.00	MIN £ 30.00	MAX £ 32.00	OPEN 1-12

FH | Buck Farm

Hanmer,
Clwyd SY14 7LX
Tel: (094 874) 339

COMMENDED

On the A525. A warm welcoming and cosy Tudor farmhouse. An excellent touring base for North Wales, Cheshire, Shropshire, Staffordshire. We provide vegetarian or vegan and meat meals on request. Always make our own muesli, Granola, hotcakes and wonderful vegetable soups (Sans M.S.G). French spoken. Library, music, cycle shelter. No smoking. Spacious interesting garden.

P	🐕	SINGLE PER PERSON B&B		DOUBLE FOR 2 PERSONS B&B		🛏 4
🏠	🍽					
		MIN £ 18.00	MAX £ 18.00	MIN £ 34.00	MAX £ 36.00	OPEN 1-12

Coed Hyrddyn, Nr. Llangollen

*T*his is the quietest holiday region in Wales, where country lanes and mountain roads wind their way tentatively through unexplored territory, and where

Inland, there's the true 'Wild Wales' of lonely high country, remote lakes, forests and traditional stone-built farmsteads. It's a little-known fact that Mid Wales has

Pony trekking on the Cader Idris Range

highlands run down to an untouched coastline. Some of Wales's – and Britain's – best-kept secrets are to be

Aberaeron harbour

found within this tranquil, timeless area of gentle hills, fresh green mountains and sweeping shores.

True to its character, the places to stay here are small and friendly. Mid Wales's 'capital' is the resort of Aberystwyth, which stands midway along Cardigan Bay, a gently curving shoreline of dunes, grassy headlands and outstandingly beautiful estuaries. Aberystwyth is a charming Victorian seaside town which doubles up as an ideally located touring centre. Other places to stay along Cardigan Bay include Barmouth, Tywyn, Aberaeron and New Quay.

the lion's share of the Snowdonia National Park – 500 of its 840 square miles, to be precise. The park extends southwards all the way to Machynlleth, and eastwards to Bala.

These two traditional towns, together with Dolgellau, are convenient centres from which to explore Mid Wales's upland wildernesses. And there's much to explore, for in addition to the Snowdonia National Park there are the Cambrian Mountains,

Harlech beach

the 'backbone' of Wales. Further east, high mountains decline to rolling, sleepy border country around Welshpool, Newtown and Llandrindod Wells.

But don't be deceived by Mid Wales's tranquillity. There's lot's going on here, including pony trekking, fishing, walking, narrow-gauge railway riding, canoeing, sailing and mountain biking.

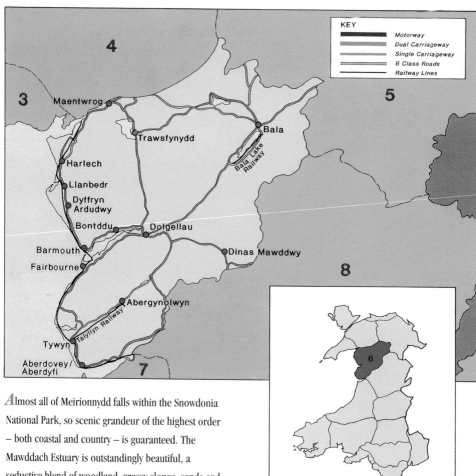

Almost all of Meirionnydd falls within the Snowdonia National Park, so scenic grandeur of the highest order – both coastal and country – is guaranteed. The Mawddach Estuary is outstandingly beautiful, a seductive blend of woodland, grassy slopes, sands and tidal riverbanks. It's the same picture along the Dovey Estuary, which meets the sea at the picturesque sailing centre of Aberdovey.

Other places to stay along the coast include the small resorts of Tywyn and Barmouth – not forgetting Harlech, home of a spectacular medieval castle. Country lovers are also spoilt for choice. Bala stands beside a lake ringed by mountains which can be explored on foot or by roads which seem to climb into the clouds. North of Dolgellau lie the remote Rhinogs,

one of Britain's last true wilderness areas. And looming above the town is mighty Cader Idris, a misty, boulder-clad mountain steeped in legend.

Meirionnydd's places to visit include narrow-gauge railways, a forest visitor centre, woollen mills, craft centres, a fascinating gold mine and a unique 'village of the future' known as the Centre for Alternative Technology – attractions that complement their surroundings perfectly.

ABERDOVEY/ABERDYFI
Map Ref: Db6

Picturesque little resort and dinghy sailor's paradise on the Dovey Estuary. All watersports, thriving yacht club, good inns looking out over the bay and 18-hole golf links. Superb views towards hills and mountains. ⇌

ABERGYNOLWYN
Map Ref: Db5

Attractively located former slate quarrying village surrounded by forests and the green foothills of Cader Idris. Narrow-gauge Talyllyn Railway runs almost to the village from Tywyn. Good choice of local walks. Visit Tal-y-llyn Lake, Bird Rock and atmospheric Castell-y-Bere.

BALA
Map Ref: Dd2

Tree-lined main street has interesting little shops and charming hotels. Narrow-gauge railway runs one side of Bala Lake, 4 miles long (the largest natural lake in Wales) and ringed with mountains. Golf, sailing, fishing, canoeing – a natural touring centre for Snowdonia.

BARMOUTH
Map Ref: Db4

Superbly located resort at the mouth of lovely Mawddach Estuary. Golden sands, miles of wonderful mountain and estuary walks nearby. Promenade, funfair, harbour and pony rides on the beach. Lifeboat and Shipwreck Centre museums. Good shops and inns. Excellent parking on seafront. ⇌

DINAS MAWDDWY
Map Ref: Dd4

Mountain village in beautiful setting with marvellous walks. On fringes of Snowdonia National Park. Visit the extensive Meirion Woollen Mill with craft shop, tea shop. Drive over the spectacular Bwlch y Groes mountain road to Bala, the highest road in Wales.

DOLGELLAU
Map Ref: Dc4

Handsome stone-built market town which seems to have grown naturally out of the mountains. The heights of Cader Idris loom above the rooftops. Interesting shops, pubs, cafes. Museum of the Quakers in town centre. Visit gold mine in nearby forest. Excellent base for touring the coast and countryside.

DYFFRYN ARDUDWY
Map Ref: Da3

Pleasant village near the coast on Barmouth - Harlech road, set between sea and mountains. Prehistoric burial chamber and stone circles nearby; also scenic Shell Island, Museum of Transport and caravan parks. ⇌

FAIRBOURNE
Map Ref: Db4

Quiet resort with 2 miles of sand south of Mawddach Estuary. Railway buffs travel far to go on its 1'3" gauge Fairbourne and Barmouth Steam Railway. Shops and accommodation. Car parks. ⇌

HARLECH
Map Ref: Ae7

Small, stone-built town dominated by remains of 13th-century castle – site of Owain Glyndŵr's last stand. Dramatically set on a high crag, the castle commands a magnificent panorama of rolling sand dunes, sea and mountains. Home of the 18-hole Royal St David's Golf Club. Shell Island nearby. Theatre and swimming pool. Visitors can explore the chambers of the Old Llanfair Slate Caverns just south of Harlech. ⇌

TYWYN
Map Ref: Da5

Seaside resort on Cardigan Bay, with beach activities, sea and river fishing and golf among its leading attractions. Good leisure centre. Narrow-gauge Talyllyn Railway runs inland from here and St Cadfan's Stone and Llanegryn Church are important Christian monuments. In the hills stands Castell-y-Bere, a native Welsh castle, and Bird Rock, a haven for birdlife. ⇌

Talyllyn

GH | 1 Trefeddian Bank

Aberdovey,
Gwynedd LL35 0RU
Tel: (0654) 767487

COMMENDED

If you are looking for a quiet relaxing break we invite you to our smoke free Edwardian home. We offer you a warm welcome, home cooked food, optional evening meal, reductions for children, safe parking, panoramic views. All bedrooms have H&C, tea/coffee facilities, some with sea views. Comfortable TV lounge and sunbathing terrace for you to enjoy.

P 🛏 🍽		SINGLE PER PERSON B&B		DOUBLE FOR 2 PERSONS B&B		🛏 3 🛁 -	
		MIN £ 14.00	MAX £ 14.00	MIN £ 26.00	MAX £ 26.00	OPEN 3-10	

GH | Bronwylfa Guest House

Llandderfel, Bala,
Gwynedd LL23 7HG
Tel: (06783) 207 or 395

HIGHLY COMMENDED

Victorian country house and garden cottage tranquil setting, large grounds. Picturesque views Berwyn mountains, River Dee, Bala town 4 miles, edge of Snowdonia National Park. Ideal touring, watersports, walking, warm friendly welcome assured. Good hearty breakfast. Excellent accommodation. Two large double, one twin (en-suite) rooms, one twin (H&C). Beverage trays, colour TV's. Ample parking. Victorian conservatory overlooking gardens.

P 🕊 C 🛏		SINGLE PER PERSON B&B		DOUBLE FOR 2 PERSONS B&B		🛏 4 🛁 3	
		MIN £ 15.00	MAX £ 19.00	MIN £ 28.00	MAX £ 34.00	OPEN 1-12	

FH | Eirianfa Farm

Sarnau,
Bala,
Gwynedd LL23 7LH
Tel: (06783) 389

3 miles north east of Bala. A mixed farm, 200 acres facing Berwyn mountains. Good centre for touring Mid and North Wales. Tea/coffee facilities in bedrooms. Full central heating. No smoking in dining room please. Ground floor bedroom. Private fishing on farm. Mrs E Jones.

P 🛏 🍽		SINGLE PER PERSON B&B		DOUBLE FOR 2 PERSONS B&B		🛏 3 🛁 -	
		MIN £ 15.00	MAX £ 16.00	MIN £ 26.00	MAX £ 28.00	OPEN 1-12	

FH | Tyddyn Rhys Farm

Aberdovey,
Gwynedd LL35 0PG
Tel: (0654) 767533

HIGHLY COMMENDED

A warm Welsh welcome awaits you at Tyddyn Rhys. A working farm of 150 acres. ½ mile from Aberdovey. With panoramic view of Cardigan Bay. All bedrooms have wash basins, tea and coffee making facilities and colour TV's. One double bedroom en-suite, one double and one single. 1 bathroom two toilets. Full central heating.

P 🛏 🍽		SINGLE PER PERSON B&B		DOUBLE FOR 2 PERSONS B&B		🛏 3 🛁 1	
		MIN £ 14.00	MAX £ -	MIN £ 27.00	MAX £ 33.00	OPEN 3-11	

GH | Erw Feurig Farm Guest House

Cefnddwysarn,
Bala,
Gwynedd LL23 7LL
Tel: (06783) 262

HIGHLY COMMENDED

Beautifully situated this farm guesthouse is the ideal centre for touring and walking. Double twin and family rooms, two with private facilities. One upstairs bathroom wc, and downstairs wc and shower room. Separate dining room and TV lounge. Excellent home cooked food served. Fire Certificate held. Private fishing. Tea/coffee facilities.

P 🛏 🍽 🐾		SINGLE PER PERSON B&B		DOUBLE FOR 2 PERSONS B&B		🛏 4 🛁 2	
		MIN £ 13.00	MAX £ 18.00	MIN £ 28.00	MAX £ 32.00	OPEN 1-12	

FH | Rhydydefaid Farm

Frongoch,
Bala,
Gwynedd LL23 7NT
Tel: (0678) 520456

 HIGHLY COMMENDED

Traditional Welsh stone farmhouse, three miles from Bala near A4212. Oak beamed lounge with inglenook fireplace. Oak beamed bedroom with en-suite facilities. Twin and single rooms. Tea/coffee facilities. Snacks available. A Welsh welcome awaits you with beautiful countryside. Ideal base for touring Snowdonia National Park. Near National White Water Centre. Brochure from Mrs Davies.

P 🛏 🍽 🐾		SINGLE PER PERSON B&B		DOUBLE FOR 2 PERSONS B&B		🛏 3 🛁 1	
		MIN £ 14.00	MAX £ 16.00	MIN £ 27.00	MAX £ 32.00	OPEN 1-12	

FH | Tanycoed Ucha

Abergynolwyn,
Tywyn,
Gwynedd LL36 9UP
Tel: (0654) 782228

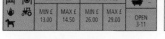 L

Located in the picturesque Dolgoch Valley overlooking the Talyllyn Gauge Railway which runs through our land, come and enjoy the warm welcome we give on our working farm. Within easy reach of Bere Castle, Bird Rock, Cader Idris and Dolgoch Falls. Perfect for bird watching. We also have deer on the farm. Home comforts. Tea/coffee in bedrooms.

P 🛏 🍽 🐾		SINGLE PER PERSON B&B		DOUBLE FOR 2 PERSONS B&B		🛏 3 🛁 -	
		MIN £ 13.00	MAX £ 14.50	MIN £ 26.00	MAX £ 29.00	OPEN 3-11	

GH | Fronderw Private Hotel

Stryd-y-Fron,
Bala,
Gwynedd LL23 7YD
Tel: (0678) 520301

COMMENDED

Charming period mansion quietly situated on hillside overlooking Bala town and lake, with magnificent views of the Berwyn Mountains. All rooms have hot and cold, central heating, tea/coffee making facilities. Lounge, separate TV lounge with colour TV. Ample parking. Dinner optional. Vegetarians catered for. Licensed. Ideal centre for touring, walking, water sport, cycling, golf.

P 🛏 🍽		SINGLE PER PERSON B&B		DOUBLE FOR 2 PERSONS B&B		🛏 8 🛁 4	
		MIN £ 17.00	MAX £ 18.00	MIN £ 26.00	MAX £ 36.00	OPEN 3-11	

GH | Endeavour Guest House

Marine Parade,
Barmouth,
Gwynedd LL42 1NA
Tel: (0341) 280271

  APPROVED

Promenade position with beautiful sandy beach. All family and double rooms have showers, five en-suite. Colour TV Satellite, tea making facilities. B & B with optional evening meal. Licensed bar. Open mid January to mid December. Weekly B & B £90.00 - £105.00 per person.

P 🛏 🍽		SINGLE PER PERSON B&B		DOUBLE FOR 2 PERSONS B&B		🛏 9 🛁 5	
		MIN £ 14.00	MAX £ 17.00	MIN £ 28.00	MAX £ 34.00	OPEN 1-12	

GH | Glyn Hefin

7 Marine Road,
Barmouth,
Gwynedd LL42 1NL
Tel: (0341) 280095

COMMENDED

Glyn Hefin assures all of a warm friendly welcome. Clean fresh rooms all with colour TV's, tea/coffee making facilities. All rooms have wash basins, vanity units. Some doubles with showers/bath wc. Ground floor double with shower, wc suitable elderly or disabled. 100 yards from beach, close to all other amenities and interest, golf, pony trekking, Snowdonia etc.

		SINGLE PER PERSON B&B		DOUBLE FOR 2 PERSONS B&B			8
							3
		MIN £	MAX £	MIN £	MAX £	OPEN 3-10	
		13.00	–	26.00	28.00		

FH | Bryncelyn Farm

Dinas Mawddwy,
Machynlleth,
Powys SY20 9JG
Tel: (0650) 531289

Situated in peaceful valley of Cywarch, at the foot of Aran Fawddwy, amidst some of the finest scenery. Excellent centre to enjoy walking, climbing and touring. Generous home cooked meals. Tea/coffee facilities. Spacious en-suite bedrooms, including colour TV and heating. The Edwards family offer a homely holiday in a comfortable farmhouse.

		SINGLE PER PERSON B&B		DOUBLE FOR 2 PERSONS B&B			2
							2
		MIN £	MAX £	MIN £	MAX £	OPEN 1-12	
		15.00	17.00	30.00	34.00		

GH | Heulwen

Llanfachreth,
Dolgellau,
Gwynedd LL40 2UT
Tel: (0341) 423085

Heulwen is situated outside the quaint village of Llanfachreth, surrounded by beautiful views. It is an ideal centre for exploring the Snowdonia National Park. Hearty breakfasts, warm and homely bedrooms, lounge with colour TV and large patio to while away the long summer evenings, all help to make your stay a memorable one.

		SINGLE PER PERSON B&B		DOUBLE FOR 2 PERSONS B&B			3
							2
		MIN £	MAX £	MIN £	MAX £	OPEN 3-10	
		16.50	–	30.00			

GH | Pen Parc Guest House

Park Road,
Barmouth,
Gwynedd LL42 1PH
Tel: (0341) 280150

HIGHLY COMMENDED

A small guest house in quiet situation overlooking park, yet only four minutes from sea. H&C in all rooms. Tea making facilities. All bedrooms on first floor. We pride ourselves on personal service and good food with traditional and vegetarian cuisine and special diets. TV lounge. Walkers welcome. Sorry no young children or pets.

		SINGLE PER PERSON B&B		DOUBLE FOR 2 PERSONS B&B			4
							–
		MIN £	MAX £	MIN £	MAX £	OPEN 1-12	
		14.00	14.00	28.00	28.00		

GH | Dwy Olwyn

Coed-y-Fronallt,
Dolgellau,
Gwynedd LL40 2YG
Tel: (0341) 422822

A comfortable guest house situated in an acre of landscaped gardens, boasting magnificent views of the Cader Idris mountain range in a peaceful position, yet only 10 minutes walk from the town. Within Snowdonia National Park, close to all amenities and numerous walks. Good home cooking, evening dinner if desired. Tea/coffee facilities, parking, lounge with colour TV.

		SINGLE PER PERSON B&B		DOUBLE FOR 2 PERSONS B&B			3
							–
		MIN £	MAX £	MIN £	MAX £	OPEN 2-12	
		12.00	–	24.00	–		

FH | Arosfyr Farm

Penycefn Road,
Dolgellau,
Gwynedd LL40 2YP
Tel: (0341) 422355

L
APPROVED

Situated on the way to Dolgellau Golf course with glorious views of Cader Idris mountains. Fairbourne and Barmouth beaches within 10 miles. Ideally situated for walking, pony trekking, narrow gauge railways, castles, gold mines and slate caverns. Double, family and twin bedrooms with wash basins and heating. TV lounge with tea/coffee making facilities and separate dining room and tables. Own free range eggs, parking. Personal attention and satisfaction assured.

		SINGLE PER PERSON B&B		DOUBLE FOR 2 PERSONS B&B			3
							–
		MIN £	MAX £	MIN £	MAX £	OPEN 1-12	
		15.00	17.50	27.00	28.00		

GH | The Sandpiper

7 Marine Parade,
Barmouth,
Gwynedd LL42 1NA
Tel: (0341) 280318

HIGHLY COMMENDED

The Sandpiper is superbly situated on Barmouth seafront. There is parking outside and we are a short level walk from the station. Most double rooms have en-suite facilities. Television and free tea/coffee in all rooms. Ground floor bedroom available. Brochure from Susan and John Palmer.

		SINGLE PER PERSON B&B		DOUBLE FOR 2 PERSONS B&B			11
							6
		MIN £	MAX £	MIN £	MAX £	OPEN 3-10	
		14.00	15.00	25.00	36.00		

GH | Y Goedlan

Brithdir,
Dolgellau,
Gwynedd LL40 2RN
Tel: (0341) 423131

This old vicarage with adjoining farm offers peaceful accommodation in pleasant rural surroundings. Ideally placed on B4416 road for walks, sea, mountains and touring. Spacious double, twin and family rooms all with H&C, colour TV, central heating, tea/coffee facilities. Bathroom with shower. Two conveniences, lounge. Comfort with homely atmosphere. Hearty breakfast. Reduction for children. Parking. Dolgellau 2 miles.

		SINGLE PER PERSON B&B		DOUBLE FOR 2 PERSONS B&B			3
							–
		MIN £	MAX £	MIN £	MAX £	OPEN 1-11	
		15.00	15.00	26.00	28.00		

FH | Cyfannedd Uchaf

Arthog,
Dolgellau,
Gwynedd LL39 1LX
Tel: (0341) 250526

HIGHLY COMMENDED

Cyfannedd Uchaf farmhouse is situated 750 ft in the foothills of the Cader Idris Mountain range. The well appointed bedrooms, two double, one twin are comfortably furnished. Guests are invited to share the beamed lounge with their hosts and the glow of a log burner on chilly evenings. Children over 14 are welcome. No pets.

		SINGLE PER PERSON B&B		DOUBLE FOR 2 PERSONS B&B			3
							–
		MIN £	MAX £	MIN £	MAX £	OPEN 1-10	
		–	–	–	32.00		

FH Cynan

Brithdir,
Dolgellau,
Gwynedd LL40 2RW
Tel: (0341) 41318

HIGHLY COMMENDED

This pretty farmhouse, with its low beams, massive stone walls and remarkably peaceful setting has a very special atmosphere - friendly, relaxed and really comfortable. Cosy, spotlessly clean en-suite bedrooms, leisurely breakfasts and scrumptious suppers make Cynan a lovely place to stay, unwind and explore all of Snowdonia.

P ▦ ✂ ❄ ¶◎ ♞	SINGLE PER PERSON B&B		DOUBLE FOR 2 PERSONS B&B		🛏 2 🛁 2
	MIN £ 19.00	MAX £ –	MIN £ 38.00	MAX £ –	OPEN 1-10

FH Tyddynmawr Farmhouse

Islawrdref,
Cader Road, Dolgellau,
Gwynedd LL40 1TL
Tel: (0341) 422331

AWARD

HIGHLY COMMENDED

Its paradise! Honestly!. A warm welcome awaits you in this lovingly restored 18th Century farmhouse. Beams, log fires. All bedrooms en-suite with superb mountain views. We farm the magnificent mountain of Cader Idris and have waterfalls, slate mines, caves and fishing on mountain lake on farm. We offer peace, tranquillity and seclusion.

P ✗ ♨ ❄ ▦	SINGLE PER PERSON B&B		DOUBLE FOR 2 PERSONS B&B		🛏 2 🛁 2
	MIN £ –	MAX £ 19.00	MIN £ 34.00	MAX £ 34.00	OPEN 4-11

H Noddfa Hotel

Lower Road, Harlech,
Gwynedd LL46 2UB
Tel: (0766) 780043
Fax: (0766) 780043

Situated in the Snowdonia National Park. Noddfa is a Victorian country house within bowshot of Harlech Castle with magnificent views of Snowdon and Tremadoc Bay. Gillian and Eric are keen historians, so why not take a castle tour with them or try a longbow. Close to beach, indoor swimming pool and theatre.

P ♨ ¶◎ ♟	SINGLE PER PERSON B&B		DOUBLE FOR 2 PERSONS B&B		🛏 4 🛁 2
	MIN £ 19.00	MAX £ 19.00	MIN £ 32.00	MAX £ 36.00	OPEN 1-12

FH Gwanas Farmhouse

Cross Foxes, Dolgellau,
Gwynedd LL40 2SH
Tel: (0341) 422624
Fax: (0341) 422624

A charming spacious farmhouse, built in 1838 situated in a peaceful setting where Tom and Mair Evans farm sheep and cattle on 1,000 acres. Delicious breakfast, twin, double, family rooms with H&C. Two bathrooms with showers. Central heating, colour TV, tea/coffee facilities. Situated 400 yards from Cross Foxes Inn off A470, three miles from Dolgellau.

P ▦ ✂ ❄ ♞	SINGLE PER PERSON B&B		DOUBLE FOR 2 PERSONS B&B		🛏 3 🐑 –
	MIN £ 16.00	MAX £ 16.00	MIN £ 26.00	MAX £ 28.00	OPEN 1-11

FH Ystumgwern Hall Farm

Dyffryn Ardudwy,
Gwynedd LL44 2DD
Tel: (0341247) 249

DE LUXE

For a traditional Welsh farmhouse holiday, Ystumgwern is ideal. Situated within the Snowdonia National Park and only one mile to golden beaches and mountain walks. All bedrooms have their own lounge and kitchen facilities, equipped and furnished to the highest of standards. Reduced rates for children and a warm welcome to all from John and Jane Williams. Luxury S/C grade 5 also available.

P ▦ ♨ ❄ ♿	SINGLE PER PERSON B&B		DOUBLE FOR 2 PERSONS B&B		🛏 4 🛁 4
	MIN £ 18.00	MAX £ –	MIN £ –	MAX £ –	OPEN 1-12

GH Fron Deg Guest House

Llanfair, Harlech,
Gwynedd LL46 2RE
Tel: (0766) 780448

L

Situated on cliff top overlooking the magnificent Harlech beach with path down through National Trust field. Traditional 18th Century Welsh cottage, beautifully renovated. Vanity units in all bedrooms. Central heating, tea making facilities. Good home cooking, dinner by prior arrangement. Central for Snowdonia National Park, golf, hill walking, bird watching.

P 📺 C ✂ ▦ ♨ ¶◎	SINGLE PER PERSON B&B		DOUBLE FOR 2 PERSONS B&B		🛏 4 🛁 –
	MIN £ 12.50	MAX £ 12.50	MIN £ –	MAX £ –	OPEN 3-11

FH Llety Nest

Brithdir,
Dolgellau,
Gwynedd LL40 2RY
Tel: (0341) 41326

COMMENDED

New bungalow, close to working farm. One family room en-suite with one double and 2 single beds, one double room and separate lounge. Separate dining room and private lounge. Fresh home cooked food with vegetarians catered for. Large garden. Beautiful scenery, quiet location. Excellent walks. 9 miles from beach. 4 miles from Dolgellau. 2 miles from Cader Idris.

P ▦ ♨ ¶◎ ♞	SINGLE PER PERSON B&B		DOUBLE FOR 2 PERSONS B&B		🛏 2 🛁 1
	MIN £ –	MAX £ –	MIN £ 26.00	MAX £ 30.00	OPEN 3-11

GH Einion House

Friog,
Fairbourne,
Gwynedd LL38 2NX
Tel: (0341) 250644

COMMENDED

Lovely old house, between mountains and sea. Set in beautiful scenery. Reputation for good home cooking. Vegetarians catered for. All rooms colour TV's, clock radios, hairdryers, teamakers. Marvellous walking, maps available. Pony trekking, fishing and bird watching. Good centre for narrow gauge railways. Castles easy reach. Safe sandy beach few minutes walk from house.

▦ ♟ ✂ ♨ ▦ 📺 ¶◎	SINGLE PER PERSON B&B		DOUBLE FOR 2 PERSONS B&B		🛏 7 🛁 4
	MIN £ 15.50	MAX £ 18.50	MIN £ 31.00	MAX £ 34.00	OPEN 1-12

GH Glanygors

Llandanwg,
Harlech,
Gwynedd LL46 2SD
Tel: (034123) 410

Small friendly guest house with 2 acres of land, situated 400 yards from sandy beach. All rooms with wash basins, TV, tea/coffee making facilities, electric blankets and central heating. Beautiful views from all bedrooms. Good home cooking. Ample parking. Private access to beach. Near train station. Golf, rambling, bird watching, sailing, fishing all to be found in the area. Warm welcome.

▦ ♨ ▦ ¶◎	SINGLE PER PERSON B&B		DOUBLE FOR 2 PERSONS B&B		🛏 3 🛁 –
	MIN £ 12.50	MAX £ 13.00	MIN £ 24.00	MAX £ 26.00	OPEN 1-12

GH | Godre'r Graig

Tan-y-Graig,
Lower Harlech,
Gwynedd LL46 2UD
Tel: (0766) 780905

Warm friendly welcome guaranteed nestling below Harlech Castle within sight of Royal St David's golf club. Childrens rates, occasional baby-sitting. Television lounge, home cooked evening meals by arrangement. Great vegetarian choice. Vanitory units, tea/coffee facilities. Convenient for all the sights of Snowdonia, pony trekking or trout and sea fishing.

P 🐕 📶 🍴 ⚓		SINGLE PER PERSON B&B		DOUBLE FOR 2 PERSONS B&B		🛏 3 🛁 –
		MIN £ 14.00	MAX £ 14.00	MIN £ 28.00	MAX £ 28.00	OPEN 1-12

FH | Bryn Celynog Farm

Cwm Prysor,
Trawsfynydd,
Gwynedd LL41 4TR
Tel: (076687) 378

 HIGHLY COMMENDED

Working farm set amid beautiful mountains in centre Snowdonia National Park. 3 miles from Trawsfynydd village. Modernised farmhouse centrally heated. Twin, double or family bedrooms, 1 en-suite, all with wash basins, tea/coffee facilities. Lounge with colour TV, log fire, separate tables in dining room. Reputation for excellent food and friendliness. Comfort and warm Welsh welcome assured. SAE please for brochure Gwladys Hughes.

P 📶 🍴 ⚓		SINGLE PER PERSON B&B		DOUBLE FOR 2 PERSONS B&B		🛏 3 🛁 1
		MIN £ 15.00	MAX £ 17.50	MIN £ 30.00	MAX £ 35.00	OPEN 1-12

FH | Cynfal Farm

Bryncrug,
Tywyn,
Gwynedd LL36 9RB
Tel: (0654) 711703

Welcome to Cynfal, 350 acre working farm with magnificent views of unspoilt countryside. Spacious bedrooms are tastefully furnished and decorated. One en-suite and two with private facilities. Residents lounge and dining room. Talyllyn narrow gauge railway runs 200 yards below the house. We are situated two miles from Tywyn and five miles from picturesque Aberdovey. Brochure available.

P 📶 C 🐾 📶 🐕		SINGLE PER PERSON B&B		DOUBLE FOR 2 PERSONS B&B		🛏 3 🛁 1
		MIN £ 13.00	MAX £ 15.00	MIN £ 26.00	MAX £ 30.00	OPEN 3-11

FH | Gwrach Ynys Country Guest House

Talsarnau,
Gwynedd LL47 6TS
Tel: (0766) 780742
Fax: (0766) 780742

  DE LUXE

Treat yourselves to a refreshingly peaceful break in the glorious setting of our country guest house. Many returning guests attest to our friendly welcome and imaginative home cooking. Bedrooms en-suite, with colour TV's and beverage facilities. Close to sea, mountains, swimming pool, golf, and lovely estuary walks. Many interesting local attractions. Illustrated brochure sent with pleasure.

P C 📶 🍴 ⚓		SINGLE PER PERSON B&B		DOUBLE FOR 2 PERSONS B&B		🛏 7 🛁 6
		MIN £ 15.00	MAX £ 18.00	MIN £ 30.00	MAX £ 36.00	OPEN 1-12

GH | Glenfield

10 Idris Villas,
Tywyn,
Gwynedd LL36 9AW
Tel: (0654) 710707

L

A warm and homely welcome awaits you at Glenfield overlooking beautiful mountain scenery. Central for shops, beach, bus and rail stations. 5 minutes walk from the famous Talyllyn Railway. Ideal for walking, fishing, sailing and golf. Personal supervision.

📶		SINGLE PER PERSON B&B		DOUBLE FOR 2 PERSONS B&B		🛏 2 🛁 –
		MIN £ 13.00	MAX £ 13.00	MIN £ 26.00	MAX £ 26.00	OPEN 3-10

Barmouth

GH | Ty Mawr

Llanfair,
Harlech,
Gwynedd LL46 2SA
Tel: (0766) 780446

A delightful 16th Century stone house overlooking Cardigan bay. Comfortable lounge with log fire and TV, tea and coffee facilities in all rooms. Llandanwg, seaside award winning beach ½ mile, historic Harlech 1 mile - castle, golf course, swimming pool, beach, restaurants etc.. An ideal centre for exploring, relaxing, walking, sailing and trekking.

P 🍴 C ⚓ 📶 📶		SINGLE PER PERSON B&B		DOUBLE FOR 2 PERSONS B&B		🛏 3 🛁 1
		MIN £ –	MAX £ –	MIN £ 26.00	MAX £ 34.00	OPEN 1-12

GH | Glenydd

Maesnewydd,
off Pier Road, Tywyn,
Gwynedd LL36 0AN
Tel: (0654) 711373
Fax: (0654) 711373

Glenydd a beautiful modernised Edwardian house in private road. Wonderful views of Cader Idris mountain range. In lovely relaxed family atmosphere, enjoy scrumptious home cooking. Famous Talyllyn steam railway, leisure centre, tennis, bowls, putting, all within 5 minutes walk. 200m from beach and surfing. Fantastic area for walking, climbing, cycling, bird watching, fishing and boating.

P 📶 📶 🐾 🍴		SINGLE PER PERSON B&B		DOUBLE FOR 2 PERSONS B&B		🛏 3 🛁 –
		MIN £ 12.50	MAX £ 12.50	MIN £ 25.00	MAX £ 25.00	OPEN 1-12

WELCOME HOST

Customer care is our top priority. It's what our Welcome Host scheme is all about. Welcome Host badge or certificate holders are part of a tradition of friendliness. The Welcome Host programme, which is open to everyone from hotel staff to taxi drivers, places the emphasis on warm Welsh hospitality and first-class service.

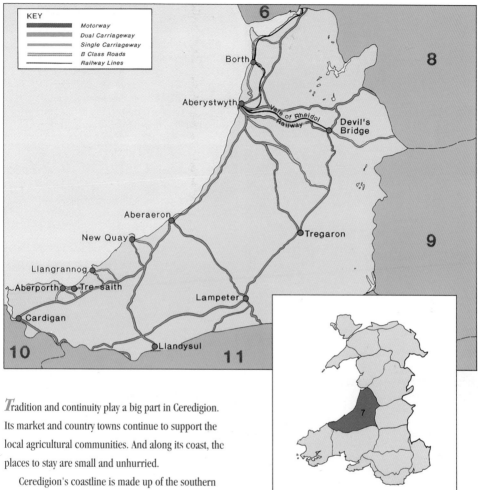

KEY

Motorway
Dual Carriageway
Single Carriageway
B Class Roads
Railway Lines

*T*radition and continuity play a big part in Ceredigion. Its market and country towns continue to support the local agricultural communities. And along its coast, the places to stay are small and unhurried.

Ceredigion's coastline is made up of the southern arc of Cardigan Bay. Aberystwyth, the area's main resort, is by no means large or loud, preferring instead to stick to its genteel Victorian roots. Its convincing period atmosphere is further enhanced by a cliff railway, camera obscura, 'museum in a music hall' and steam-powered narrow-gauge trains.

Further south there's a string of charming little centres – Aberaeron, New Quay, Llangrannog and Aberporth – ideal for a relaxing seaside holiday. The pace of life can hardly be described as hectic inland – except perhaps during market days, when farmers invade places like Tregaron and Lampeter for busy buying and selling. From Tregaron, you can follow in the footsteps of the drovers by driving across the Abergwesyn Pass, one of Wales's most spectacular roads. And for a spectacular train ride, take the Vale of Rheidol Railway from Aberystwyth to Devil's Bridge.

ABERAERON
Map Ref: Fc4

Most attractive little town on Cardigan Bay, with distinctive Georgian-style architecture. Pleasant harbour, marine aquarium, coastal centre, re-creation of Aeron Express, an extraordinary aerial ferry across harbour first built in 1885. Sailing popular, good touring centre for coast and inland.

ABERYSTWYTH
Map Ref: Fe2

Premier resort on the Cardigan Bay coastline. Fine promenade, cliff railway, camera obscura, harbour and many other seaside attractions. Excellent museum in restored Edwardian theatre. University town, lively arts centre with theatre and concert hall. National Library of Wales stands commandingly on hillside. Good shopping. Vale of Rheidol narrow-gauge steam line runs to Devil's Bridge falls. ≥

BORTH
Map Ref: Db7

Popular holiday village with a marvellous expanse of firm sands, ideal for beach games. Fine views from Ynyslas dunes to north across Dovey Estuary. Golf links, promenade 2 miles long. 'Animalarium' farm attraction. ≥

CARDIGAN
Map Ref: Fa5

Market town on mouth of River Teifi close to beaches and resorts. Good shopping facilities, accommodation, inns. Golf and fishing. Base for exploring inland along wooded Teifi Valley and west to the Pembrokeshire Coast National Park. Y Felin Corn Mill and ruined abbey at neighbouring St Dogmael's. Wildlife park nearby.

LAMPETER
Map Ref: Fe5

Farmers and students mingle in this distinctive small central Dyfed town in the picturesque Teifi Valley. Concerts are often held in St David's University College, and visitors are welcome. Golf and angling, range of small shops and some old inns. Visit the landscaped Cae Hir Gardens, Cribyn.

LLANDYSUL
Map Ref: Fc6

Pleasant Teifiside village in a historic textile-producing area where woollen mills still work - and welcome visitors. Salmon fishing very popular; canoeing at certain times of year.

NEW QUAY
Map Ref: Fc4

Picturesque little resort with old harbour on Cardigan Bay. Lovely beaches and coves around and about. Good for sailing and fishing. Resort sheltered by protective headland.

TREGARON
Map Ref: Ga3

Small traditional market town with good pony trekking. Anglers and naturalists delight in this area: the great bog nearby is a nature reserve with rare flowers and birds. Wildlife centre at nearby Penuwch. On the doorstep of remote uplands – follow old drovers' road across the spectacular Abergwesyn Pass.

Cors Caron, Tregaron

GH Arosfa

8 Cadwgan Place,
Aberaeron,
Dyfed SA46 0BU
Tel: (0545) 570120

COMMENDED

Real Welsh hospitality, home cooking and occasional song. Georgian guest house and cottage overlooking pretty yachting harbour. Central but quiet. Free parking at adjacent car park. Tea making. En-suite rooms have TV's. Family suite. Ground floor bedroom. Three course evening meal for £8.00 with fresh meat and vegetables. Excellent choice of breakfast. No smoking. Wine licence.

		SINGLE PER PERSON B&B		DOUBLE FOR 2 PERSONS B&B			6
		MIN £ 15.00	MAX £ 19.00	MIN £ 26.00	MAX £ 36.00	OPEN 1-12	3

H Southgate Hotel

Antaron Avenue,
Penparcau, Aberystwyth,
Dyfed SY23 1SF
Tel: (0970) 611550

APPROVED

Family run licensed small hotel. Approximately one mile from town on A487. En-suite twin, double, family rooms with TV, tea and coffee facilities. Dinner optional. Bar meals available. Two ground floor bedrooms. Pool table. Access, Visa. Prop. J.C. and J. Morgan.

		SINGLE PER PERSON B&B		DOUBLE FOR 2 PERSONS B&B			8
		MIN £ –	MAX £ –	MIN £ –	MAX £ 38.00	OPEN 1-12	8

GH Pantgwyn

Llanfarian,
Aberystwyth,
Dyfed SY23 4DE
Tel: (0970) 612031

This family run guest house is quietly situated in rural countryside in its own five acres of grounds on the A487 just outside the village of Llanfarian. Private parking. All rooms have hot and cold, colour TV, tea/coffee making facilities, central heating. Some rooms en-suite. Ideal for a touring or relaxing holiday.

		SINGLE PER PERSON B&B		DOUBLE FOR 2 PERSONS B&B			3
		MIN £ 14.00	MAX £ 18.00	MIN £ 28.00	MAX £ 36.00	OPEN 1-12	2

GH Moldavia

7 and 8 Bellevue Terrace,
Aberaeron,
Dyfed SA46 0BB
Tel: (0545) 570107

HIGHLY COMMENDED

Comfortable period house on quiet side of picturesque harbour. Relax in lovely garden and flower filled conservatory. Featured in Country Living 1993. Children/single travellers welcome. No single supplement. Fresh coffee, locally baked bread, homemade marmalade. Expert help to plan your days. Lots of maps/walks/brochures to lend. Beach, shops, restaurants, an easy walk.

		SINGLE PER PERSON B&B		DOUBLE FOR 2 PERSONS B&B			4
		MIN £ 16.50	MAX £ 19.00	MIN £ 33.00	MAX £ 38.00	OPEN 1-12	2

GH Ael-y-Bryn Guest House

Capel Bangor,
Aberystwyth,
Dyfed SY23 3LR
Tel: (097084) 681

COMMENDED

Long established family guest house. Set in its own grounds, situated on the A44 road five miles east of Aberystwyth. Ideal touring centre. All rooms have hot and cold, TV, tea/coffee making facilities. Centrally heated. Sorry no pets. Stamped addressed envelope for brochure. Proprietor: Mrs. Enid Jones.

		SINGLE PER PERSON B&B		DOUBLE FOR 2 PERSONS B&B			3
		MIN £ 14.50	MAX £ –	MIN £ 29.00	MAX £ –	OPEN 1-12	

FH Tycam Farm

Capel Bangor,
Aberystwyth,
Dyfed SY23 3NA
Tel: (097084) 662

Peaceful dairy and sheep farm in glorious Rheidol Valley. 7½ miles Aberystwyth, 2½ miles off A44. Real home comfort and farmhouse cooking is offered in traditional Cardiganshire farmhouse. Lounge, dining room, separate tables, colour TV. Perfect walking, birdwatching, sightseeing ¼ mile. Superb salmon, sewin, trout fishing on farm plus nearby lakes. Golf.

		SINGLE PER PERSON B&B		DOUBLE FOR 2 PERSONS B&B			2
		MIN £ 15.00	MAX £ 17.00	MIN £ 30.00	MAX £ 34.00	OPEN 1-12	

H The Halfway Inn

Devil's Bridge Road (A4120),
Pisgah, Aberystwyth,
Dyfed SY23 4NE
Tel: (0970) 84631
Fax: (0970) 84631

COMMENDED

Halfway between Aberystwyth and Devil's Bridge, 700 feet up on the A4120. This traditional hostelry is world famous for real ales and fine food. Relax in old fashioned ambience of flagstone floors, log fires and candles. Extensive grounds with magnificent views of the Rheidol Valley. Outdoor pursuits in the heart of Red Kite country.

		SINGLE PER PERSON B&B		DOUBLE FOR 2 PERSONS B&B			2
		MIN £ –	MAX £ –	MIN £ 37.00	MAX £ 37.00	OPEN 1-12	2

GH Myrddin

1 Rheidol Terrace,
Aberystwyth,
Dyfed SY23 1JU
Tel: (0970) 612799

Comfortable friendly family run guest house. Experienced in providing excellent service and good food. 100 yards from South Promenade, castle and harbour. All bedrooms have hot and cold, shaver points and central heating, colour TV lounge, separate dining room. Packed lunches available on request, vegetarian meals available. A warm welcome awaits you, see for yourselves. Brochure available, please contact Lisa Bumford.

		SINGLE PER PERSON B&B		DOUBLE FOR 2 PERSONS B&B			3
		MIN £ 12.00	MAX £ 16.00	MIN £ 24.00	MAX £ 32.00	OPEN 7-9	–

GH Ty-Gwylan Guest House

Francis Road,
Borth,
Dyfed SY24 5NJ
Tel: (0970) 871434

COMMENDED

Overlooking miles of safe sandy beach. Swimming boating, fishing and all water sports within few minutes easy walk. Golf course and pony trekking nearby. Proprietor provides warm friendly welcome and homely atmosphere throughout the year. Double and twin bedded rooms all en-suite with colour television, tea/coffee making facilities. Central heating. In fact every home comfort.

		SINGLE PER PERSON B&B		DOUBLE FOR 2 PERSONS B&B			3
		MIN £ 18.00	MAX £ 19.00	MIN £ 36.00	MAX £ 38.00	OPEN 1-12	3

H — Morlan Motel

Aberporth,
Cardigan,
Dyfed SA43 2EN
Tel: (0239) 810611

Modern motel with bar, lounge and restaurant. All bedrooms en-suite with tea and coffee making facilities, colour TV and central heating. Seven miles from Cardigan and thirty miles from Aberystwyth, 300 yards from two sandy beaches. In centre of village near shops. Home cooking and vegetarian menu available. Children welcome, pool table and game machines available.

P	▼	SINGLE PER PERSON B&B		DOUBLE FOR 2 PERSONS B&B		🛏	16
🛏	🛏					🛁	16
⚐	🍽	MIN £ 17.00	MAX £ 18.00	MIN £ 34.00	MAX £ 36.00	OPEN 1-12	

GH — Maes-a-Môr

Park Place,
Gwbert Road, Cardigan,
Dyfed SA43 1AE
Tel: (0239) 614929

  HIGHLY COMMENDED

Well established non-smoking family run guest house. High standard of comfort and good food always assured. Situated in a pleasant area of town opposite King George V Park. Ideal centre for the whole of Wales. Including beautiful beaches, rugged mountains. All rooms en-suite with colour TV, tea/coffee facilities. Private parking. RAC Acclaimed, The Jones family offer a memorable holiday in their comfortable home. Warm Welsh welcome assured. Croeso cynnes gan y teulu i bawb.

P	🛏	SINGLE PER PERSON B&B		DOUBLE FOR 2 PERSONS B&B		🛏	3
🛏	🐾	MIN £ –	MAX £ –	MIN £ 27.00	MAX £ 36.00	OPEN 1-12	🛁 3

FH — Abermeuring Mansion

Lampeter,
Dyfed SA48 8PP
Tel: (0570) 470216

 HIGHLY COMMENDED

Four poster en suite bedroom, canopy bedroom and bedroom shower en-suite. Ancestral home, listed Welsh farmhouse breakfast and friendly hospitality. "How to find us:" From Lampeter take A482 road for 4 miles, turn right on B4337, follow for 1 mile, take 1st right, follow for 1 mile. On entering Abermeurig village pass a chapel on right, take next left and entrance gates are immediately in front . We are 1 mile from "Lampeter University".

P	⚐	SINGLE PER PERSON B&B		DOUBLE FOR 2 PERSONS B&B		🛏	3
✂	🛏	MIN £ 18.00	MAX £ 18.00	MIN £ 36.00	MAX £ 36.00	OPEN 1-12	🛁 2

H — Berwyn

St Dogmaels,
Cardigan,
Dyfed SA43 3HS
Tel: (0239) 613555

Privately situated in 2 acres delightful grounds with magnificent views overlooking Teifi River, central to beautiful beaches, historic places, golf fishing. Enjoy breakfast with gorgeous views. En-suite with private entrance from grounds. All bedrooms vanity suites, tea/coffee facilities, colour TV, guest lounge, payphone. Private parking. Warm Welsh welcome. Croeso Cynnes I Berwyn.

P	🛏	SINGLE PER PERSON B&B		DOUBLE FOR 2 PERSONS B&B		🛏	3
🛏	🐾					🛁	3
🛏		MIN £ 15.50	MAX £ 18.00	MIN £ 30.00	MAX £ 36.00	OPEN 4-10	

FH — Talywerydd

Penbryn,
Sarnau, Llandysul,
Dyfed SA44 6QY
Tel: (0239) 810322

 COMMENDED

Farmhouse overlooking beautiful Cardigan Bay. 1 double en-suite plus 1 double, 1 twin with wash basins, colour TV, and tea making facilities in all rooms. Heated swimming pool. Childrens play area, private parking. Regret no smoking. Friendly atmosphere.

P	🛏	SINGLE PER PERSON B&B		DOUBLE FOR 2 PERSONS B&B		🛏	3
⚐	🐾	MIN £ 16.00	MAX £ 18.00	MIN £ 32.00	MAX £ 36.00	OPEN 4-9	🛁 1

FH — Brynog Mansion

Felinfach,
Lampeter,
Dyfed SA48 8AQ
Tel: (0570) 470266

 COMMENDED

Spacious 250 year old mansion. Situated in the beautiful Vale of Aeron, midway between Lampeter university town and unique Aberaeron seaside resort 15 minutes by car. Approached by ¼ mile rhododendron lined drive off the A482 main road and village of Felinfach. 2 spacious en-suite bedrooms, other near bathroom, tea making facilities, central heating. Full breakfast served in the grand old furnished dining room.

P	🛏	SINGLE PER PERSON B&B		DOUBLE FOR 2 PERSONS B&B		🛏	3
🛏	🛏					🛁	2
⚐	🐾	MIN £ 16.00	MAX £ 18.00	MIN £ 32.00	MAX £ 36.00	OPEN 1-12	

GH — Brynhyfryd Guest House

Gwbert Road,
Cardigan,
Dyfed SA43 1AE
Tel: (0239) 612861

  HIGHLY COMMENDED

One of Cardigan's longest established guest houses, where a high standard of comfort, cleanliness and good food is always assured. Situated in a pleasant area of the town, within two miles of the coast. All bedrooms have colour television and tea/coffee facilities, en-suites available. Guests lounge, evening meals, easy parking. AA QQQ, RAC Acclaimed. Brochure.

🛏	🛏	SINGLE PER PERSON B&B		DOUBLE FOR 2 PERSONS B&B		🛏	7
⚐	🍽	MIN £ 14.00	MAX £ 15.00	MIN £ 28.00	MAX £ 33.00	OPEN 1-12	🛁 2

GH — Penwern Old Mills

Cribyn,
Lampeter,
Dyfed SA48 7QH
Tel: (0570) 470762

Ⓛ

A former rural woollen mill set in a quiet valley alongside a small stream. Double, twin and single rooms, cot and highchair available. Central heating. Large comfortable elevated lounge with television. Trout lakes nearby. Many Mid Wales attractions within reasonable distance. Well behaved pets, children and non smokers welcome.

P	🛏	SINGLE PER PERSON B&B		DOUBLE FOR 2 PERSONS B&B		🛏	3
🛏	🐾					🛁	2
⚐	🍽	MIN £ 13.00	MAX £ 13.00	MIN £ 26.00	MAX £ 26.00	OPEN 1-12	

FH — Bryn Castell Farm

Llanfair Road,
Lampeter,
Dyfed SA48 8JY
Tel: (0570) 422447

  HIGHLY COMMENDED

Bilingual Welsh family on 140 acre riverside farm; Panoramic views of Teifi Valley. Excellent cuisine featuring authentic Welsh recipes and homemade wines. Combined traditional Welsh hospitality with comfort of modern conveniences. One mile from Lampeter town centre. Half mile from Pioneer Co-op store. Signposted Llanfair Clydogau. Opposite W.D. Lewis Agricultural Merchants. Taste of Wales Member.

P	🛏	SINGLE PER PERSON B&B		DOUBLE FOR 2 PERSONS B&B		🛏	3
Ⓒ	🐾					🛁	2
🛏	🍽	MIN £ 15.00		MIN £ 30.00	MAX £ 32.00	OPEN 1-12	
♿	🚳						

FH Nantymedd Farm

Llanfair Clydogau,
Lampeter,
Dyfed SA48 8JZ
Tel: (0570) 45208

COMMENDED

Nantymedd is situated in quiet countryside overlooking the River Teifi, 350 acre dairy and sheep farm with free trout and salmon fishing and riding ponies on the farm. Within easy driving distances seaside resorts of Aberaeron, New Quay, Aberystwyth, market town of Carmarthen, Lampeter, Llanybydder horse fair. Good home cooked food from fresh Welsh produce. Taste of Wales Member.

P C		SINGLE PER PERSON B&B		DOUBLE FOR 2 PERSONS B&B		🛏 2 🛁
		MIN £ 15.00	MAX £ 18.00	MIN £ 30.00	MAX £ 36.00	OPEN 3-11

GH Glanrhyd Isaf

Stags Head,
Llangeitho, nr. Tregaron,
Dyfed SY25 6QU
Tel: (0974) 298762

DE LUXE

A modern bungalow situated on an elevated site surrounded by beautiful countryside. Comfortably furnished. Centrally heated. Double room en-suite, twin room bathroom, both rooms have colour TV and tea/coffee facilities. Ideal walking, touring, bird watching country, pony trekking, golf, fishing in area. 10 miles from coast. OS ref: Sheet 146 Ref: 637-591. Mrs. W.R. Owen.

P C		SINGLE PER PERSON B&B		DOUBLE FOR 2 PERSONS B&B		🛏 2 🛁 1
		MIN £ 16.00	MAX £ 19.00	MIN £ 28.00	MAX £ 34.00	OPEN 1-12

GH Neuaddlas Guest House

Tregaron,
Dyfed SA25 6LJ
Tel: (0974) 298905

COMMENDED

Enjoy the timeless beauty of Wales. Neuaddlas offers you a comfortable relaxing holiday. Large separate lounge with a log fire. Dining room offers home cooked food, overlooking Cors Caron Nature Reserve. Accommodation tastefully furnished. Ground floor bedrooms. Suitable for disabled. Special diets catered for. Fire Certificate held. Located in own spacious grounds. Informative brochure available. AA QQQ

P		SINGLE PER PERSON B&B		DOUBLE FOR 2 PERSONS B&B		🛏 4 🛁 3
TW		MIN £ 16.50	MAX £ 18.50	MIN £ 33.00	MAX £ 37.00	OPEN 1-12

GH Pellorwel

Bwlch-y-Groes,
Ffostrasol, Llandysul,
Dyfed SA44 5JU
Tel: (0239) 851226

L HIGHLY COMMENDED

A friendly welcome awaits our guests. Comfortable accommodation. H&C all rooms, double four poster bed. Charming Victorian style house, conveniently situated for touring, 10 miles Cardigan Bay resorts. Meals freshly cooked using available garden and local produce. Special diets by prior arrangement. Reduced rates for three nights or more. Only house rule " Please close the gate".

P TW		SINGLE PER PERSON B&B		DOUBLE FOR 2 PERSONS B&B		🛏 3 🛁 –
		MIN £ 12.50	MAX £ –	MIN £ 25.00	MAX £ –	OPEN 1-12

GH Arfon View

Francis Street,
New Quay,
Dyfed SA45 9QL
Tel: (0545) 560837

HIGHLY COMMENDED

Arfon View is an old Victorian house, full of character. Excellent views of Cardigan Bay to Snowdonia. Situated above New Quay looking down on harbour and village. Quiet, secluded in private grounds. Five minutes from the sea. Ample parking. Large rooms with H&C, shaver points, guest lounge. Warm Welsh welcome with personal service recommended highly.

P C		SINGLE PER PERSON B&B		DOUBLE FOR 2 PERSONS B&B		🛏 3 🛁 –
		MIN £ 16.00	MAX £ 18.00	MIN £ 32.00	MAX £ 36.00	OPEN 4-9

Cwm Tudu, Nr. New Quay

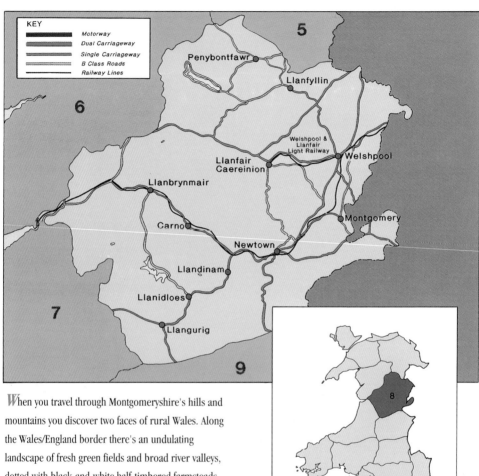

When you travel through Montgomeryshire's hills and mountains you discover two faces of rural Wales. Along the Wales/England border there's an undulating landscape of fresh green fields and broad river valleys, dotted with black-and-white half-timbered farmsteads that might have been transplanted from Shakespeare Country. But head further west, into Montgomeryshire's untamed highlands, and the scene changes dramatically. These mountains and moors, with their thin scattering of sturdy, stone-built dwellings, are the home of the hardy hill-sheep farmer.

Montgomeryshire is also home to some of Wales's most scenic lakes – remote Lake Vyrnwy, almost lost in thickly wooded uplands, and Llyn Clywedog, surrounded by rolling hills and forests.

Explore the area from market towns and country villages. Stay, for example, at Welshpool, Llanidloes or Machynlleth, three handsome, historic towns. Or choose somewhere smaller, such as Montgomery with its pretty Georgian buildings and ruined castle. Nearby Powis Castle is anything but a ruin. Don't miss this sumptuous National Trust house, which stands in magnificent grounds on the outskirts of Welshpool.

CARNO
Map Ref: De6

Located in the middle of Mid Wales - an excellent touring base for exploring Southern Snowdonia, the Cardigan Bay coast, Cambrian Mountains and border country. Only a small village, but famous as the base for Laura Ashley fabrics and fashions.

LLANBRYNMAIR
Map Ref: De5

Scattered mountain-ringed village on Afon (River) Twymyn, a tributary of the Dovey. Travel south from here on the B4518 to the huge man-made lake of Llyn Clywedog – an inspiring mountain route.

LLANDINAM
Map Ref: Ea7

Beautifully kept country village with black-and-white half- timbered houses, noted for its flower displays. Statue of David Davies (1818-90), the archetypal 'local boy made good', who made his fortune from coal. Good base from which to explore undulating border country and the wilder hills, mountains and lakeland to the west.

LLANFAIR CAEREINION
Map Ref: Eb5

Pleasant town set amid rolling hills and forest in lovely Vale of Banwy. Best known as terminus for narrow-gauge Welshpool and Llanfair Light Railway.

LLANFYLLIN
Map Ref: Eb3

Historic small country town, in rolling peaceful Powys farmlands. Lake Vyrnwy and 240ft Pistyll Rhaeadr waterfall are popular beauty spots nearby. Visit the Bird and Butterfly World, an attraction with birds from all over the world.

LLANIDLOES
Map Ref: Gd1

Historic and attractive market town at confluence of Severn and Clywedog rivers; excellent touring centre. Noted for its 16th-century market hall, now a museum, and other fine half-timbered buildings. Interesting shops. Massive Clywedog dam and lake 3 miles away on B4518. Take the scenic drive around lakeside and visit the Bryn Tail Lead Mine beneath the dam.

MACHYNLLETH
Map Ref: Dc5

Historic market town near beautiful Dovey Estuary. Owain Glyndŵr's Parliament House in the wide handsome main street is now a museum and brass rubbing centre. Superbly equipped Bro Dyfi Leisure Centre offers wide range of activities. Ancient and modern meet here; the inventive Centre for Alternative Technology is 3 miles away, just off A487 to Dolgellau. Felin Crewi Flour Mill is off A489 2 miles to the east. ⇌

MONTGOMERY
Map Ref: Ec6

Hilltop market town of distinctive Georgian architecture beneath the ruins of a 13th-century castle. Offa's Dyke, which once marked the border, runs nearby. Not far from Welshpool and Powis Castle.

NEWTOWN
Map Ref: Eb6

Busy Severn Valley market town and one-time home of Welsh flannel industry. Textile history recalled in small museum; another museum based around Robert Owen, pioneer socialist, who lived here. Town also has interesting WH Smith Museum, solid old buildings, river promenade, street market and the lively Theatr Hafren. ⇌

Pistyll Rhaeadr

PENYBONTFAWR
Map Ref: Eb3

Secluded village amid forests and lakes, near the spectacular 240ft Pistyll Rhaeadr waterfalls. Pony trekking and walking country, with hills and woods all around. Lake Vyrnwy Visitor Centre nearby.

WELSHPOOL
Map Ref: Ec5

Old market town of the borderlands, full of character, with half-timbered buildings and welcoming inns. Attractive canalside museum. Good shopping centre; golf and angling. Powis Castle is an impressive stately home with a Clive of India Museum and outstanding gardens. Ride the narrow-gauge Welshpool and Llanfair Light Railway, visit the Moors Wildlife Collection. ⇌

Llyn Clywedog

FH Pentre Uchaf

Carno,
Montgomeryshire
Powys SY17 5JP
Tel: (0686) 420663

A warm welcome awaits you at this family run farm, set amidst glorious countryside. Situated ½ mile off the A470 coast road. Traditional stone farmhouse. Colour TV, log fires. Dining room. En-suite bedroom - colour TV, tea/coffee facilities, central heating. Ideal base for touring Mid Wales, walking, cycling, golf, shooting. Mrs. Gwyneira Bound.

P		SINGLE PER PERSON B&B		DOUBLE FOR 2 PERSONS B&B			1
C							1
		MIN £	MAX £	MIN £	MAX £	OPEN 4-10	
		–	24.00	28.00			

FH Trewython Farm

Llandinam,
Powys SY17 5BQ
Tel: (0686) 688444

AWARD HIGHLY COMMENDED

Trewython is a mixed farm set in beautiful countryside in peaceful surroundings. A traditional beamed farmhouse comfortably furnished with a warm welcome and good home cooking. En-suite bedrooms with tea making facilities. An ideal location for touring Mid Wales. Brochure available.

P		SINGLE PER PERSON B&B		DOUBLE FOR 2 PERSONS B&B			3
							2
		MIN £	MAX £	MIN £	MAX £	OPEN 5-10	
		15.00	16.00	34.00	38.00		

H Lloyds

Cambrian Place,
Llanidloes,
Powys SY18 6BX
Tel: (0686) 412284
Fax: (0686) 412666

In a quiet part of the centre of Llanidloes, Lloyds has been a hotel and restaurant for over 120 years. An ideal centre for walking, cycling or touring, most of the delights of Wales are within reach: from moor and mountain to sea and sand. Tom and Roy will keep a welcome for you.

C		SINGLE PER PERSON B&B		DOUBLE FOR 2 PERSONS B&B			10
		MIN £	MAX £	MIN £	MAX £	OPEN 1-12	
		13.50	16.00	27.50	32.00		

H Star Inn

Dylife, nr. Staylittle,
Llanbrynmair,
Powys SY19 7BW
Tel: (0650) 521345

APPROVED

Set in some of Britain's most breathtaking countryside the Star Inn is an idyllic venue for exploring the superb local areas. All rooms have H&C. There are two en-suite. We are famous for our excellent home cooking and real ales. Own residents lounge. TV. Relaxed ambience and a warm and friendly welcome always guaranteed.

P		SINGLE PER PERSON B&B		DOUBLE FOR 2 PERSONS B&B			7
							2
		MIN £	MAX £	MIN £	MAX £	OPEN 1-12	
		17.00	19.00	34.00	38.00		

FH Madog's Wells

Llanfair Caereinion,
Welshpool,
Powys SY21 0DE
Tel: (0938) 810446

Warm welcome awaits visitors to our small hill farm in secluded valley. Ideal for touring Mid Wales. Wash basins in rooms. Visitors bathroom. Families welcome. Reduced rates for under 12's. TV, games room, also two fully equipped 6/8 berth caravans £115.00 - £140.00 per week. £25.00 per day. Astronomical observatory with superb 16" dobsonian telescope. Brochure available.

P		SINGLE PER PERSON B&B		DOUBLE FOR 2 PERSONS B&B			3
							–
		MIN £	MAX £	MIN £	MAX £	OPEN 1-12	
		–	13.50	–	27.00		

GH Severn View Guest House

China Street,
Llanidloes,
Powys SY18 6AB
Tel: (0686) 412207

This licensed guest house is set in the centre of the first town on the River Severn. Llanidloes is a small market town on the main Midland-Aberystwyth road and is quite near to the coast. All bedrooms have H&C and are centrally heated. There are numerous glorious walks, golf course and fishing nearby.

P		SINGLE PER PERSON B&B		DOUBLE FOR 2 PERSONS B&B			7
							–
		MIN £	MAX £	MIN £	MAX £	OPEN 1-12	
		15.00	18.00	28.00	30.00		

GH Cyfeiliog Guest House

Bont Dolgadfan,
Llanbrynmair,
Powys SY19 7BB
Tel: (0650) 521231

COMMENDED

Licensed guest house in pretty hamlet beside River Twymyn. Centrally heated throughout. Open fire, beamed lounge. Relaxed friendly atmosphere. TV, books, information maps. Wonderful holiday centre. Walking, birdwatching, castles, lakes, touring, golf. Sea 25 miles, Machynlleth, Centre for Alternative Technology 15 miles. Evening meal, packed lunches, vegetarians welcome. Ideal cosy winter breaks.

P		SINGLE PER PERSON B&B		DOUBLE FOR 2 PERSONS B&B			3
							1
TW		MIN £	MAX £	MIN £	MAX £	OPEN 1-12	
		13.50	15.00	27.00	30.00		

FH Delwyn Farm

Derlwyn Lane,
Llanfyllin,
Powys SY22 5LB
Tel: (0691) 648249

Delwyn offers one family, one twin bedded room on first floor, double bedded en suite ground floor. Situated 300 yards down Derwlwyn Lane off the A490 at Southern approach. Opposite 30 mph sign to Llanfyllin. Warm welcome guaranteed. Ideal base for walking, cycling, touring. Ample parking. Quiet peaceful homely atmosphere. Dining room. Comfortable lounge.

P		SINGLE PER PERSON B&B		DOUBLE FOR 2 PERSONS B&B			3
							1
		MIN £	MAX £	MIN £	MAX £	OPEN 4-10	
		16.00	16.00	30.00	30.00		

FH Esgairmaen

Y Fan,
Llanidloes,
Powys SY18 6UT
Tel: (05516) 272

Esgairmaen is a farmhouse situated 1 mile from the Clywedog Reservoir, where fishing and sailing can be enjoyed. An ideal base for walking, bird watching and exploring the nearby forests. The farmhouse commands magnificent views and the atmosphere is peaceful. Guests can be sure of a warm welcome.

P		SINGLE PER PERSON B&B		DOUBLE FOR 2 PERSONS B&B			2
							1
		MIN £	MAX £	MIN £	MAX £	OPEN 3-10	
		–	–	28.00	32.00		

FH | The Drewin Farm

Churchstoke,
Montgomery,
Powys SY15 6TW
Tel: (0588) 620325

This friendly family run farmhouse was featured on BBC Travel Show 1993. Overlooking panoramic views. Bedrooms have TV, hairdryer and drinks facilities. En-suite available. Games room with snooker table. Good home cooking is served in the oak beamed dining room. Vegetarian by request. Offa's Dyke footpath runs through farm. A warm welcome awaits. AA.

		SINGLE PER PERSON B&B		DOUBLE FOR 2 PERSONS B&B			2
		MIN £	MAX £	MIN £	MAX £		1
		–	28.00	–	34.00	OPEN 3-10	

GH | Melin-y-Wig Guest House

Aberystwyth Road,
Machynlleth,
Powys SY20 8ET
Tel: (0654) 703933

L

Comfortable guest house in historic market town. Convenient for walking, touring and golf. Leisure centre nearby, including swimming pool. Coast, nature reserves and centre for alternative technology. Few minutes drive. Parking facilities. Wash basins, TV, central heating and tea/coffee facilities in all rooms. Parking facilities. Contact Pat or Peter Eley.

		SINGLE PER PERSON B&B		DOUBLE FOR 2 PERSONS B&B			2
		MIN £	MAX £	MIN £	MAX £		–
		–	–	26.00	28.00	OPEN 3-11	

FH | Mathafarn

Llanwrin,
Machynlleth,
Powys SY20 8QJ
Tel: (0650) 511226

HIGHLY COMMENDED

Henry VII is reputed to have stayed here en-route to the battle of Bosworth. Now this 16th Century elegant country house is part of a working farm. Inglenook fire, central heating, television lounge. One twin, private bathroom, double en-suite, one single, tea/coffee making facilities. Close to Machynlleth, Centre for Alternative Technology and beautiful coastline of Aberdovey.

		SINGLE PER PERSON B&B		DOUBLE FOR 2 PERSONS B&B			2
		MIN £	MAX £	MIN £	MAX £		2
		16.00	17.00	32.00	34.00	OPEN 1-12	

GH | Caeheulon

Aberhosan,
Machynlleth,
Powys SY20 8UR
Tel: (0654) 703243

HIGHLY COMMENDED

Quiet comfortable 17th Century converted farmhouse off mountain road south Machynlleth, near Glyndwr's Way. Good centre for walking, touring and golf. Close to coast, nature reserves, little trains, Centre for Alternative Technology and Leisure Centre. One double/family and one twin room. Private facilities. Large interesting garden. Views. Non smoking. Contact Wendy Morgan.

		SINGLE PER PERSON B&B		DOUBLE FOR 2 PERSONS B&B			2
		MIN £	MAX £	MIN £	MAX £		2
		–	–	32.00	32.00	OPEN 4-10	

FH | Bacheiddon Farm

Aberhosan,
Machynlleth,
Powys SY20 8SG
Tel: (0654) 702229

850 acre beef and sheep farm. Six miles from the market town of Machynlleth and within easy reach of the sea and Snowdonia National Park. Three double en-suite bedrooms with tea/coffee facilities, home cooking, own spring water. Lounge with TV and reading material. Brochure from Mrs. A. Lewis.

		SINGLE PER PERSON B&B		DOUBLE FOR 2 PERSONS B&B			3
		MIN £	MAX £	MIN £	MAX £		3
		17.00	19.00	34.00	38.00	OPEN 5-10	

GH | Greenfields Guest House

Kerry, Newtown,
Powys SY16 4LH
Tel: (0686) 670596
Fax: (0686) 670354

A warm welcome awaits you at Greenfields situated on the A489 ¼ mile east of Kerry. Our bedrooms have picturesque views of the rolling hills of Kerry. Lounge has colour TV and open log fire. Good stopping point for one night stops, weekends or longer breaks, while exploring beautiful Mid Wales and the borderlands. Your contact Vi Madeley.

		SINGLE PER PERSON B&B		DOUBLE FOR 2 PERSONS B&B			3
		MIN £	MAX £	MIN £	MAX £		–
		13.00	15.00	26.00	30.00	OPEN 1-12	

GH | Maenllwyd

Newtown Road,
Machynlleth,
Powys SY20 8EY
Tel: (0654) 702928
Fax: (0654) 702928

HIGHLY COMMENDED

Licensed guest house. Some en-suite rooms all tastefully decorated. TV's, tea/coffee all rooms. Noted for our breakfasts. Large garden, off road parking. Bike storage. Will collect from station. Credit cards accepted. Telephone or fax to Margaret or Nigel Vince.

		SINGLE PER PERSON B&B		DOUBLE FOR 2 PERSONS B&B			7
		MIN £	MAX £	MIN £	MAX £		4
		–	–	28.00	34.00	OPEN 1-12	

FH | Cefn Farm

Darowen,
Machynlleth,
Powys SY20 8NS
Tel: (0650) 511336 or 511273

Lies at the end of small peaceful village amidst beautiful hill farm country, central for touring North and Mid Wales and west coast. A country lovers paradise with excellent walking from the house. Bird watching, wild flowers etc. Oak beamed lounge, dining room with spectacular views. Quiet dogs by arrangement. En-suite bedroom, wash basins in rooms. Personal service and attention.

		SINGLE PER PERSON B&B		DOUBLE FOR 2 PERSONS B&B			3
		MIN £	MAX £	MIN £	MAX £		1
		14.00	–	28.00	–	OPEN 1-12	

FH | Dyffryn

Aberhafesp,
Newtown,
Powys SY16 3JD
Tel: (0686) 688817

DE LUXE

Lovingly restored 17th Century half timbered barn on 200 acre sheep and beef farm. Three en-suite bedrooms, colour TV's, centrally heated. Guest lounge and dining room. Guests welcome to watch all farm activities, lovely walks, lakes, bird watching and golf nearby. Delicious evening meals including vegetarian. Warm welcome guaranteed from David and Sue Jones.

		SINGLE PER PERSON B&B		DOUBLE FOR 2 PERSONS B&B			3
		MIN £	MAX £	MIN £	MAX £		3
		19.00	19.00	38.00	38.00	OPEN 1-12	

FH | Llettyderyn

Mochdre,
Newtown,
Powys SY16 4JY
Tel: (0686) 626131

AWARD — HIGHLY COMMENDED

Restored farmhouse with exposed beams, inglenook fireplace, traditional parlour. All rooms en-suite and drinks trays. Vegetarians catered for. Excellent farmhouse cooking including home baked bread. We are 2 miles from Newtown A489/470 and have superb views from our working farm rearing sheep and beef. Ample parking. Central heating.

		SINGLE PER PERSON B&B		DOUBLE FOR 2 PERSONS B&B			3
							3
		MIN £ 18.00	MAX £ 19.00	MIN £ 28.00	MAX £ 32.00	OPEN 1-12	

GH | Glyndwr

Penybontfawr,
Powys SY10 0NT
Tel: (0691 74) 430

COMMENDED

17th Century stone cottage in the beautiful Tanat Valley. Oak beams, open fires. Bedrooms have private bathrooms, tea/coffee facilities. Dining room/television lounge. Also cosy cottage suite, double bedroom, en-suite shower, private lounge, colour TV, Midi Hi-fi, stable door to garden and riverside patio. Good home cooking and a warm friendly welcome. Ideal walking, touring.

		SINGLE PER PERSON B&B		DOUBLE FOR 2 PERSONS B&B			3
							3
		MIN £ —	MAX £ —	MIN £ 28.00	MAX £ 32.00	OPEN 1-12	

FH | Wernddu Farm

Penybontfawr,
via Oswestry,
Powys SY10 0HW
Tel: (069174) 221

COMMENDED

One double, one twin family with wash basins, tea/coffee making facilities. A friendly homely atmosphere awaits you at Wernddu Farm which is a working farm surrounded by beautiful countryside from which to tour the area, many attractions, gardens, walking, fishing, bird watching, waterfalls and lakes. Enquiries to Enid Roberts.

		SINGLE PER PERSON B&B		DOUBLE FOR 2 PERSONS B&B			2
		MIN £ 15.00	MAX £ 20.00	MIN £ 24.00	MAX £ —	OPEN 1-11	

FH | Lower-Gwestydd

Llanllwchaiarn,
Newtown,
Powys SY16 3AY
Tel: (0686) 626718

AWARD — HIGHLY COMMENDED

Beautiful half timbered 17th Century listed farmhouse, just off B4568, 1½ miles north Newtown. 2 rooms en-suite, all centrally heated, beverage trays. Separate dining room, lounge with colour TV. Large garden providing fresh produce for table. Lovely views and country walks from this 200 acre farm. Only 1 hour drive from sea. 20 minutes Powis Castle, narrow gauge railway with trekking, golf, leisure centre nearby.

		SINGLE PER PERSON B&B		DOUBLE FOR 2 PERSONS B&B			3
							2
		MIN £ 15.50	MAX £ 16.00	MIN £ 31.00	MAX £ 32.00	OPEN 1-12	

FH | Glanhafon

Penybontfawr,
Powys SY10 0EW
Tel: (0691 74) 377

COMMENDED

Glanhafon is a traditional Welsh farmhouse situated in the upper Tanat Valley close to Lake Vyrnwy and Pistyll Falls. A working sheep farm with rock climbing and hill walks on farm. One twin private bathroom, double and family en-suite, own sitting room with log fire, central heating. Children welcome. Enquiries to Anne Evans.

		SINGLE PER PERSON B&B		DOUBLE FOR 2 PERSONS B&B			3
							3
		MIN £ 14.00	MAX £ 18.00	MIN £ 26.00	MAX £ 30.00	OPEN 4-10	

GH | Peniarth

10 Cefn Hawys (off Adelaide Drive),
Red Bank, Welshpool,
Powys SY21 7RH
Tel: (0938) 552324

A warm friendly welcome awaits you. Detached house situated at the end of a quiet cul-de-sac. On the outskirts of a small market town. No smoking. Special rates for children. Parking, central heating. One of the bedrooms is en-suite.

		SINGLE PER PERSON B&B		DOUBLE FOR 2 PERSONS B&B			3
							1
		MIN £ 13.00	MAX £ 13.00	MIN £ 26.00	MAX £ 32.00	OPEN 4-10	

GH | Blaen Hirnant Guest House

Hirnant, Penybontfawr,
Powys SY10 0HR
Tel: (0691 73) 330

HIGHLY COMMENDED

14/15th Century Welsh farmhouse, peacefully situated in Montgomeryshire hills. Tastefully renovated exposing original cruck beam construction, inglenook fireplace. En-suite rooms have TV/radio, tea/coffee, central heating. Comfortable lounge, oak beamed dining room. Pre-booked dinner available. Special diets catered for. Own produce. 3 miles Lake Vyrnwy. Walking, bird watching, touring. Easy reach of many places of interest.

		SINGLE PER PERSON B&B		DOUBLE FOR 2 PERSONS B&B			3
							3
		MIN £ —	MAX £ —	MIN £ 28.00	MAX £ 30.00	OPEN 1-12	

FH | Penyceunant

Penybontfawr,
Powys SY10 0PF
Tel: (069 174) 459

COMMENDED

Old farmhouse in elevated position above Tanat Valley. Substantial rooms with spectacular views, wash basins, colour TV, and easy chair. Also guests garden, lounge. Ideal as a secluded retreat, yet well placed for touring. We specialise in walking holidays offering half board packages for week long or weekend breaks. Information given, routecard loan. Enquiries and brochures from Anna Francis.

		SINGLE PER PERSON B&B		DOUBLE FOR 2 PERSONS B&B			2
							3
		MIN £ 16.00	MAX £ 16.00	MIN £ 28.00	MAX £ 28.00	OPEN 2-11	

WELSHPOOL

GH	Tresi-Aur

Brookfield Road,
Welshpool,
Powys SY21 7PZ
Tel: (0938) 552430

Family or double room with own bathroom and shower. Car parking. Children under 14 reduction. Central heating, TV, tea or coffee, telephone available. Open January until November. No smoking. Shaving points. Warm friendly welcome awaits. Golf, fishing, pony trekking, walking facilities in area.

		SINGLE PER PERSON B&B		DOUBLE FOR 2 PERSONS B&B			1
							1
		MIN £ 13.00	MAX £ 13.00	MIN £ 26.00	MAX £ 26.00	OPEN 1-11	

FH	Tynllwyn Farm

Welshpool,
Powys SY21 9BW
Tel: (0938) 553175

Tynllwyn is a family farm and farmhouse with a friendly welcome. Good farmhouse food and bar licence. All bedrooms have central heating, colour TV, tea and coffee facilities, hot and cold wash units. 1 mile from the lovely market town of Welshpool (on the A490 north). Very quiet and pleasantly situated on a hillside with beautiful views. 2 day short bargain break available October-March. Pets by arrangement. Taste of Wales member.

		SINGLE PER PERSON B&B		DOUBLE FOR 2 PERSONS B&B			5
		MIN £ 14.00	MAX £ 14.00	MIN £ 28.00	MAX £ 28.00	OPEN 1-12	

Powis Castle

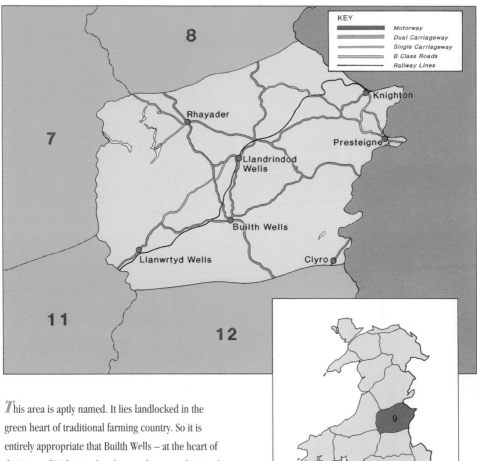

*T*his area is aptly named. It lies landlocked in the green heart of traditional farming country. So it is entirely appropriate that Builth Wells – at the heart of the Heart of Wales! – plays host each year to the Royal Welsh Show, the premier gathering of farming folk.

Builth is one of four 'Wells' towns in the Heart of Wales. Of the others – Llandrindod, Llanwrtyd and Llangammarch – Llandrindod is the largest. All prospered during the heyday of the spa town. Llandrindod Wells, in particular, preserves memories of those fashionable times gone by – in its impressive Victorian streets, parklands and boating lake, and also during its annual Victorian Festival. Llanwrtyd Wells, Britain's smallest town, is busy again as a pony

trekking, walking and mountain biking centre.

Water seems to be a dominant theme here. The Wye, a famous fishing river, flows through the middle of the area. And in the hills above Rhayader there are the Elan Valley lakes, Wales's first – and possibly most scenic – man-made reservoirs. Call in at the Elan Valley Visitor Centre for an introduction to these beautiful lakelands and their prolific wildlife.

BUILTH WELLS
Map Ref: Ge4

Solidly built old country town which plays host every July to the Royal Welsh Agricultural Show, Wales's largest farming gathering. Lovely setting on River Wye amid beautiful hills. Lively sheep and cattle markets. Good shopping for local products, touring centre for Mid Wales and border country. River walk, Wyeside Arts Centre.

KNIGHTON
Map Ref: Hb2

Tref y Clawdd, 'the town on the dyke', stands in a deep wooded valley where the 8th-century Offa's Dyke defines the ancient border between Wales and England. Some of the best- preserved stretches of the earthen dyke can be found in the undisturbed hills near the town's Offa's Dyke Centre. ⇌

LLANDRINDOD WELLS
Map Ref: Ge3

Victorian spa town with spacious street and impressive architecture. Victorian-style visitor centre and excellent museum tracing the history of spa. Magic Lantern Theatre. A popular inland resort with golf, fishing, bowling, boating and tennis available. Good selection of hotels. Excellent touring centre for Mid Wales hills and lakes. Annual Victorian Festival in August. ⇌

Mountain biking, nr. Llanwrtyd Wells

LLANWRTYD WELLS
Map Ref: Gc5

One-time spa encircled by wild and beautiful countryside, now a centre for pony trekking, walking and fishing. Cambrian Woollen Factory is a popular attraction. For spectacular views explore nearby Abergwesyn Pass/Llyn Brianne area. Mountain bike centre. Diverse programme of events throughout the year. ⇌

RHAYADER
Map Ref: Gd2

Country market town full of character, with inviting inns and Welsh craft products in the shops. Excellent base for exploring mountains and lakes (Elan Valley and Claerwen), with opportunities for pony trekking, mountain biking and fishing. Small museum. An interesting walk through the country on the nearby Gigrin Farm Trail.

Lear's Magic Lantern Theatre, Llandrindod Wells

H | Griffin Inn

Cwm Owen,
Builth Wells,
Powys LD2 3HY
Tel: (0982) 552778

 COMMENDED

Step back in time on an adventure into the past - The Griffin Inn, gas lit bar and restaurant. All rooms en-suite, centrally heated, tea/coffee facilities, TV Sky. Our own trout fishing on premises free for guests. Trout up to 5lbs. Draught ale, fine wines, splendid walks and views. 15th Century Drovers Inn, original stone flagged floors. Pets by arrangement.

		SINGLE PER PERSON B&B		DOUBLE FOR 2 PERSONS B&B			3
		MIN £	MAX £	MIN £	MAX £	OPEN	3
		–	–	38.00	38.00	1-12	

FH | Caepandy Farm

Garth Road,
Builth Wells,
Powys LD2 3NS
Tel: (0982) 553793

L

A warm welcome awaits guests to Caepandy Farm. This modernised 17th Century house stands 1 mile from Builth Wells with magnificent views of the Irfon Valley and surrounding countryside. Guests TV lounge, tea/coffee all rooms. Within easy reach of Black mountains, Brecon Beacons, Hay-on-Wye. A good base from which to tour Mid Wales.

		SINGLE PER PERSON B&B		DOUBLE FOR 2 PERSONS B&B			3
		MIN £	MAX £	MIN £	MAX £	OPEN	–
		12.00	13.00	24.00	26.00	1-12	

FH | Fairview

Green Lane,
Onibury, Craven Arms,
Shropshire SY7 9BL
Tel: (0584) 77505

 HIGHLY COMMENDED

300 year old small holding on Shropshire/Welsh borders. Non smoking residence. Log fires. Panoramic views. Lounge with TV. Fresh home cooked evening meals using own or local produce. Tea and coffee facilities. Hot and cold all rooms. One room en-suite. 1½ miles off main road. Reduced rates three day or one week breaks. Comfortable family home.

		SINGLE PER PERSON B&B		DOUBLE FOR 2 PERSONS B&B			3
		MIN £	MAX £	MIN £	MAX £	OPEN	1
		15.00	16.50	30.00	33.00	4-10	

GH | The Cedars Guest House

Hay Road,
Builth Wells,
Powys LD2 3BP
Tel: (0982) 553356

 COMMENDED

Family run guest house situated on A470 just outside Builth Wells. Good views overlooking Royal Welsh Showground. Home cooking, vegetables fresh from garden. Comfortable lounge bar. En-suite bedrooms. Ideally situated for day trips covering Mid Wales. Builth Wells supports 18 hole golf course, bowls, many walks along River Wye and many more activities. Ideal for weekend or holiday.

		SINGLE PER PERSON B&B		DOUBLE FOR 2 PERSONS B&B			7
		MIN £	MAX £	MIN £	MAX £	OPEN	5
		14.00	16.00	34.00	36.00	1-12	

FH | Gwern-y-Mynach Farm

Llanafan Fawr,
Builth Wells,
Powys LD2 3PN
Tel: (0597) 89256

L

Gwern-y-Mynach is a mixed sheep and dairy farm situated in heart of Wales, near the three famous wells within easy reach of the Elan Valley reservoir. Which make a lovely walk from the farm across the mountains. A most friendly welcome awaits all visitors. Cricket, golf, bowling, swimming at Builth Wells Sports Hall.

		SINGLE PER PERSON B&B		DOUBLE FOR 2 PERSONS B&B			2
		MIN £	MAX £	MIN £	MAX £	OPEN	1
		12.00	16.00	15.00	30.00	1-12	

H | Drovers Arms

Howey,
Llandrindod Wells,
Powys LD1 5PT
Tel: (0597) 822508

L

Quiet Inn in picturesque village just off A483. 2 bars, real ales. Camra and Egon Ronay Food Guide recommended. Light meals and full à la Carte menu freshly cooked. Patio garden, ideal spot for golf, fishing, walking. Reduction for 2 nights or more. Half an hour to Brecon Beacons, close to Elan Valley dams.

		SINGLE PER PERSON B&B		DOUBLE FOR 2 PERSONS B&B			3
		MIN £	MAX £	MIN £	MAX £	OPEN	1
		19.00	19.00	30.00	38.00	4-10	

GH | Old Vicarage

Erwood,
Builth Wells,
Powys LD2 3EX
Tel: (0982) 560680

Beautiful situation in peaceful grounds just off A470 near Erwood. Breathtaking views over Wye Valley to Black Mountains. Elegant decoration, spacious throughout. Beverage tray, H&C all rooms, one colour TV. Guests own bathroom, separate wc. Private TV lounge, adequate comfort and indoor games. Separate dining room. Traditional roasts with veg from our garden. Farm animals. Children/ pets welcome. Ideal to tour Mid/South Wales.

		SINGLE PER PERSON B&B		DOUBLE FOR 2 PERSONS B&B			3
		MIN £	MAX £	MIN £	MAX £	OPEN	–
		12.00	13.00	24.00	26.00	1-12	

FH | Cwmgilla

Knighton,
Powys LD7 1PG
Tel: (0547) 528387

 HIGHLY COMMENDED

Cwmgilla is a mixed farm set in a secluded valley with beautiful views of surrounding hills and woods. It is a comfortable modern farmhouse with TV lounge, dining room. All bedrooms with H&C. Traditional farmhouse breakfast. Large garden. Trout pool. Wildlife. Glyndwr's Way footpath runs through farm. Offa's Dyke nearby. Ideal spot for walking, touring or just relaxing. Open all year (closed Christmas and New Year).

		SINGLE PER PERSON B&B		DOUBLE FOR 2 PERSONS B&B			3
		MIN £	MAX £	MIN £	MAX £	OPEN	–
		15.00	17.00	30.00	30.00	1-11	

GH | Corven Hall

Howey,
Llandrindod Wells,
Powys LD1 5RE
Tel: (0597) 823368

  HIGHLY COMMENDED

Victorian country house in large grounds, peaceful setting surrounded by beautiful countryside. 1½ miles south of Llandrindod Wells off A483 at Gwesty sign. The house is licensed, centrally heated and spacious. TV lounge, bar. Traditional home cooking freshly prepared. Most bedrooms en-suite, tea/coffee facilities. Ground floor accommodation. Walking, bird watching country. Dinners by arrangement. Brochure available.

		SINGLE PER PERSON B&B		DOUBLE FOR 2 PERSONS B&B			10
		MIN £	MAX £	MIN £	MAX £	OPEN	8
		–	–	30.00	35.00	2-11	

GH | Pen-y-Cae

Church Fields,
Cregrina, Llandrindod Wells,
Powys LD1 5SF
Tel: (0982) 570270

A warm welcome awaits you in our modern single storey accommodation. Situated in beautiful secluded valley, near the market town of Builth Wells and the Spa town of Llandrindod Wells. Ideal for exploring the many attractions Mid Wales has to offer. All rooms colour TV, tea/coffee making facilities. En-suite available. Use of garden.

		SINGLE PER PERSON B&B		DOUBLE FOR 2 PERSONS B&B		2
		MIN £	MAX £	MIN £	MAX £	1
		–	–	28.00	32.00	OPEN 4-9

FH | Highbury Farm

Llanyre,
Llandrindod Wells,
Powys LD1 6EA
Tel: (0597) 822716

  HIGHLY COMMENDED

A small holding situated one mile west of Llandrindod Wells on the edge of the village of Llanyre. A warm welcome awaits you. Comfortable spacious rooms. Beverage trays in bedrooms. Firm beds guaranteed. Full central heating. TV lounge. Separate dinning room. Evening meal optional. Large garden. Brochure and enquiries to Mrs. Shirley Evans.

		SINGLE PER PERSON B&B		DOUBLE FOR 2 PERSONS B&B		3
		MIN £	MAX £	MIN £	MAX £	1
		13.00	16.00	26.00	32.00	OPEN 4-10

GH | Cerdyn Country Guest House

Cerdyn Villa,
Llanwrtyd Wells,
Powys LD5 4RS
Tel: (0591) 3635

Peace, pure air and dramatic scenery to enjoy with comfortable accommodation and plentiful good home cooked food to return to. Family run guest house in large Victorian House. Quiet location half mile from town near BR station. Lounge, dining room, private facilities, beverage trays. Children welcome. Pony trekking, cycling, guided walks, bird watching, fishing nearby.

		SINGLE PER PERSON B&B		DOUBLE FOR 2 PERSONS B&B		4
		MIN £	MAX £	MIN £	MAX £	2
		–	–	29.00	35.00	OPEN 1-12

GH | Ty Clyd

Park Terrace,
Llandrindod Wells,
Powys LD1 6AY
Tel: (0597) 822122

Tea and coffee making facilities in lounge. One bath, two showers, three toilets, to service maximum eleven guests. Quiet cul-de-sac overlooking wooded park. Easy on road parking. Garage available for push bikes etc. Close to train station.

		SINGLE PER PERSON B&B		DOUBLE FOR 2 PERSONS B&B		7
		MIN £	MAX £	MIN £	MAX £	–
		14.00	14.00	28.00	28.00	OPEN 1-12

FH | Holly Farm

Howey,
Llandrindod Wells,
Powys LD1 5PP
Tel: (0597) 822402

  HIGHLY COMMENDED

Holly Farm set in beautiful countryside offering guests a friendly welcome. 1½ miles south of Llandrindod Wells. Excellent base for exploring lakes, mountains and bird watching. Some rooms en-suite, beverage trays, TV lounge, log fire, dining room separate tables and superb meals, using home produce. AA listed. Safe car parking. Brochure Mrs. Ruth Jones.

		SINGLE PER PERSON B&B		DOUBLE FOR 2 PERSONS B&B		3
		MIN £	MAX £	MIN £	MAX £	2
		17.00	19.00	30.80	36.00	OPEN 4-11

GH | Brynteg

East Street,
Rhayader,
Powys LD6 5EA
Tel: (0597) 810052

Friendly Edwardian guest house over looking hills and gardens. Close to town centre. We have double, twin/family or single rooms with en-suite, central heating, tea/coffee facilities, TV lounge and separate breakfast room. Special rates for 5 nights or more, children sharing half price. Ideally situated for exploring the beautiful Elan Valley and Cambrian Mountains. Croeso.

		SINGLE PER PERSON B&B		DOUBLE FOR 2 PERSONS B&B		3
		MIN £	MAX £	MIN £	MAX £	3
		14.00	15.00	26.00	28.00	OPEN 1-12

FH | Brynhir Farm

Chapel Road,
Howey, Llandrindod Wells,
Powys LD1 5PB
Tel: (0597) 822425

  HIGHLY COMMENDED

Charming olde worlde farmhouse situated 1 mile off A483, in magnificent mountain setting. Traditional inglenook fireplace, exposed oak beams. Ideal relaxing holiday, good walking area. Trout fishing lake. Pied flycatchers, Redstarts and Buzzards commonly seen. Conducted badger sett tours. Beverage trays. Delicious cuisine. 1 mile off A483 through Howey Village, turn right up Chapel Road. Evening meal by arrangement.

		SINGLE PER PERSON B&B		DOUBLE FOR 2 PERSONS B&B		6
		MIN £	MAX £	MIN £	MAX £	3
		15.00	17.00	30.00	34.00	OPEN 4-11

H | Carlton House Hotel

Dolycoed Road,
Llanwrtyd Wells,
Powys LD5 4SN
Tel: (05913) 248

Bow-windowed Edwardian villa at the foot of Cambrian Mountains and lakes of mid Wales. Comfortable wood panelled lounge with log fire. Excellent dinners in small dining room with French doors onto terrace. Golf, pony trekking, riding, mountain biking and bird watching nearby. Special short break rates available. Access and Visa cards are accepted.

		SINGLE PER PERSON B&B		DOUBLE FOR 2 PERSONS B&B		6
		MIN £	MAX £	MIN £	MAX £	2
		17.00	19.00	34.00	38.00	OPEN 1-12

GH | Liverpool House

East Street,
Rhayader,
Powys LD6 5EA
Tel: (0597) 810706

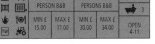

Family run guest house where friendliness and service go hand in hand. Private car parking. Bedrooms have colour TV, clock/radio, tea making facilities and most have en-suite. Full central heating. Spacious lounge. Reduced rates for children. Cot available. Three miles from the beautiful Elan Valley reservoirs. Ideally central for walking, bird watching, fishing and touring.

		SINGLE PER PERSON B&B		DOUBLE FOR 2 PERSONS B&B		4
		MIN £	MAX £	MIN £	MAX £	3
		14.00	–	25.00	–	OPEN 1-12

FH	Beili Neuadd Farmhouse

Beili Neuadd,
Rhayader,
Powys LD6 5NS
Tel: (0597) 810211

AWARD / HIGHLY COMMENDED

Set amidst glorious countryside, beside a trout pool, 2 miles from the market town of Rhayader, best known as the gateway to "The lakeland of Wales". The stonebuilt 16th Century farmhouse has central heating, log fires, well appointed en-suite bedrooms with beverage trays. We offer good imaginative meals using farm and garden produce.

		SINGLE PER PERSON B&B		DOUBLE FOR 2 PERSONS B&B			3
							3
		MIN £ 16.50	MAX £ 17.50	MIN £ 33.00	MAX £ 35.00	OPEN 1-12	

FH	Downfield Farm

Rhayader,
Powys LD6 5PA
Tel: (0597) 810394

Welcome to Downfield, situated one mile east of Rhayader on the A44 with ample parking space. 3 bedrooms all with hot and cold water and shaver points. All bedrooms have tea/coffee making facilities. 2 bathrooms, 1 with shower. Lounge with colour television, dining room with separate tables. Fully centrally heated. Three miles Elan Valley.

		SINGLE PER PERSON B&B		DOUBLE FOR 2 PERSONS B&B			3
							-
		MIN £ 14.00	MAX £ 15.00	MIN £ 26.00	MAX £ 28.00	OPEN 2-10	

AWARD-WINNING GUEST HOUSES AND FARMHOUSES

AWARD

Look out for the Wales Tourist Board Award on the pages of this brochure. Award-winners offer extra-special standards of comfort, furnishings and surroundings. They're as good as many a hotel. And proprietors will have completed college training in tourism.

Elan Valley

It's impossible to summarise South Wales in a sentence, simply because the region – which extends from the borderland Wye Valley across to the western tip of Pembrokeshire – is so full of contrasts. For a

spectacular headlands, and the endless sands of Carmarthen Bay.

Inland, the Brecon Beacons National Park is an exhilarating landscape of open spaces, grassy summits

Worm's Head on the Gower Peninsula

start, there are two very different national parks, the Pembrokeshire Coast and the Brecon Beacons. Add to these the splendid Gower Peninsula, Carmarthen Bay, the Glamorgan Heritage Coast, the characterful Welsh Valleys and the wooded Wye Valley, and you have a multiplicity of holiday choices.

Pembrokeshire is one of Europe's finest stretches of coastal natural beauty. Stay at Tenby or Saundersfoot (you'll find an excellent choice of holiday accommodation here) or at one of the many smaller resorts along this magnificent coastline. Wherever you travel in South Wales, you'll come across attractive seashores – the cliffs and dunes of Glamorgan's Heritage Coast, the popular resorts of Barry Island and Porthcawl, Gower's sheltered bays and

and big skies, popular with walkers and pony trekkers. Abergavenny, Llandovery and, of course, Brecon, are good centres from which to explore the park.

Brecon Beacons

Cardiff Castle

Cardiff, Wales's capital, is a cosmopolitan city of museums, theatres and green spaces, with an architecturally magnificent Civic Centre, ornate castle and exciting new waterfront development. Swansea's stylish marina and Maritime Quarter have been praised

Oakwood Park, nr Narberth

for bringing new life to old docklands. The city's success story is one of the many surprises you'll come across in South Wales, a region of grand castles and 'Great Little Trains', wildlife parks and showcaves, Roman remains and mining museums.

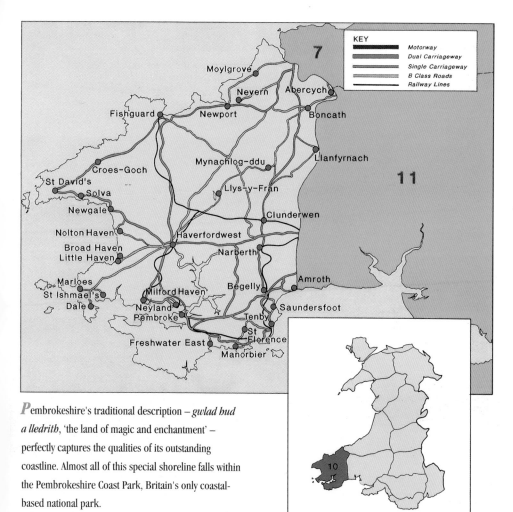

*P*embrokeshire's traditional description – *gwlad hud a lledrith*, 'the land of magic and enchantment' – perfectly captures the qualities of its outstanding coastline. Almost all of this special shoreline falls within the Pembrokeshire Coast Park, Britain's only coastal-based national park.

The park's 225 square miles, running from near Tenby in the south to Cardigan in the north, are indeed extraordinary – they contain everything from towering cliffs to sheltered harbours, huge beaches to secluded coves, wildlife sanctuaries to wooded creeks. The park's boundary, which shadows the coastline for most of the way, even ventures inland between Fishguard and Cardigan to encompass the Preseli Hills, a haunting area scattered with prehistoric sites.

Much of the holiday accommodation is found around stylish Tenby and Saundersfoot. If you're looking for somewhere smaller, there's an excellent choice – Broad Haven, Dale, Solva or St David's to name but a few. There are also many places to stay inland – the old county town of Haverfordwest, for example – which are convenient for exploring all parts of the coast.

71

BEGELLY
Map Ref: Je5

South Pembrokeshire village close to Tenby and Saundersfoot. Excellent beaches and wonderful coastal scenery only a short drive away. Local family attractions include Folly Farm (based at a large working dairy farm), and the Manor House Wildlife and Leisure Park.

BONCATH
Map Ref: Fa6

Small village in foothills of Preseli Mountains on the edge of the Pembrokeshire Coast National Park. Also convenient for exploring southern Cardigan Bay and lovely Teifi Valley.

BROAD HAVEN
Map Ref: Jb5

Sand and green hills cradle this holiday village on St Bride's Bay in the Pembrokeshire Coast National Park. Good beach, accommodation, shops. National Park Information Centre.

CLUNDERWEN
Map Ref: Je4

Centrally located for all of Pembrokeshire. The national park's northern, western and southern shores are all within easy reach of this village, which stands in countryside just south of the Preseli Hills. Llawhaden Castle, Black Pool Mill Caverns and Oakwood Park - one of Wales's top family attractions - all close by. ⇌

CROES-GOCH
Map Ref: Jb3

Small village, useful spot for touring Pembrokeshire Coast National Park - especially its peaceful, rugged northern shores and nearby holiday centres of St David's and Fishguard.

FISHGUARD
Map Ref: Jc2

Lower Fishguard is a cluster of old wharfs and cottages around a beautiful harbour. 'Under Milk Wood' with Richard Burton was filmed here in 1971. Shopping in Fishguard town. Good walks along Pembrokeshire Coast Path and in the country. Nearby Goodwick is the Irish ferry terminal, with a direct link from London. Excellent range of craft workshops in area including Tregwynt Woollen Mill. Music Festival in July. ⇌

FRESHWATER EAST
Map Ref: Jd6

Sheltered sandy bay south-east of Pembroke backed by dunes. Good swimming, access for boats, limited car parking.

HAVERFORDWEST
Map Ref: Jc5

Ancient town – now a good base for exploring the Pembrokeshire Coast National Park – and the administrative and shopping centre for the area. Medieval churches and narrow streets. Museum in the castle grounds, which occupy an outcrop overlooking the town. Most attractive redeveloped riverside and old wharf buildings. Graham Sutherland art collection in Picton Castle, a few miles east. Many other attractions nearby, including Scolton Manor Country Park, 'Motormania' exhibition, Selvedge Farm Museum and Nant-y-Coy Mill. ⇌

LITTLE HAVEN
Map Ref: Jb5

Combines with Broad Haven - just over the headland - to form a complete family seaside holiday centre in the Pembrokeshire Coast National Park. The village dips down to a pretty sandy beach. Popular spot for sailing, swimming and surfing.

LLANFYRNACH
Map Ref: Fa7

Away-from-it-all village in maze of country lanes on the borders of Pembrokeshire. An appealing range of country and coastal attractions close by - the bare, history-laden Preseli Hills, the wooded Teifi Valley, Cardigan Bay and the rugged North Pembrokeshire shoreline.

MARLOES
Map Ref: Jb5

Village near to Marloes Sands, a remote stretch of the Pembrokeshire Coast National Park - one of its finest beaches - overlooking Skomer Island, a haven for puffins and other seabirds. Safe for surfing and swimming; boat trips to the island from nearby Martin's Haven.

MILFORD HAVEN
Map Ref: Jc6

Important port on edge of Pembrokeshire Coast National Park; Nelson called it one of the best natural harbours he had seen. Marina in redeveloped docks has maritime museum and other attractions. Fine walks and gardens. Torch Theatre, and leisure centre. Excellent touring base. ≷

MYNACHLOG-DDU
Map Ref: Je3

On southern approach to Preseli Hills off A478. Prehistoric stone circle nearby together with site of famous 'Bluestones' used in the construction of Stonehenge. Centrally located village for rugged North Pembrokeshire coast and beaches of the south.

NARBERTH
Map Ref: Je5

Small market town, ancient castle remains (private). Charming local museum. Convenient for beaches of Carmarthen Bay and resorts of Tenby and Saundersfoot. Many attractions nearby, including activity-packed Oakwood Park, Heron's Brook Country Park, Folly Farm and Blackpool Mill. ≷

NEWPORT
Map Ref: Jd2

Ancient castled village on Pembrokeshire coast. Fine beaches – bass and sea trout fishing. Pentre Ifan Burial Chamber is close by. Backed by heather-clad Preseli Hills and overlooked by Carn Ingli Iron Age Fort.

NEYLAND
Map Ref: Jc6

Old seafaring village on north bank of Milford Haven waterway opposite Pembroke Dock. Attractive new marina. Superb sailing centre. Easy access to Pembrokeshire's south and west coasts.

PEMBROKE
Map Ref: Jc6

Ancient borough built around Pembroke Castle, birthplace of Henry VII. Fascinating Museum of the Home and next-door Sea Historic Gallery. In addition to impressive castle, well-preserved sections of old town walls. Sandy bays within easy reach, yachting, fishing – all the coastal activities associated with estuaries. Plenty of things to see and do in the area, including visit to beautiful Upton Castle Grounds. ⇌

ST DAVID'S
Map Ref: Ja4

Smallest cathedral city in Britain, shrine of Wales's patron saint. Magnificent ruins of a Bishop's Palace beside ancient cathedral nestling in hollow. Set in Pembrokeshire Coast National Park, with fine beaches nearby; superb scenery on nearby headland. Craft shops, sea life centres, painting courses, boat trips to Ramsey Island, farm parks and museums; ideal for walking and birdwatching.

ST FLORENCE
Map Ref: Je6

South Pembrokeshire village, in the country but only a stone's throw from popular Tenby. Explore some of Britain's most beautiful coastline from this charming spot - Manorbier with its beach-side castle, Stackpole and Barafundle Bay. Local attractions include Folly Farm and Manor House Wildlife and Leisure Park.

ST ISHMAEL'S
Map Ref: Jb6

Village in far-flung south-west of the Pembrokeshire Coast National Park, close to sailing centre of Dale on the Milford Haven waterway. Some of Pembrokeshire's loveliest coastline close by - the unexplored Dale Peninsula, Marloes Sands, and boat trips to Skomer Island from Martin's Haven.

SAUNDERSFOOT
Map Ref: Je6

Popular resort on South Pembrokeshire coast within the national park. Picturesque harbour and sandy beach. Very attractive sailing centre. Good sea fishing. In the wooded hills to the north is the fascinating Stepaside Industrial Heritage Centre. ⇌

SOLVA
Map Ref: Jb4

Picturesque Pembrokeshire coast village with small perfectly sheltered harbour and excellent craft shops. Pembrokeshire Coast Path offers good walking. Famous cathedral at nearby St David's.

TENBY
Map Ref: Je6

Popular, picturesque South Pembrokeshire resort with two wide beaches. Fishing trips from the attractive Georgian harbour and boat trips to nearby Caldy Island. The medieval walled town has a maze of charming narrow streets and fine old buildings, including Tudor Merchant's House (National Trust). Galleries and craft shops, excellent museum on headland, good range of amenities. Attractions include Manor House Leisure Park and 'Silent World' Aquarium. ⇌

GH Chestnut Villa

Begelly, Kilgetty,
Pembrokeshire,
Dyfed SA68 0XE
Tel: (0834) 813292

Centrally situated for South Pembrokeshire beaches. In the beautiful countryside of Begelly near Tenby and Saundersfoot. Good home cooking. Dining room with separate tables, TV lounge, bathroom, shower. Children, small dogs welcome. Private parking. Fire certificate. No smoking.

		SINGLE PER PERSON B&B		DOUBLE FOR 2 PERSONS B&B		🛏 4
		MIN £	MAX £	MIN £	MAX £	OPEN 6-9
		10.50	12.50	21.00	25.00	

GH Glenfield

5 Atlantic Drive, Broad Haven,
Haverfordwest,
Dyfed SA62 3JA
Tel: (0437) 781502

A warm welcome awaits you at my comfortable guest house with ample home cooked meals and friendly service. Hot and cold, tea making facilities in all rooms. Full central heating, colour television, own key. 300 yards to beach and coastal path.

		SINGLE PER PERSON B&B		DOUBLE FOR 2 PERSONS B&B		🛏 3
		MIN £	MAX £	MIN £	MAX £	OPEN 4-9
		12.00	12.50	24.00	25.00	

FH Plas-y-Brodyr

Rhydwilym,
Llandissilio, Clunderwen,
Dyfed SA66 7QH
Tel: (0437) 563771

Peaceful Pembrokeshire farmhouse in historic valley of Rhydwilym. An ideal holiday base. Wildlife, bird watching, pony trekking, woodland walks, farm trail, ¼ mile private fishing, local lakes. Within easy reach of Preseli hills and all coasts. Comfortable, pretty bedrooms with H&C, tea making. Original Inglenooked sitting room. Good home cooking. Reduced rates for children. Low season breaks. O.S. REF 115 246.

		SINGLE PER PERSON B&B		DOUBLE FOR 2 PERSONS B&B		🛏 2
		MIN £	MAX £	MIN £	MAX £	OPEN 3-11
		12.50	13.50	25.00	27.00	

GH Awel-y-Grug

Boncath,
Dyfed SA37 0JP
Tel: (0239) 841260

HIGHLY COMMENDED

Rural licensed guest house. Ample off street parking. One double, one twin en-suite with colour TV. Two twin. All with tea and coffee making facilities. Guest lounge, separate dining room, wide menu, many vegetarian dishes. Large pretty garden with furniture. Games room, laundry room. Near to beaches, golf, riding, walking, fishing.

		SINGLE PER PERSON B&B		DOUBLE FOR 2 PERSONS B&B		🛏 4
		MIN £	MAX £	MIN £	MAX £	OPEN 1-12
		15.00	19.00	30.00	38.00	2

GH Ringstone Guest House

Haroldston Hill, Broad Haven,
Haverfordwest,
Dyfed SA62 3JP
Tel: (0437) 781051

Friendly family run B&B, tea facilities, TV, en-suite. Sea views. Patio lounge, pool and parking. Packed lunches. Ideal coastal path, walking, 3 minutes large sandy beach. Windsurfing, diving, sailing, bird watching and local boat trips Skomer/Grassholm bird islands. Few minutes walk to restaurants, shops, cafe, etc. Fire certificate. HHH Recommended. Please write or telephone for brochure to Mrs Morgan.

		SINGLE PER PERSON B&B		DOUBLE FOR 2 PERSONS B&B		🛏 3
		MIN £	MAX £	MIN £	MAX £	OPEN 1-11
		15.00	–	30.00	–	3

GH Llainpropert Cottage

Treffynnon, Croes-Goch,
Haverfordwest,
Dyfed SA62 5JY
Tel: (0348) 831135

COMMENDED

Comfortable 200 year old Pembrokeshire character cottage, recently modernised. Warm and friendly atmosphere in rural setting, close to beaches. Coastal path and within easy reach of St David's and Fishguard. Attractive dining room and lounge with exposed beams throughout. Pleasant gardens. Ample parking. H & C available in both bedrooms, with tea/coffee making facilities.

		SINGLE PER PERSON B&B		DOUBLE FOR 2 PERSONS B&B		🛏 2
		MIN £	MAX £	MIN £	MAX £	OPEN 1-12
		14.00	15.00	28.00	30.00	–

GH Barley Villa

Walwyns Castle, Broad Haven,
Haverfordwest, Pembrokeshire,
Dyfed SA62 3EB
Tel: (0437) 781254

Bed and breakfast in our comfortable spacious house situated in peaceful countryside, near coastal paths, island bird sanctuaries and sandy beaches which are suitable for sailing, surfing and swimming. Guests own television lounge. Ample parking. Tea making facilities in bedrooms, one en-suite. Enquiries to Mrs. Davies.

		SINGLE PER PERSON B&B		DOUBLE FOR 2 PERSONS B&B		🛏 2
		MIN £	MAX £	MIN £	MAX £	OPEN 4-10
		13.50	15.00	27.00	30.00	1

FH The Bower Farm

Little Haven,
Haverfordwest,
Dyfed SA62 3TY
Tel: (0437) 781554

COMMENDED

Warm comfortable and peaceful farm guest house in Pembrokeshire Coast National Park. Working sheep farm. Overlooking Broad Haven sandy beach (one mile) and off-shore islands famous for their beauty and birds. Ideal situation for walking, hunting (livery available), shooting, fishing and all watersports. Pets and children welcome. Ample safe parking. Farm trail. Gardens. etc., etc.

		SINGLE PER PERSON B&B		DOUBLE FOR 2 PERSONS B&B		🛏 3
		MIN £	MAX £	MIN £	MAX £	OPEN 1-12
		–	–	36.00	38.00	3

GH Trearched Farm

Croes-Goch,
Haverfordwest,
Dyfed SA62 5JP
Tel: (0348) 831310

HIGHLY COMMENDED

Enjoy a relaxing break in our 18th century listed farmhouse on arable farm. Long farm drive entrance by lodge cottage on A487 at village outskirts. Sorry no dogs or smoking inside. Spacious grounds with small lake. Double, twin or single rooms. B&B only. Footpath link to coast approx 2¼ miles. Ideal walking and bird watching area.

		SINGLE PER PERSON B&B		DOUBLE FOR 2 PERSONS B&B		🛏 6
		MIN £	MAX £	MIN £	MAX £	OPEN 1-12
		15.00	15.00	30.00	30.00	

H | Seaview Hotel

Seafront, Fishguard,
Dyfed SA65 9PL
Tel: (0348) 874282
Fax: (0348) 874282

Small friendly family run hotel on seafront, adjacent to Pembrokeshire National Park coastal path. Super home cooking. Well behaved children welcome. All rooms en-suite all with tea making facilities and colour TV's. Convenient for Irish ferry passengers. Large car park. Excellent coastal views. Restaurant open to non residents. Bar and restaurant menu. Fully licensed. Welcome.

	SINGLE PER PERSON B&B	DOUBLE FOR 2 PERSONS B&B		14
				14
MIN £ 18.00	MAX £ 19.00	MIN £ 36.00	MAX £ 38.00	OPEN 1-12

GH | Hamilton Guest House

21 23 Hamilton Street,
Fishguard,
Dyfed SA65 9HL
Tel: (0348) 873834

COMMENDED

Close to the coastal footpath and picturesque harbour of lower town, Fishguard and the beginning of the Gwaun Valley. Family run, offering you a comfortable stay with separate bathroom and shower room. Babysitting available and drying facilities. Fresh wholesome food, including vegetarian, provided by qualified cook. Bookings welcome for late night ferry arrivals.

	SINGLE PER PERSON B&B	DOUBLE FOR 2 PERSONS B&B		5
				–
MIN £ 14.00	MAX £ 15.00	MIN £ 26.00	MAX £ 28.00	OPEN 1-12

FH | Berry-Hill

Goodwick,
nr. Fishguard,
Pembrokeshire,
Dyfed SA64 0HG
Tel: (0348) 872260

AWARD

HIGHLY COMMENDED

We welcome you to our small holding magnificently positioned overlooking Fishguard Harbour and Preseli Hills. 2 minutes walk from coastal path, bedrooms have sea views. En-suite, tea/coffee facilities. Award winning. Full central heating. Car parking. Farm pets. Most activities nearby. Brochure from Mrs. Rees.

	SINGLE PER PERSON B&B	DOUBLE FOR 2 PERSONS B&B		2
				2
MIN £ 16.00	MAX £ 17.00	MIN £ 32.00	MAX £ 34.00	OPEN 1-12

GH | Cefn-y-Dre

Fishguard,
Pembrokeshire,
Dyfed SA65 9QS
Tel: (0348) 874499

HIGHLY COMMENDED

Ideal touring base within two miles of town centre in quiet secluded country house setting with artist's coach house studio in spacious grounds. Open all year, licensed dining room, TV lounge, tea making facilities in all bedrooms, two double and one twin/triple family room. Home cooked evening meals, including vegetarian, served in peaceful surroundings.

	SINGLE PER PERSON B&B	DOUBLE FOR 2 PERSONS B&B		3
				1
MIN £ –	MAX £ –	MIN £ 33.00	MAX £ 38.00	OPEN 1-12

GH | Heathfield

Mathry Road,
Letterston,
Dyfed SA62 5EG
Tel: (0348) 840263

Our exclusive Georgian country house in its tranquil setting of pastures and woodlands is the perfect place to relax and be spoilt. It is ideally situated to explore Pembrokeshire's treasures. The comfortable rooms with beautiful views over rolling countryside, the friendly atmosphere and the excellent food and wines make for a truly enjoyable holiday.

	SINGLE PER PERSON B&B	DOUBLE FOR 2 PERSONS B&B		4
				–
MIN £ 12.50	MAX £ 18.00	MIN £ –	MAX £ –	OPEN 3-12

FH | Gilfach Goch Farmhouse

Garn Gelli Hill, Fishguard,
Pembrokeshire,
Dyfed SA65 9SR
Tel: (0348) 873871
Fax: (0348) 873871

AWARD

HIGHLY COMMENDED

Enjoy peace and quiet on our 30 acre farm in National Park. Beautiful countryside, magnificent views. Near coastal path, beaches. Attractive beamed rooms, with antiques/books. Pretty bedrooms - TV, H&C, tea/coffee. "Real" home cooking. Pay phone. Licensed. Fire certificate. Grid ref. SM982373 (three miles British Rail, bus stop at gate). For brochure ring June Devonald.

	SINGLE PER PERSON B&B	DOUBLE FOR 2 PERSONS B&B		6
				3
MIN £ 16.00	MAX £ 19.00	MIN £ 32.00	MAX £ 38.00	OPEN 3-10

GH | Cri'r Wylan

Pen Wallis, Fishguard,
Pembrokeshire,
Dyfed SA65 9HR
Tel: (0348) 873398

HIGHLY COMMENDED

Relax in comfort in homely atmosphere. Tea/coffee always available. Attractive rooms, TV and/or radio in bedrooms. Drying facilities. Vanity basins all rooms. Detached stone house with superb views overlooking Fishguard Bay. Central for Preseli Hills and coastal paths, beaches etc. Short stroll town centre. Ample parking, peaceful surroundings. Late night ferry bookings welcome. Children welcome.

	SINGLE PER PERSON B&B	DOUBLE FOR 2 PERSONS B&B		3
				–
MIN £ 14.00	MAX £ 15.00	MIN £ 26.00	MAX £ 30.00	OPEN 1-12

GH | Rhos Felen

Scleddau, Fishguard,
Pembrokeshire,
Dyfed SA65 9RD
Tel: (0348) 873711
Fax: (0348) 873711

HIGHLY COMMENDED

Family run house in 3 acres. Quiet rural setting. Golf putting green. 2 miles from Fishguard. 3 miles from Goodwick (Stena Sealink Ferry and B.R.). Family and self contained 2 bedroom unit (sleeping 4/5) available. Reduced rates for children. Late ferry bookings. Home cooking in our restaurant including special diets and vegetarian. Ideal for coastal path, beaches, Preseli Hills and St David's.

	SINGLE PER PERSON B&B	DOUBLE FOR 2 PERSONS B&B		4
				1
MIN £ 13.00	MAX £ 16.00	MIN £ 26.00	MAX £ 32.00	OPEN 1-12

GH | Seahorses

Freshwater East,
Pembrokeshire,
Dyfed SA71 5LA
Tel: (0646) 672405

COMMENDED

A welcoming comfortable guest house. Ideal touring centre within Pembrokeshire Coast National Park and close to coastal path, castles nearby. The many sandy beaches of Pembrokeshire are within easy reach. Good food and friendly service. All bedrooms have H & C, TV lounge. Parking.

	SINGLE PER PERSON B&B	DOUBLE FOR 2 PERSONS B&B		2
				–
MIN £ 13.00	MAX £ 14.00	MIN £ 26.00	MAX £ 28.00	OPEN 5-9

FH | East Trewent Farm

Freshwater East,
Pembrokeshire,
Dyfed SA71 5LR
Tel: (0646) 672127

Birds, flowers, fresh air in abundance. East Trewent Farm adjoins the coastal footpath. Beach 400 yards. Fishing and riding nearby. Ideal for those who love the outdoor life. In the evening relax in the bar and enjoy the excellent cuisine in the Chough Restaurant. Open all the year round.

P 🛏 ⚒ 🐕 🍽 TW	SINGLE PER PERSON B&B		DOUBLE FOR 2 PERSONS B&B		🛏 6 🛁
	MIN £ 15.50	MAX £ 15.50	MIN £ 31.00	MAX £ 31.00	OPEN 1-12

GH | Greenways

Shoal Hook Lane,
Haverfordwest, Pembrokeshire,
Dyfed SA61 2XN
Tel: (0437) 762345

HIGHLY COMMENDED

Set in two acres, picturesque gardens, picnic area, sun terrace, overlooking golf course, Preseli mountains, Greenways is central to Tenby, Oakwood, St David's, Ferry terminals and coastal paths. Relax in comfort, bedrooms en-suites on ground floor. All have service trays, hairdryers and colour TV. Private parking a quiet retreat home from home. Children and pets welcome.

P 🛏 ⚒ 🐕 🍽	SINGLE PER PERSON B&B		DOUBLE FOR 2 PERSONS B&B		🛏 3 🛁 3
	MIN £ 13.00	MAX £ 19.00	MIN £ 26.00	MAX £ 38.00	OPEN 1-12

FH | Cuckoo Mill Farm

Pelcomb Bridge, St. David's Road,
Haverfordwest, Pembrokeshire,
Dyfed SA62 6EA
Tel: (0437) 762139

Peacefully situated central Pembrokeshire. Two miles out of Haverfordwest, six miles coastline walks, beaches. Mixed livestock working farm. Three comfortable bedrooms, each with storage heaters, wash-basins, tea making facilities. Lounge with TV and open fire. Two bathrooms with toilets, showers. Personal attention. Good home cooking using home produce. Evening meal. Children welcome.

P 🛏 🐕 🍽 🐓	SINGLE PER PERSON B&B		DOUBLE FOR 2 PERSONS B&B		🛏 3 🛁
	MIN £ 13.00	MAX £ 15.50	MIN £ 26.00	MAX £ 31.00	OPEN 1-12

GH | The Fold

Cleddau Lodge,
Camrose, Haverfordwest,
Pembrokeshire,
Dyfed SA62 6HY
Tel: (0437) 710640

Converted 15th Century farmhouse in secluded garden overlooking River Cleddau. Private fishing available. Central to Pembrokeshire coast 6 miles. Double bedroom, H&C, TV, tea/coffee. Own shower, toilet. Separate entrance. Homely welcome as one of the family. Part of 50 acre estate with gardens, woodlands and river. View of the Preseli hills.

P 🐕 ⚒ 🛏	SINGLE PER PERSON B&B		DOUBLE FOR 2 PERSONS B&B		🛏 1 🛁 -
	MIN £ 15.00	MAX £ 15.00	MIN £ 26.00	MAX £ 30.00	OPEN 4-10

GH | Redstock Guest House

Johnston,
Haverfordwest, Pembrokeshire,
Dyfed SA62 3HW
Tel: (0437) 890287

Mrs. Boyett's guest house has been caring for its guests for over 30 years giving excellent value for money, all home comforts. Situated 2 miles from Milford Haven and 4 miles from Haverfordwest. Redstock is very convenient for touring West Wales. Comfort and guest satisfaction are ensured. Ample car parking just off the A4076 past Johnston.

P 🛏 ⚒ 🐕	SINGLE PER PERSON B&B		DOUBLE FOR 2 PERSONS B&B		🛏 10 🛁 2
	MIN £ 14.50	MAX £ 14.50	MIN £ 27.00	MAX £ 27.00	OPEN 1-12

FH | Knock Farm

Camrose, Haverfordwest,
Pembrokeshire,
Dyfed SA62 6HW
Tel: (0437) 762208

Peacefully situated in a scenic valley. Ten minutes from Pembrokeshire beaches. Two miles from Haverfordwest. Children welcome, lots of farm animals to see. Good home cooking, homely atmosphere. TV lounge available all day. Central heating, log fires in winter. Tea coffee facilities in bedrooms. Family room en-suite.

P 🛏 🐕 🍽 🐓	SINGLE PER PERSON B&B		DOUBLE FOR 2 PERSONS B&B		🛏 2 🛁 1
	MIN £ 13.00	MAX £ 15.50	MIN £ 26.00	MAX £ 31.00	OPEN 1-12

GH | Greenacre Guest House

Spittal, Haverfordwest,
Pembrokeshire,
Dyfed SA62 5RE
Tel: (0437) 731201

Quiet guest house one mile from Scolton Manor Country Park. Three miles from Llys-y-Fran Reservoir, convenient for the coast. Large well kept grounds and a field for games etc. Guests may come and go throughout the day. A warm welcome and a comfortable relaxed holiday is guaranteed.

P 🛏 ⚒ 🐕 🍽	SINGLE PER PERSON B&B		DOUBLE FOR 2 PERSONS B&B		🛏 3 🛁 -
	MIN £ 13.00	MAX £ 15.00	MIN £ 26.00	MAX £ 30.00	OPEN 1-12

FH | Crossways

Spittal Cross Farm, Spittal,
Haverfordwest, Pembrokeshire,
Dyfed SA62 5DB
Tel: (0437) 87253

DE LUXE

Our stylish farmhouse offers bed and breakfast in en-suite bedrooms with TV and beverage trays. Relax in the guests lounge which overlooks the terrace attractive garden and beautiful Treffgarne Valley. Four miles north of Haverfordwest. We're ideally located for visiting Pembrokeshire. A warm welcome awaits you at this dairy farm. Your enquiries for a brochure are welcomed. Mrs. M. Evans.

P 🛏 🐕 🚜	SINGLE PER PERSON B&B		DOUBLE FOR 2 PERSONS B&B		🛏 2 🛁 2
	MIN £ -	MAX £ -	MIN £ 35.00	MAX £ 38.00	OPEN 3-10

FH | Lower Haythog

Spittal, Haverfordwest,
Pembrokeshire,
Dyfed SA62 5QL
Tel/Fax: (0437) 731279

AWARD | HIGHLY COMMENDED

For a taste of the real country life, stay on our working farm, 5 miles north of Haverfordwest. Tasteful and comfortable accommodation with a friendly atmosphere, the 300 year old farmhouse has charm and character - with inglenook, exposed stonework and beams. Excellent cuisine. Lovely gardens - imaginatively landscaped. Well appointed bedrooms - all facilities. Full central heating - log fires. Trout fishing - pony rides, mini-golf.

P 🛏 ⚒ 🐕 🍽 🐓	SINGLE PER PERSON B&B		DOUBLE FOR 2 PERSONS B&B		🛏 4 🛁 4
	MIN £ 17.50	MAX £ 19.00	MIN £ 35.00	MAX £ 38.00	OPEN 1-12

GH Whitegates

Little Haven,
Pembrokeshire,
Dyfed SA62 3LA
Tel: (0437) 781552
Fax: (0437) 781552

On the Pembrokeshire coastal path in lovely fishing village. Beautiful sea views, heated swimming pool, en-suite most rooms, tea/coffee, radio all rooms. TV lounge, access all times. Ideal walking, windsurfing, bird watching on four islands or family beach holidays. Local sea food/produce in several reasonably priced pubs - restaurants within comfortable walking distance.

		SINGLE PER PERSON B&B		DOUBLE FOR 2 PERSONS B&B		🛏 4 🛁 3
		MIN £ –	MAX £ –	MIN £ 35.00	MAX £ 38.00	OPEN 3-12

FH Castle Pill Farm

Steynton,
Milford Haven,
Dyfed SA73 1HE
Tel: (0646) 692906

A warm welcome over a cup of tea (or something stronger!) awaits you at Castle Pill Farm. Our secluded sheep, arable and fruit farm adjacent to woodland and tidal estuary. The end of lane location belies our nearness to Pembrokeshire's beaches, walks and historical towns. Beverage tray, colour TV. Ample private parking and own access.

		SINGLE PER PERSON B&B		DOUBLE FOR 2 PERSONS B&B		🛏 2 🛁 1
		MIN £ 14.00	MAX £ 15.00	MIN £ 25.00	MAX £ 30.00	OPEN 1.12

FH Highland Grange Farm Guest House

Robeston Wathen,
Narberth, Pembrokeshire,
Dyfed SA67 8EP
Tel: (0834) 860952
Fax: (0834) 860952

Large beef and sheep farm. Centrally situated on A40 amidst lovely countryside. Ideal for touring West Wales. Ground floor accommodation, disabled access. 2 en-suite bedrooms. Delicious home cooking, dinner available. Walks on farm, panoramic views, woodland trail. Many amenities in area. Beach 7 miles. Every comfort assured. Extensive local knowledge, history and information provided by host.

		SINGLE PER PERSON B&B		DOUBLE FOR 2 PERSONS B&B		🛏 5 🛁 2
		MIN £ 13.50	MAX £ 16.50	MIN £ 26.00	MAX £ 33.00	OPEN 1-12

GH Bron-y-Gaer

Llanfyrnach,
Dyfed SA35 0DA
Tel: (0239) 831265

Our peaceful small holding near Preseli mountains offers an ideal touring base for exploring West Wales. Accommodation is in pretty en-suite bedrooms within the house or adjacent cottage, all with tea/coffee making facilities. Guests have their own lounge with colour TV. We have a craft shop, beautiful gardens and friendly farm animals.

		SINGLE PER PERSON B&B		DOUBLE FOR 2 PERSONS B&B		🛏 2 🛁 2
		MIN £ 15.00	MAX £ 15.00	MIN £ 30.00	MAX £ 30.00	OPEN 1-12

FH Dolau Isaf Farm

Mynachlog-ddu, Clunderwen,
Pembrokeshire,
Dyfed SA66 7SB
Tel: (0994) 419327

Personal service awaits you on our family farm in the Pembrokeshire Coast National Park and every effort is made to provide for your comfort. Come and see our angora goats grazing with our sheep and cattle, for this is the home of Preseli mohair. Lounge, TV, home cooking. Ideal for riding, walking, bird watching, fishing, relaxing.

		SINGLE PER PERSON B&B		DOUBLE FOR 2 PERSONS B&B		🛏 3 🛁 2
		MIN £ 13.00	MAX £ 14.00	MIN £ 26.00	MAX £ 28.00	OPEN 1-12

GH Grove Park Guest House

Pen-y-Bont,
Newport, Pembrokeshire,
Dyfed SA42 0LT
Tel: (0239) 820122

HIGHLY COMMENDED

Grove Park is situated on the outskirts of Newport only one hundred yards from Pembrokeshire coastal path. 19th century house which has been completely refurbished but retains original character, estuary views. Easy distance from large sandy beach and Preseli Hills. Imaginative four course dinner menu. Two rooms en-suite. Colour TV in all bedrooms. Winter breaks available.

		SINGLE PER PERSON B&B		DOUBLE FOR 2 PERSONS B&B		🛏 3 🛁 2
		MIN £ 17.00	MAX £ 17.00	MIN £ 34.00	MAX £ 38.00	OPEN 1-12

GH Foxdale Guest House and Camping

Glebe Lane, Marloes,
Haverfordwest, Pembrokeshire,
Dyfed SA62 3AX
Tel: (0646) 636243

Foxdale is a large comfortable detached house. Three spacious rooms, one en-suite all with tea/coffee making facilities etc. Ideal base for all seawater sports, walking, bird watching and spectacular coastal scenery and flora. Close to Skomer and Grassholm islands and Marloes sands. Bed & breakfast, camping facilities, campers breakfasts and swimming pool. Fully licensed.

		SINGLE PER PERSON B&B		DOUBLE FOR 2 PERSONS B&B		🛏 3 🛁 1
		MIN £ 16.00	MAX £ 18.00	MIN £ 30.00	MAX £ 34.00	OPEN 4-10

FH Yethen Isaf

Mynachlog-ddu, Clunderwen,
Pembrokeshire,
Dyfed SA66 7SN
Tel: (0437) 532256

Traditional welcoming 300 year old farmhouse - inglenook fireplace and beams, enjoying spectacular views within Preseli Hills. Working sheep and beef farm, 12 miles coast. Three double/twin rooms, 1 with en-suite facilities, tea/coffee making facilities and radios all rooms. Bathroom with shower. Fishing, riding, walking, bird watching, crafts. Packed lunches and dinners.

		SINGLE PER PERSON B&B		DOUBLE FOR 2 PERSONS B&B		🛏 3
		MIN £ 16.00	MAX £ 19.00	MIN £ 32.00	MAX £ 37.00	OPEN 1-12

GH Llysmeddyg Guest House

East Street,
Newport, Pembrokeshire,
Dyfed SA42 0SY
Tel: (0239) 820008

Listed Georgian house. Spacious rooms furnished mainly with antiques. Ideal base for walkers or beach holiday. Close to coastal path, mountains and amenities of historic coastal town. Dining room with separate tables. Excellent home cooking. Small wine list. Guide book recommendations. Log fire in winter. Extensive library. Self catering flat available with optional evening meal.

		SINGLE PER PERSON B&B		DOUBLE FOR 2 PERSONS B&B		🛏 3
		MIN £ 17.00	MAX £ 17.00	MIN £ 34.00	MAX £ 34.00	OPEN 1-12

GH Church Lakes Guest House

88 Church Road, Llanstadwell,
Neyland, Milford Haven,
Pembrokeshire, Dyfed SA73 1EA
Tel: (0646) 600840

Comfortable, detached house alongside the Cleddau Estuary foreshore and coastal footpath. Haven views from all rooms and terrace with yachts from nearby Neyland Marina, the Irish ferries, etc., often adding interest. Tea/coffee facilities and H & C in bedrooms. Good food. Near Haven Bridge linking Preseli and South Pembrokeshire. Details from Barry and Sylvia Fieldhouse.

		SINGLE PER PERSON B&B	DOUBLE FOR 2 PERSONS B&B		3
		MIN £ 14.00	MAX £ 15.00	MIN £ 28.00	MAX £ 30.00	OPEN 1-12

FH Bangeston Farm

Stackpole, Pembroke,
Dyfed SA71 5BX
Tel: (0646) 683986

Homely farmhouse in peaceful countryside with coast outlook three miles from Pembroke. Close to Bosherston Lily Ponds. Clean beaches, coastal walks and bird life. Good home cooking. Hearty breakfasts. Separate dining tables, lounge with colour TV. Tea making facilities and H&C in all bedrooms. Clean and comfortable accommodation. A warm and friendly welcome awaits.

		SINGLE PER PERSON B&B	DOUBLE FOR 2 PERSONS B&B		3
		MIN £ 12.00	MAX £ 12.00	MIN £ 24.00	MAX £ 24.00	OPEN 4-9

GH Glan-y-Môr Guest House

Caerfai Road, St David's,
Dyfed SA62 6QT
Tel: (0437) 721788
Fax: (0437) 721342

Magnificent views over St Brides Bay. We are just a short walk from Pembrokeshire Coastal path and nearby St David's. All rooms have wash-basins, shaver points and central heating. (3 rooms with en-suite facilities). TV lounge, restaurant and residents licensed bar. Private parking, large gardens. We are open 12 months of the year.

		SINGLE PER PERSON B&B	DOUBLE FOR 2 PERSONS B&B		9
		MIN £ 16.00	MAX £ –	MIN £ –	MAX £ –	OPEN 1-12	3

FH Nolton Haven Farmhouse

Nolton Haven, Haverfordwest,
Pembrokeshire,
Dyfed SA62 8NH
Tel: (0437) 710263
Fax: (0437) 710263

Beside the beach this comfortable farmhouse offers you a good base to see the heart of the Pembrokeshire Coast National Park. The farmhouse situated on a 200 acre beef, corn farm has a large lounge with coal and log fire which is open to guests all day as are the bedrooms.

		SINGLE PER PERSON B&B	DOUBLE FOR 2 PERSONS B&B		7
		MIN £ 14.00	MAX £ 16.00	MIN £ 28.00	MAX £ 32.00	OPEN 1-12	2

H Ynys Barry Holiday Centre

Porthgain,
St David's, Pembrokeshire,
Dyfed SA62 5BH
Tel: (0348) 831180
Fax: (0348) 831800

COMMENDED

Ynys Barry located adjacent to famous Welsh coastal path. Facilities include lounge bar, games room, restaurant, snacks, cream teas. Home cooking. Self contained holiday cottages, Motel room. All in the midst of Pembrokeshire with its glorious rugged coastline and sweeping beaches is literally on your doorstep. B&B available and room only.

		SINGLE PER PERSON B&B	DOUBLE FOR 2 PERSONS B&B		14
		MIN £ 19.00	MAX £ 19.00	MIN £ 38.00	MAX £ –	OPEN 1-12	14

GH The Mount

66 New Street,
St David's, Haverfordwest,
Dyfed SA62 6SU
Tel: (0437) 720276

A 200 year old ex farmhouse with character. Situated in own grounds. A few minutes from the city centre. Double and twin rooms. Hot and cold water and shaver points all bedrooms. Electric heating all rooms. Large lounge with colour TV. Dining room with separate tables. Private car park behind house. Fire certificated granted.

		SINGLE PER PERSON B&B	DOUBLE FOR 2 PERSONS B&B		3
		MIN £ –	MAX £ –	MIN £ 24.00	MAX £ –	OPEN 4-10

GH The Old Rectory

Cosheston, Pembroke,
Pembrokeshire,
Dyfed SA72 4UJ
Tel: (0646) 684960

Believed to date from Norman times, the Old Rectory is set in two acre gardens. Tastefully furnished bedrooms with H&C and tea/coffee facilities. Spacious lounge with colour TV. Upstairs dining room where meals are served at times to suit you. Ideal base for beaches and castles, village walks. Pembroke two miles. Reduced rates for children.

		SINGLE PER PERSON B&B	DOUBLE FOR 2 PERSONS B&B		3
		MIN £ 15.00	MAX £ 17.00	MIN £ 30.00	MAX £ 34.00	OPEN 3-11

GH Awel-Môr Guest House

Penparc, Trevine,
nr. St David's, Pembrokeshire,
Dyfed SA62 5AG
Tel: (0348) 837865

DE LUXE

Luxury "non smoking" accommodation. Magnificent view overlooking National Park and coastline. Three large bedrooms with central heating, soft chairs, colour TV, H&C, tea/coffee facilities. En-suite available. Delicious food from breakfast/dinner menu. Table licence. Optional evening meal. Car park. No hidden extras. "Best Guest House in Wales", Wales Tourist Board Hospitality Award. Map grid ref. SM845312.

		SINGLE PER PERSON B&B	DOUBLE FOR 2 PERSONS B&B		3
		MIN £ 18.00	MAX £ 18.00	MIN £ 36.00	MAX £ 36.00	OPEN 3-10	2

GH Ramsey House

Lower Moor,
St David's, Pembrokeshire,
Dyfed SA62 6RP
Tel: (0437) 720321

HIGHLY COMMENDED

Our award winning Welsh cuisine, using traditional recipes and local produce, will be the highlight of your stay at Ramsey House. Individually furnished rooms (en-suite £3 - £4 pppn supplement), cosy bar and lounge. Congenial hospitality and personal service. Quiet convenient location for touring or walking, ½ mile from Cathedral and coastal path. Les Routiers. AA QQQ. RAC Acclaimed. Great value!

		SINGLE PER PERSON B&B	DOUBLE FOR 2 PERSONS B&B		7
		MIN £ 18.00	MAX £ 19.00	MIN £ 36.00	MAX £ 38.00	OPEN 1-12	5

GH Ty Olaf

Mount Gardens,
St David's,
Dyfed SA62 6BS
Tel: (0437) 720885
Fax: (0437) 720314

HIGHLY COMMENDED

Family home in quiet position on edge of Britain's smallest Cathedral city in Pembrokeshire Coast National Park. Double and family rooms, central heating, H&C, shaver points, tea/coffee facilities, TV lounge, no stairs, off-road parking. Five minutes walk to Cathedral and good restaurants. Convenient for coastal path, boat trips, beaches etc.

P		SINGLE PER PERSON B&B		DOUBLE FOR 2 PERSONS B&B		🛏 3
		MIN £	MAX £	MIN £	MAX £	OPEN 4-10
		–	–	26.00	30.00	

GH Parsonage Farm Inn

St. Florence, nr. Tenby,
Pembrokeshire,
Dyfed SA70 8LR
Tel: (0834) 871436

An attractive Village Inn. Featured on TV's 'Wish You Were Here' and Which magazines 'Good Pub Guide'. Set in the picturesque village of St. Florence. Offering good food and a friendly atmosphere. Summer breaks, Christmas, New Year, Easter, all at special rates. Please phone for our own brochure and more information. An ideal friendly family break.

P		SINGLE PER PERSON B&B		DOUBLE FOR 2 PERSONS B&B		🛏 8
		MIN £	MAX £	MIN £	MAX £	7
		16.00	18.00	32.00	36.00	OPEN 1-12

H Cliff House

Wogan Terrace, Saundersfoot,
Pembrokeshire,
Dyfed SA69 9HA
Tel: (0834) 813931

Quality, comfort, service, welcome - words our guests tell us really mean something at Cliff House. In the heart of the village, with superb sea and harbour views, ideal accommodation for relaxation, sporting holidays or exploring beautiful Pembrokeshire. Luxury en-suite facilities in several rooms (supplement payable). Personal service from resident proprietors. Ring for colour brochure.

		SINGLE PER PERSON B&B		DOUBLE FOR 2 PERSONS B&B		🛏 6
		MIN £	MAX £	MIN £	MAX £	3
		–	–	30.00	36.00	OPEN 1-12

FH Tresiencyn Farm

Croes-Goch, Haverfordwest,
Pembrokeshire,
Dyfed SA62 5AD
Tel: (0348) 831314

Bed and breakfast on a working Dairy Farm. Situated near the village of Croes-Goch, three miles from Abereiddy beach, Porthgain harbour and the coastal path. Five miles from St David's. H&C and tea making facilities in bedrooms. TV Lounge. Good home produced food. Families welcome. Enquiries to Mrs. L.A. Thomas.

P		SINGLE PER PERSON B&B		DOUBLE FOR 2 PERSONS B&B		🛏 2
		MIN £	MAX £	MIN £	MAX £	–
		13.00	–	26.00	–	OPEN 3-10

FH Bicton Farm

St Ishmael's, Haverfordwest,
Pembrokeshire,
Dyfed SA62 3DR
Tel: (0646) 636215
Fax: (0646) 636215

Comfortable farmhouse, one mile from the village of St Ishmael's, within easy access to several beaches, coastal footpath and the bird sanctuaries of Skomer and Skokholm. Two double rooms, one with wc, shower en-suite. One twin. Sitting room with TV, central heating.

P		SINGLE PER PERSON B&B		DOUBLE FOR 2 PERSONS B&B		🛏 3
		MIN £	MAX £	MIN £	MAX £	1
		–	–	28.00	30.00	OPEN 3-10

H The Grange Hotel

Wooden,
Saundersfoot,
Dyfed SA69 9DY
Tel: (0834) 812809

COMMENDED

Family run licensed hotel close to Saundersfoot, Tenby and the Pembrokeshire coastal path. All rooms have tea/coffee, colour TV and central heating and there is a large car park. An ideal base for beach and water sports holidays, bird watching, walking and fishing. Reductions are available for weekly booking and children. Brochure Mrs. S. Griffin - Proprietor.

P		SINGLE PER PERSON B&B		DOUBLE FOR 2 PERSONS B&B		🛏 6
		MIN £	MAX £	MIN £	MAX £	2
		12.00	19.00	24.00	38.00	OPEN 2-11

FH Trevaccoon Farm

St David's,
Haverfordwest,
Dyfed SA62 6DP
Tel: (0348) 831418

A warm welcome awaits you in our 17th century farmhouse in peaceful country and coastal setting with spectacular sea views. En-suite bathrooms. Friendly farm pets. Relaxed atmosphere. Licensed for that glass of wine to complement Vikki's farmhouse cooking. Sandy beaches and coastal path nearby. Children half price. Tea/coffee making facilities. Pets, vegetarians, walkers welcome. Free golf.

P		SINGLE PER PERSON B&B		DOUBLE FOR 2 PERSONS B&B		🛏 6
		MIN £	MAX £	MIN £	MAX £	5
		16.00	19.00	32.00	38.00	OPEN 1-12

FH Skerryback

Sandy Haven, St. Ishmael's,
Haverfordwest,
Dyfed SA62 3DN
Tel: (0646) 636598

HIGHLY COMMENDED

A traditional Pembrokeshire welcome on coastal path. A haven for walkers and bird lovers. Ideal for visiting Skomer and Skokholm. Fishing, sailing and exploring Pembrokeshire's beautiful coast. Children welcome. Central heating, drying facilities, open fires in winter. TV lounge. Double and twin rooms with H&C and tea/coffee facilities.

P		SINGLE PER PERSON B&B		DOUBLE FOR 2 PERSONS B&B		🛏 2
TW		MIN £	MAX £	MIN £	MAX £	
		14.00	15.00	28.00	30.00	OPEN 2-??

GH Dalwood

The Ridgeway, Saundersfoot,
Pembrokeshire,
Dyfed SA69 9LD
Tel: (0834) 813342

A warm and friendly welcome assured in attractive homely surroundings. Quiet situation with views over countryside and sea, ½ mile from harbour and beaches. Family room with vanity unit and hospitality tray. Comfortable lounge with TV. Private parking. Mrs. A. Etherington.

P		SINGLE PER PERSON B&B		DOUBLE FOR 2 PERSONS B&B		🛏 1
		MIN £	MAX £	MIN £	MAX £	–
		–	–	22.00	26.00	OPEN 5-9

GH Pinewood

Cliff Road, Wiseman's Bridge,
Narberth,
Dyfed SA67 8NU
Tel: (0834) 811082

We offer comfortable quiet accommodation in our large detached dormer bungalow, surrounded by gardens and overlooking a small peaceful caravan park on the coastal path between Saundersfoot and Amroth, beach 350 yards. Both the twin and double rooms are en-suite with colour television and tea/coffee facilities. Ideal for sightseeing and walking.

P ⚓	⛉	SINGLE PER PERSON B&B		DOUBLE FOR 2 PERSONS B&B		🛏 2 🛁 2	
		MIN £ 13.00	MAX £ 16.00	MIN £ 26.00	MAX £ 32.00	OPEN 1-12	

FH Llanddinog Old Farmhouse

Solva, Haverfordwest,
Pembrokeshire,
Dyfed SA62 6NA
Tel: (0348) 831224

This peaceful 16th century farmhouse situated only 3 miles from sandy beaches and coastal paths, can offer excellent facilities including roaring fires on cooler nights. Children enjoy the large garden, rope swings and small animals. Substantial farmhouse food using local ingredients. Packed lunches. Riding, golf, mountain bikes, all watersports nearby. Close Solva Harbour, St David's Cathedral. Mrs. S. Griffiths. SAE.

P		SINGLE PER PERSON B&B		DOUBLE FOR 2 PERSONS B&B		🛏 2 🛁 2	
		MIN £ 16.00	MAX £ 16.00	MIN £ 32.00	MAX £ 32.00	OPEN 1-12	

H Ashby House Hotel

Victoria Street,
Tenby, Pembrokeshire,
Dyfed SA70 7DY
Tel: (0834) 842867

COMMENDED

A small family run hotel catering for people who require a more relaxing holiday. Superbly situated close to South beach, town centre and public car park. Most rooms en-suite some with sea views, all with colour TV, tea maker, central heating and furnished to a high standard. 10% senior citizen discount all season. RAC Acclaimed.

		SINGLE PER PERSON B&B		DOUBLE FOR 2 PERSONS B&B		🛏 9 🛁 8	
		MIN £ 14.00	MAX £ 18.00	MIN £ 28.00	MAX £ 36.00	OPEN 3-10	

FH Carne Mountain Farm

COMMENDED

Reynalton, Begelly,
Kilgetty, Pembrokeshire,
Dyfed SA68 0PD
Tel: (0834) 860546

A warm welcome awaits you at our lovely 200 year old farmhouse. Set amidst the peace and tranquillity of the beautiful Pembrokeshire countryside. Distant views Preseli Hills, yet only 3½ miles from Saundersfoot. Picturesque bedroom with TV, teasmade, wash hand basins, central heating, separate dining room with interesting plate collection. Delicious farmhouse food. Welcome Host Award. S.A.E. Mrs. Joy Holgate.

P ❄	⛉	SINGLE PER PERSON B&B		DOUBLE FOR 2 PERSONS B&B		🛏 2	
		MIN £ 13.00	MAX £ 14.50	MIN £ 26.00	MAX £ 29.00	OPEN 1-12	

FH Lochmeyler Farm

AWARD

DE LUXE

Llandeloy, Pen-y-Cwm,
nr. Solva, Haverfordwest,
Pembrokeshire,
Dyfed SA62 6LL
Tel/Fax: (0348) 837724

220 acre dairy farm centre St David's Peninsula. 4 miles Solva Harbour. 3 miles coastal path. Luxury facilities, some 4 poster. Excellent menus of fresh farm produce, tastefully prepared by proprietor. Dinner 7 pm. Choice of menus. Traditional and vegetarian. Children over 10 welcomed. Guests provided with folder of walks, places of interest. Credit cards accepted. "RAC Guest House of the Year 1993"

P	⛉	SINGLE PER PERSON B&B		DOUBLE FOR 2 PERSONS B&B		🛏 10 🛁 10	
TW		MIN £ 19.00	MAX £ 19.00	MIN £ 38.00	MAX £ 38.00	OPEN 1-12	

H Buckingham Hotel

Esplanade,
Tenby,
Dyfed SA70 7DU
Tel: (0834) 842622

Superbly situated overlooking the sunny South Beach and only 5 minutes from Tenby town centre. Relaxing family run hotel offering fine food, wine and service. All rooms heated, colour TV, beverage facilities and en-suite. Two day breaks from £45.00, weekly rates from £157.00 (above rates include dinner).

⛉		SINGLE PER PERSON B&B		DOUBLE FOR 2 PERSONS B&B		🛏 8 🛁 8	
		MIN £ 19.00	MAX £ 19.00	MIN £ 32.00	MAX £ 38.00	OPEN 4-11	

GH White House

Penycwm, nr. Solva,
Haverfordwest, Pembrokeshire,
Dyfed SA62 6LA
Tel: (0437) 720959
Fax: (0437) 720959

The combination of comfort and a peaceful setting will make your stay a memorable experience. Enjoy a rural location, surrounded by lawns and green fields, yet only 1.5 miles from the coastal path. Ideally situated for exploring the many facets of Pembrokeshire. Also available excellent family room with en-suite. "Taste of Wales" a speciality.

P	⛉	SINGLE PER PERSON B&B		DOUBLE FOR 2 PERSONS B&B		🛏 4 🛁 1	
TW		MIN £ 13.00	MAX £ 13.00	MIN £ 26.00	MAX £ 32.00	OPEN 1-12	

FH Upper Vanley Farmhouse

AWARD

COMMENDED

Llandeloy, nr. Solva,
Haverfordwest,
Pembrokeshire,
Dyfed SA62 6LJ
Tel: (0348) 831418

Friendly farmhouse central for St David's Peninsula. Three miles from coastal path, Solva Harbour, safe sandy beaches. Spectacular walks, bird watching, wild flowers, water sports. Pretty rooms all en-suite, colour TV, tea making. Children welcome, garden play area. Attractive restaurant serving traditional and vegetarian dishes. Licensed. Pets welcome. Free ample parking.

P	⛉	SINGLE PER PERSON B&B		DOUBLE FOR 2 PERSONS B&B		🛏 7 🛁 7	
		MIN £ 16.50	MAX £ 19.00	MIN £ 33.00	MAX £ 38.00	OPEN 2-12	

H Clarence House Hotel

COMMENDED

Esplanade, Tenby,
Pembrokeshire,
Dyfed SA70 7DU
Tel: (0834) 844371
Fax: (0834) 844372

Tenby Town, Centre Esplanade, South Beach sea front.

Send for free colour brochure. Full information. All you need to know.

⛉		SINGLE PER PERSON B&B		DOUBLE FOR 2 PERSONS B&B		🛏 29 🛁 29	
		MIN £ 17.00	MAX £ 19.00	MIN £ 30.00	MAX £ 36.00	OPEN 4-10	

H	Ripley St Mary's Hotel

St Mary's Street, Tenby,
Pembrokeshire,
Dyfed SA70 7HN
Tel: (0834) 842837

Situated in quiet "floral" street within walled town. 75 yards Sea Front and Paragon Gardens. Car Parks within short distance. All bedrooms have colour TV and tea makers. Supplements for en-suite facilities. Personally run by Alan and Kath Mace who enjoy a high reputation for their friendly welcome and good home cooking. RAC Acclaimed and AA listed.

		SINGLE PER PERSON B&B		DOUBLE FOR 2 PERSONS B&B		14
						8
		MIN £ 18.00	MAX £ 19.00	MIN £ 36.00	MAX £ 38.00	OPEN 3-10

GH	High Seas

8 The Norton, Tenby,
Dyfed SA70 8AA
Tel: (0834) 843611/842491

COMMENDED

This Georgian terraced house is in an ideal position with beautiful views of the beach and harbour. Close to the town centre and only a few steps from the sands and safe bathing of the North beach. There are six bedroom, four with private bathroom. All rooms have colour TV and tea making facilities.

		SINGLE PER PERSON B&B		DOUBLE FOR 2 PERSONS B&B		6
						4
		MIN £ 14.00	MAX £ 19.00	MIN £ 28.00	MAX £ 38.00	OPEN 4-10

GH	Sutherlands

3 Picton Road,
Tenby,
Dyfed SA70 7DP
Tel: (0834) 842522

Small family run guest house, ideally situated for all the delights of this beautiful walled town. Golf links, bowling green and beautiful unspoilt beaches, all within easy reach. Noted for our hospitality and "rich" breakfasts. The discerning palate will also appreciate our evening meals.

		SINGLE PER PERSON B&B		DOUBLE FOR 2 PERSONS B&B		3
						1
		MIN £ 13.00	MAX £ 16.00	MIN £ 26.00	MAX £ 32.00	OPEN 1-12

H	Strathmore Hotel

23 Victoria Street, Tenby,
Pembrokeshire,
Dyfed SA70 7DY
Tel: (0834) 842323

Discover Tenby from our conveniently situated hotel, close to amenities, beaches, parking, town centre. With a reputation as one of Tenby's leading good food/accommodation hotels. We offer choice of menus. All rooms en-suite with TV, tea/coffee bar, radio, heating, smoke alarms. Some sea views, 10% senior citizens discount. Midweek and mini breaks available.

		SINGLE PER PERSON B&B		DOUBLE FOR 2 PERSONS B&B		7
						7
		MIN £ 13.00	MAX £ 17.00	MIN £ 26.00	MAX £ 36.00	OPEN 4-9

GH	Flemish Court

St. Florence,
Tenby,
Dyfed SA70
Tel: (0834) 871413

COMMENDED

Lovely house in beautiful gardens and village. Where hospitality, good food, excellent accommodation are the key words. You'll enjoy the informal atmosphere of our home where you will be made to feel welcome as friends. Try us and you won't be disappointed. Plenty of food to enjoy! before going to explore the lovely area of South Pembrokeshire which I assure you is hard to beat!! Telephone or write. June Taylor.

		SINGLE PER PERSON B&B		DOUBLE FOR 2 PERSONS B&B		3
						3
		MIN £ 14.00	MAX £ 15.00	MIN £ 28.00	MAX £ 30.00	OPEN 1-12

Tenby

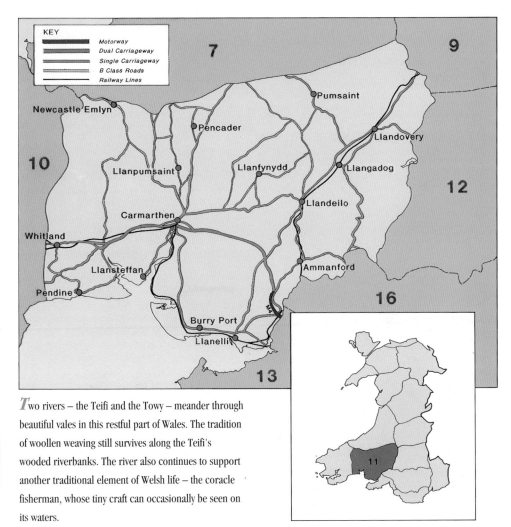

*T*wo rivers – the Teifi and the Towy – meander through beautiful vales in this restful part of Wales. The tradition of woollen weaving still survives along the Teifi's wooded riverbanks. The river also continues to support another traditional element of Welsh life – the coracle fisherman, whose tiny craft can occasionally be seen on its waters.

The Towy's broad vale cuts a swathe through rich farming country, flowing past the pleasant country towns of Llandovery, Llandeilo and Carmarthen. Don't miss Carmarthen's busy market (Wednesday is the best day) when farmers and shoppers pour in for the livestock sales and the fresh food stalls. Flanking the vale are the brooding Black Mountain, western outpost of the Brecon Beacons National Park, and the silent Brechfa Forest.

The Towy meets the sea at Carmarthen Bay. This sandy coastline, and the sleepy little seatown of Laugharne, inspired some of Dylan Thomas's best work (the poet's Boathouse home at Laugharne is open to the public). Elsewhere along this uncrowded coastline there's more sand – miles and miles of it – at Pendine and the splendid Pembrey Country Park.

AMMANFORD
Map Ref: Ke2

Bustling valley town, good for Welsh crafts and products, on western edge of Brecon Beacons National Park. Spectacular mountain routes over nearby Black Mountain to Llangadog. ⇌

CARMARTHEN
Map Ref: Kc2

County town of Dyfed in pastoral Vale of Towy. Lively market and shops, livestock market. Carmarthen Castle was an important residence of the native Welsh princes but only the gateway and towers remain. Golf, fishing, tennis and well-equipped leisure centre. Remains of Roman amphitheatre. Immaculate museum in beautiful historic house on outskirts of town. Gwili Railway and ornamental Middleton Hall amenity area nearby. ⇌

LLANDEILO
Map Ref:Ga7

Farming centre at an important crossing on River Towy, and handy as touring base for Carreg Cennen Castle, impressively set on high crag, and remains of Dryslwyn Castle. Limited access to Dinefwr Castle in parklands on edge of town. Gelli Aur Country Park nearby has 90 acres, including a nature trail, arboretum and deer herd. ⇌

LLANDOVERY
Map Ref: Gb6

An important market town on the A40 with a ruined castle; its Welsh name Llanymddyfri means 'the church among the waters'. Nearby is the cave of Twm Siôn Cati - the Welsh Robin Hood. Good touring centre for Brecon Beacons and remote Llyn Brianne area. ⇌

LLANPUMSAINT
Map Ref: Fc7

Small village off the main A485 Carmarthen - Lampeter road, nestling in a quiet valley between Cynwyl Elfed and the western edge of Brechfa Forest. Take a ride on the steam-powered Gwili Railway from Bronwydd Arms.

LLANSTEFFAN
Map Ref: Kc3

Beautifully sited at the mouth of the River Towy, with an imposing castle. Beaches nearby and sailing in the estuary. Cockle picking and sea angling.

PENCADER
Map Ref: Fc6

Peaceful country village ideal for walking, pony trekking, fishing - or simply relaxing. Rolling hills and wooded valleys all around. On doorstep of the Brechfa Forest and the beautiful Teifi Valley, with its woollen mills. Nearby market and country towns of Carmarthen, Lampeter, Llandysul and Llanybydder full of character.

Dylan Thomas' Boat House, Laugharne

PUMSAINT
Map Ref: Ga5

Famous for the Roman gold mines at Dolaucothi - now a National Trust site open to visitors. The village is attractively sited on the river Cothi in peaceful farmlands near the Caeo Forest. There are nature trails to follow and the ruins of Talley Abbey are 6 miles south. Also visit Felin Newydd Flour Mill at Crugybar.

WHITLAND
Map Ref: Ka2

Market town with remains of 12th-century abbey. Touring centre. Canolfan Hywel Dda is a visitors' centre, with thematic gardens, which tells the story of the Welsh King Hywel the Good, who devised a famous legal code. ⇌

Carreg Cennen Castle, nr Llandeilo

GH Mount Pleasant

Pontarddulais Road,
Garnswllt, Ammanford,
Dyfed SA18 2RT
Tel: (0269) 591722

 APPROVED

Enjoy the best of both worlds. Relax in peaceful surroundings with magnificent views over Loughor Valley and enjoy the convenient location. Situated 2½ miles from Ammanford market town and 5 miles from M4 Junction 48. In easy reach of Swansea shopping and leisure facilities and many tourist attractions. A warm welcome awaits you.

	SINGLE PER PERSON B&B		DOUBLE FOR 2 PERSONS B&B			5
						2
	MIN £	MAX £	MIN £	MAX £	OPEN	
	14.00	–	–	–	1-12	

GH Old Priory Guest House

20 Priory Street,
Carmarthen,
Dyfed SA31 1NE
Tel: (0267) 237471

Family run guest house situated five minutes from town centre. Comfortable TV lounge, à la carte restaurant and bar. Bus and train station within easy walking distance.

		SINGLE PER PERSON B&B		DOUBLE FOR 2 PERSONS B&B			16
							–
		MIN £	MAX £	MIN £	MAX £	OPEN	
		17.50	19.00	29.00	38.00	1-12	

FH Trebersed Farmhouse

Trebersed, Travellers Rest,
St Peters, Carmarthen,
Dyfed SA31 3RR
Tel: (0267) 238182

COMMENDED

A warm welcome awaits you at our working Dairy Farm. Overlooking the thriving market town of Carmarthen, only two miles from its centre. Plenty of parking space. Excellent touring base, just off main A40. Comfortable rooms, double or twin en-suite facilities. Tea/coffee making, central heating, radio/alarms and colour TV lounge.

	SINGLE PER PERSON B&B		DOUBLE FOR 2 PERSONS B&B			2
						2
	MIN £	MAX £	MIN £	MAX £	OPEN	
	16.00	18.00	32.00	32.00	1-12	

GH Gardde-y-Rebecca Guest House

High Street, Lower St. Clears,
Carmarthen,
Dyfed SA33 4DY
Tel: (0994) 230617

A 17th Century house, four miles from Carmarthen Bay and Dylan Thomas's "Sun-Honeyed", Laugharne. Spacious rooms with wash basins, tea making trolleys, central heating, ample parking. Fishing, rambling, trekking, good restaurants, shops nearby. Television lounge. Once the home of Horniman, the tea magnate, later of Hugh Williams, the Chartist and Rebecca Figurehead.

		SINGLE PER PERSON B&B		DOUBLE FOR 2 PERSONS B&B			6
							–
		MIN £	MAX £	MIN £	MAX £	OPEN	
		16.00	16.00	27.00	27.00	1-12	

FH Pantgwyn Farm Guest House

Whitemill,
Carmarthen,
Dyfed SA32 7ES
Tel: (0267) 290247

   HIGHLY COMMENDED

A warm welcome awaits you at our 200 year old farmhouse. Relax in luxuriously appointed bedrooms. Residents inglenook lounge, large dining room. Superb Welsh home cooking. Wales winners " Best breakfast in Britain". Donkey rides. Wildlife conservation valley and pond. 4 miles Carmarthen. 8 miles sandy beach. Ideally situated for touring West Wales.

		SINGLE PER PERSON B&B		DOUBLE FOR 2 PERSONS B&B			3
							3
		MIN £	MAX £	MIN £	MAX £	OPEN	
		–	–	36.00	38.00	1-12	

VISITOR'S GUIDE TO SOUTH WALES

Don't visit South Wales without this full-colour, information-packed guide.

Where to go and what to see.

Descriptions of towns, villages and resorts.

Hundreds of attractions and places to visit

Detailed maps and plans.

Scenic drives, beaches, narrow-gauge railways, what to do on a rainy day.

£3.55 inc. p&p (see page 118)

GH Glasfryn Guest House

Brechfa,
Carmarthen,
Dyfed SA32 7QY
Tel: (0267) 202306

HIGHLY COMMENDED

Situated in the heart of Brechfa Forest, surrounded by moss covered hills, a small family owned guest house. Ideally located for salmon and sewin fishing, pony trekking, walking, bird watching, forestry mountain bike trails. All rooms en-suite. Excellent home cooking. 20 minutes from Carmarthen, 45 minutes from nearest blue flag beach. Please ring for colour brochure.

		SINGLE PER PERSON B&B		DOUBLE FOR 2 PERSONS B&B			3
							3
		MIN £	MAX £	MIN £	MAX £	OPEN	
		16.50	18.00	33.00	36.00	1-12	

FH Plas Farm

Llangynog,
Carmarthen,
Dyfed SA33 5DB
Tel: (0267) 211492

Ideally situated in the quiet countryside, yet within easy reach of the South and West coastline. Friendly run family working farm, all rooms are centrally heated with H&C, tea making facilities and colour TV. One hours drive from the Fishguard and Pembroke Ferries to Ireland. Good evening meals available nearby at local Country Inn or Restaurant.

		SINGLE PER PERSON B&B		DOUBLE FOR 2 PERSONS B&B			2
							2
		MIN £	MAX £	MIN £	MAX £	OPEN	
		16.00	–	25.00	30.00	1-12	

GH Brynawel Guest House

19 New Road,
Llandeilo,
Dyfed SA19 6DD
Tel: (0558) 822925

COMMENDED

Family run guest house in convenient central location. Centrally heated, Fire Certificate. Television, H & C, shaving, tea making facilities in all rooms. En-suite available. Quiet comfortable lounge. Ideal for Golf, riding, fishing, historic buildings, delightful country walks. Close to Brecon Beacons National Park. Leisurely drive to Gower, Pembrokeshire coasts, Pembrey Country Park and motor sports centre.

		SINGLE PER PERSON B&B		DOUBLE FOR 2 PERSONS B&B			5
							3
		MIN £	MAX £	MIN £	MAX £	OPEN	
		19.00	–	29.00	35.00	1-12	

GH — Tygwyn Bach

Gwynfe Road, Ffairfach,
Llandeilo
Dyfed SA19 6UY
Tel: (0558) 823546

COMMENDED

Spacious, attractive and comfortable rooms. Central heating, H & C, tea making facilities. One bed sitting room with en-suite shower. The house is set in an acre of landscaped gardens. Outdoor swimming pool, heated in summer. Ideally located for touring, walking, golf, bird watching, fishing etc. Within easy reach of Brecon Beacons, Gower Peninsula and M4. Very peaceful location.

		SINGLE PER PERSON B&B		DOUBLE FOR 2 PERSONS B&B		2 1
		MIN £ 12.00	MAX £ 15.00	MIN £ 24.00	MAX £ 28.00	OPEN 1-12

FH — Llanerchindda Farm

Cynghordu, Llandovery,
Dyfed SA20 0NB
Tel: (05505) 274
Fax: (05505) 274

L

The west wing of our traditional farmhouse provides 7 very comfortable en-suite bedrooms, residents lounge with log fire and bar. We have a wonderful, quiet, pretty, location overlooking the Brecon Beacons and Towi Valley. Very friendly hosts, excellent home made food. We are adjacent to bird reserves, Cambrian Way footpath. Riding and fishing available.

		SINGLE PER PERSON B&B		DOUBLE FOR 2 PERSONS B&B		7 7
		MIN £ –	MAX £ 19.00	MIN £ –	MAX £ 38.00	OPEN 1-12

GH — Arlandir

Pencader
Dyfed SA39 9AN
Tel: (0559) 384872

HIGHLY COMMENDED

Friendly family welcome at our comfortable home, which enjoys extensive views over the surrounding countryside. Ideal central location for touring countryside and coasts of Ceredigion and Carmarthenshire. One bedroom with en-suite facilities, colour television, peaceful situation with ample parking. Large garden and excellent home cooking using fresh local produce. Pony rides available. Enquiries Mrs Jackie Wonfor.

		SINGLE PER PERSON B&B		DOUBLE FOR 2 PERSONS B&B		2 1
C		MIN £ 13.00	MAX £ 16.00	MIN £ 26.00	MAX £ 30.00	OPEN 1-12
TW						

GH — Myrtle Hill Guest House

Llansadwrn,
Llanwrda,
Dyfed SA19 8HL
Tel: (0550) 777530

COMMENDED

Old farmhouse with magnificent views in beautiful, unspoilt countryside. All bedrooms with en-suite bathrooms, tea/coffee facilities. Two sitting rooms, one "no smoking". Access at all times. Excellent food, freshly prepared using own garden produce. Ideally situated for exploring South, West and Mid Wales. Abundant wildlife, fishing, pony trekking locally, lovely walking country.

		SINGLE PER PERSON B&B		DOUBLE FOR 2 PERSONS B&B		3 3
		MIN £ 17.00	MAX £ 17.00	MIN £ 34.00	MAX £ 34.00	OPEN 1-12

FH — Fferm-y-Felin

Llanpumsaint,
Dyfed SA33 6DA
Tel: (0267) 253498

A warm welcome awaits you at our 18th Century stone farmhouse, with oak beams and log fires. Situated in 15 acres of conserved countryside. You can enjoy long walks, bird watching and trout fishing. Pony rides available for the children. Excellent home cooking, en-suite facilities. Traditional Welsh breakfasts, a delight. Ample parking. Pets by arrangement. Ideal for the discerning traveller.

		SINGLE PER PERSON B&B		DOUBLE FOR 2 PERSONS B&B		5 2
C		MIN £ 15.00	MAX £ 18.00	MIN £ 30.00	MAX £ 36.00	OPEN 1-12

FH — Llystroiddyn Home Farm

Pumsaint, Llanwrda,
Dyfed SA19 8YU
Tel: (05585) 482
Fax: (0550) 21397

L

Situated in beautiful countryside with scenic views. Only 9 miles drive to market towns of Lampeter and Llandovery. Nearest coast is only 40 minutes. Farmhouse of much character with all modern conveniences and a warm welcome is assured. Many walks abound with pony trekking and fishing facilities nearby. TV and hand basins in all rooms.

		SINGLE PER PERSON B&B		DOUBLE FOR 2 PERSONS B&B		3 3
		MIN £ 16.00	MAX £ 16.00	MIN £ 30.00	MAX £ 30.00	OPEN 1-12

FH — Cwmgwyn Farm

Llangadog Road,
Llandovery,
Dyfed SA20 0EQ
Tel: (0550) 20410

HIGHLY COMMENDED

Welcome to our 17th Century farmhouse with oak beams and stone fireplaces, overlooking the River Towy. Peaceful ideal for walking. A working livestock farm two miles from Llandovery Market town on A4069 road. Ideal for touring Mid and South Wales. All bedrooms en-suite, hairdryers, colour TV and tea and coffee facilities.

		SINGLE PER PERSON B&B		DOUBLE FOR 2 PERSONS B&B		3 3
		MIN £ 16.00	MAX £ 18.00	MIN £ 32.00	MAX £ 36.00	OPEN 4-10

GH — Brig-y-Don

The Green, Llansteffan,
Carmarthen,
Dyfed SA33 5LW
Tel: (0267) 83349

L

Sea front accommodation, mouth of estuary beneath Norman Castle. Friendly village with choice of eating places. Lounge with TV. Tea and coffee making facilities in bedrooms. Home baked bread. Personal care.

		SINGLE PER PERSON B&B		DOUBLE FOR 2 PERSONS B&B		3 3
C		MIN £ 15.00	MAX £ 15.00	MIN £ 30.00	MAX £ 30.00	OPEN 1-12

FH — Brunant Farm

Whitland,
Dyfed SA34 0LX
Tel: (0994) 240421

COMMENDED

We offer a warm friendly welcome at Brunant Farm, where guests may relax in the garden or walk around the farm. Ideally situated for touring, walking, riding or visiting beaches. Four comfortable bedrooms, all en-suite with tea/coffee facilities. Full central heating. Comfortable lounge, separate dining room. Home cooking. Full English breakfast. Licence applied for.

		SINGLE PER PERSON B&B		DOUBLE FOR 2 PERSONS B&B		4 4
		MIN £ 16.00	MAX £ 17.00	MIN £ 30.00	MAX £ 32.00	OPEN 3-10

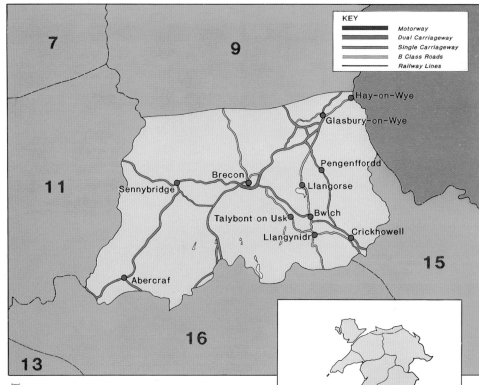

KEY
Motorway
Dual Carriageway
Single Carriageway
B Class Roads
Railway Lines

7

9

Hay-on-Wye

Glasbury-on-Wye

Pengenffordd

Brecon

11

Sennybridge

Llangorse

Bwlch

Talybont on Usk

Crickhowell

Llangynidr

15

Abercraf

16

13

12

The 519-square-mile Brecon Beacons National Park covers much of this area. Grassy slopes and smooth, ice-sculpted hillsides spread themselves out beneath Pen-y-fan, at 2,907ft the highest peak in South Wales. In addition to the Beacons' plentiful open spaces, there are beautiful river valleys, lakes and forests – all in all, a landscape which might have been purpose-built for lovers of the great outdoors.

Walking, pony trekking, fishing, watersports and canal cruising are all popular here – some visitors are even content just to look at the scenery! Explore Pen-y-fan, Llangorse Lake and the central Beacons from the charming old town of Brecon or pretty Crickhowell in the Usk Valley.

Further west, the moorlands of Fforest Fawr lead to the wildernesses of the Black Mountain. Don't confuse this Black Mountain with the Black Mountains at the other end of the park. This latter chain of hills straddles the Wales/England border, running almost to Hay-on-Wye, the world-famous 'town of books'. Hay is a magnet for bibliophiles, especially during its annual Festival of Literature. And music fans from far and wide flock to Brecon each summer for its Jazz Festival.

ABERCRAF
Map Ref: Lc2

In the Upper Tawe Valley on the edge of the Brecon Beacons National Park. Honeycombed with limestone caves, the area boasts the Dan-yr-Ogof Showcaves - the largest in western Europe - a complex which also has a Dinosaur Park and dry ski slope. The beautiful Craig-y-nos Country Park is on the opposite side of the valley.

BRECON
Map Ref: Ge6

Main touring centre for the 519 square miles of the Brecon Beacons National Park. Handsome old town with thriving market, ruined castle, cathedral, priory and interesting Brecknock and South Wales Borderers' museums. Wide range of inns, guest houses and hotels, and good shopping. Centre for walking and pony trekking. Golf, fishing and canal cruising also available. Very popular summer Jazz Festival.

CRICKHOWELL
Map Ref: Hb7

Small, pleasant country town beautifully situated on the River Usk. Walking, fishing, pony trekking and riding facilities. Remains of Norman castle, 14th-century Tretower Court and earlier castle worth a visit.

HAY-ON-WYE
Map Ref: Hb5

Small market town on the Offa's Dyke Path, nestling below the Black Mountains on a picturesque stretch of the River Wye. A mecca for book lovers - there are antiquarian and second-hand bookshops, some huge, all over the town. Attractive crafts centre. Literature Festival in early summer attracts big names.

PENGENFFORDD
Map Ref: Ha6

Tiny settlement on scenic road between Tretower and Talgarth, which cuts through edge of Black Mountains. Wonderful views from Castell Dinas Iron Age Hillfort. Popular with walkers and pony trekkers - good selection of trekking centres locally. Llangorse Lake nearby.

SENNYBRIDGE
Map Ref: Gd6

Quiet village on the edge of Brecon Beacons National Park. Pony trekking, fishing and walking country. Eppynt mountain ranges to the north. Brecon Beacons National Park Visitor Centre close by.

Pony Trekking in the Brecon Beacons

BRECON AND THE BEACONS

ABERCRAF • BRECON

GH — Maes-y-Gwernen

School Road, Abercraf,
Swansea Valley
Powys SA9 1XD
Tel: (0639) 730218
Fax: (0639) 730765

HIGHLY COMMENDED

Maes-y-Gwernen is a large country house in its own well kept grounds on the National Park border and close to the Gower coastline. Guests have their own private lounges. Conservatory and bar and each room has colour TV, coffee and tea making facilities. We pride ourselves on our food and service and provide quality accommodation at realistic prices.

		SINGLE PER PERSON B&B		DOUBLE FOR 2 PERSONS B&B		4
						2
		MIN £ 18.00	MAX £ –	MIN £ 28.00	MAX £ 35.00	OPEN 1-12

GH — Beacons Guest House

16 Bridge Street,
Brecon,
Powys LD3 8AH
Tel: (0874) 623339

COMMENDED

A friendly atmosphere is assured in our family Georgian guest house. Close to town centre, River Usk and Brecon Beacons. En-suite rooms with beverage tray, colour TV. Cosy bar, resident lounge and private parking. Ideal location for attractions and outdoor activities. Groups, pets and children welcome! Excellent home cooking "Taste of Wales" recommended. AA listed. Credit cards accepted. Please write or phone for brochure.

		SINGLE PER PERSON B&B		DOUBLE FOR 2 PERSONS B&B		10
						7
		MIN £ 16.00	MAX £ 19.00	MIN £ 32.00	MAX £ 38.00	OPEN 1-12

GH — Glascwm

Talyllyn,
Brecon,
Powys LD3 7SY
Tel: (0874) 84649

HIGHLY COMMENDED

Edwardian house situated 4½ miles from Brecon in lovely countryside near Llangorse Lake, Brecon Beacons, Black Mountains, Big Pit, Pony trekking, fishing, caving. H&C in all rooms. Tea and coffee. TV lounge. Near Inns for good food. Private car park.

		SINGLE PER PERSON B&B		DOUBLE FOR 2 PERSONS B&B		3
						2
		MIN £ 16.00	MAX £ 17.00	MIN £ 30.00	MAX £ 32.00	OPEN 1-12

H — Red Lion Hotel

Llangorse,
Brecon,
Powys LD3 7TY
Tel: (0874) 84238

COMMENDED

Friendly 18th Century Inn, six miles east of Brecon near Llangorse Lake between Black Mountains and Brecon Beacons. Comfortable bedrooms with showers. Real ales and good food served in bars and informal candlelit restaurant. Ideal base for touring and outdoor activities including walking, fishing, horseriding. Two night breaks available. Please telephone for brochure and tariff.

		SINGLE PER PERSON B&B		DOUBLE FOR 2 PERSONS B&B		3
						–
		MIN £ –	MAX £ –	MIN £ 38.00	MAX £ 38.00	OPEN 1-12

GH — The Coach Guest House

Orchard Street,
Brecon,
Powys LD3 8AN
Tel: (0874) 623803

AWARD — HIGHLY COMMENDED

"Hotel standards at guest house prices". Six bedrooms all en-suite, three with bath, three with shower. Four double rooms, two twin. All have colour TV, Hairdryer, clock/radio, telephone and beverage tray. Whole house completely non smoking. Ideal base for touring Brecon Beacons National Park, close to Brecon town centre. RAC Highly Acclaimed. AA Listed QQQ.

		SINGLE PER PERSON B&B		DOUBLE FOR 2 PERSONS B&B		6
						6
		MIN £ –	MAX £ –	MIN £ 36.00	MAX £ 38.00	OPEN 1-12

GH — Glasfryn House

Church Street,
Brecon,
Powys LD3 8BY
Tel: (0874) 623014

COMMENDED

Clean, comfortable, warm and friendly. Hearty breakfasts and imaginative and freshly cooked evening meals (by arrangement). Situated in the heart of the National Park, close to Brecon centre with its Cathedral, castle, museums and river. We take pleasure in helping our visitors enjoy this very beautiful area. Your hosts Peter and Barbara Jackson.

		SINGLE PER PERSON B&B		DOUBLE FOR 2 PERSONS B&B		9
						–
		MIN £ 15.00	MAX £ –	MIN £ 30.00	MAX £ –	OPEN 1-12

H — Tai'r Bull Inn

Libanus,
Brecon,
Powys LD3 8EL
Tel: (0874) 625849

COMMENDED

With Panoramic views of the Brecon Beacons, Tai'r Bull lies in the lea of Pen-y-Fan at the heart of the National Park. All rooms are en-suite with colour TV and tea making facilities. After a day packed with attractions enjoy a meal and drink in our oak beamed bar or dining room. Private car park. A warm welcome awaits.

		SINGLE PER PERSON B&B		DOUBLE FOR 2 PERSONS B&B		5
						5
		MIN £ –	MAX £ –	MIN £ 36.00	MAX £ 36.00	OPEN 1-12

GH — Drostre House

Talyllyn,
Brecon,
Powys LD3 7SY
Tel: (0874) 84231

COMMENDED

Off the beaten track but only 1½ miles from A40 Abergavenny to Brecon road. Large Edwardian House in two acres landscaped gardes with views to Black Mountains, Llangorse Lake, Brecon Beacons. 2 spacious well furnished rooms with shared luxury bathroom and shower. Comfortable lounge/dining room with colour TV. Paradise for walker, bird watcher and country lover. No children under 10 years.

		SINGLE PER PERSON B&B		DOUBLE FOR 2 PERSONS B&B		2
						1
		MIN £ –	MAX £ –	MIN £ 35.00	MAX £ –	OPEN 1-12

GH — The Old Rectory

Llanfilo,
Brecon,
Powys LD3 0RE
Tel: (0874) 711237

HIGHLY COMMENDED

Come and relax in peaceful country surroundings where a warm and friendly welcome is assured. A beautiful Georgian Rectory adjacent to one of the oldest parish churches in Wales. Situated between the Brecon Beacons and the Black Mountains, this idyllic area offers many country and sporting activities. Television in all rooms, books and games.

		SINGLE PER PERSON B&B		DOUBLE FOR 2 PERSONS B&B		4
						1
		MIN £ 13.50	MAX £ 15.00	MIN £ 27.00	MAX £ 29.00	OPEN 1-12

90

GH | Tir Bach Guest House

13 Alexandra Road,
Brecon,
Powys LD3 7PD
Tel: (0874) 624551

Comfortable, homely, family run guest house on quiet road overlooking the town. Two minute walk from centre, panoramic views of Brecon Beacons. Lounge with colour TV, central heating and car park. Plentiful hot water, traditional British breakfast. Three bedrooms, family, twin, double. Special rates for children. Well travelled friendly host.

		SINGLE PER PERSON B&B		DOUBLE FOR 2 PERSONS B&B			3
		MIN £ 13.00	MAX £ 14.50	MIN £ 26.00	MAX £ 28.00	OPEN 2-10	-

FH | Cwmcamlais Uchaf Farm

Cwmcamlais,
Sennybridge, Brecon,
Powys LD3 8TD
Tel: (0874) 636376

HIGHLY COMMENDED

Cwmcamlais Uchaf is situated in the Brecon Beacons National Park, 1 mile off the A40 between Brecon and Sennybridge. Our spacious 16th Century farmhouse has exposed beams, log fires and 3 tastefully decorated bedrooms. 1 double en-suite and one double and one twin with private bathrooms. Good food and a warm Welsh welcome of prime importance.

		SINGLE PER PERSON B&B		DOUBLE FOR 2 PERSONS B&B			3
							1
		MIN £ 16.00	MAX £ 18.00	MIN £ 30.00	MAX £ 34.00	OPEN 1-12	

FH | Llwyncynog Farm

Felinfach,
Brecon,
Powys LD3 0NG
Tel: (0874) 623475

Family run farm set in peaceful countryside. Commanding splendid views of the Brecon Beacons and Black Mountains. Well situated for many leisure activities. 17th century farmhouse with original oak beams. 3 comfortable bedrooms with tea/coffee making facilities. Guests lounge and dining room with colour television. 1 family room, plus twin room, en-suite, double bedroom with private bathroom.

		SINGLE PER PERSON B&B		DOUBLE FOR 2 PERSONS B&B			3
C							2
		MIN £ 15.00	MAX £ 16.00	MIN £ 26.00	MAX £ 28.00	OPEN 4-10	

FH | Aberbran Fawr Farm

Aberbran,
Brecon,
Powys LD3 9NG
Tel: (0874) 623301

Our 16th Century farmhouse is situated in the beautiful Usk Valley, within the Brecon Beacons National Park and 3 miles from the market town of Brecon. Spacious centrally heated bedrooms with private facilities. TV's and beverage trays. Farmhouse breakfast served in panelled dining room. A good centre for walking, golf, pony trekking, wildlife and touring.

		SINGLE PER PERSON B&B		DOUBLE FOR 2 PERSONS B&B			2
							1
		MIN £ 19.00	MAX £ 19.00	MIN £ 27.00	MAX £ 30.00	OPEN 4-11	

FH | Cilfodig Farm

Ponde, Llandefalle,
Brecon,
Powys LD3 0NR
Tel: (0874) 754207

L

A 17th Century beamed farmhouse set in some of the most beautiful countryside of Mid Wales. In the heart of the Brecon Beacons, Black Mountains, Wye Valley country. Sleeping accommodation is flexible with double, single and family rooms. Dinner is served in our log fired dining room. The interesting market towns of Brecon, Hay-on-Wye town of books and Builth Wells are all within an easy 15 minutes drive.

		SINGLE PER PERSON B&B		DOUBLE FOR 2 PERSONS B&B			3
							-
		MIN £ 13.00	MAX £ 15.00	MIN £ 26.00	MAX £ 30.00	OPEN 4-9	

FH | Llwynhir Farm

Cray,
Brecon,
Powys LD3 8YW
Tel: (0874) 636563

L

Mixed 500 acre hill farm. Panoramic mountain views. Peaceful, near to Dan yr Ogof Caves, National Park centre, waterfalls, Brecon Beacons, Black Mountains, National Trust properties, Penscynor Bird Gardens. Nearby attractions, fishing, pony trekking, dry ski slope, Castles, pottery, art gallery, indoor swimming pool, Brecon 12 miles. Swansea 24 miles. Established over 20 years.

		SINGLE PER PERSON B&B		DOUBLE FOR 2 PERSONS B&B			3
C							-
		MIN £ 14.00	MAX £	MIN £ 26.00	MAX £ -	OPEN 3-10	

FH | Brynfedwen Farm

Trallong Common,
Sennybridge, Brecon,
Powys LD3 8HW
Tel: (0874) 636505

AWARD

HIGHLY COMMENDED

Brynfedwen meaning "Hill of the Birch Trees", is a family farm set high above the Usk Valley, commanding splendid views of the Brecon Beacons. Well situated for all country pursuits or just relaxing. Period, centrally heated farmhouse, all three rooms are en-suite including self contained flat designed for disabled visitors. Good home cooking. Children welcome.

		SINGLE PER PERSON B&B		DOUBLE FOR 2 PERSONS B&B			3
							3
		MIN £ 16.00	MAX £	MIN £ 32.00	MAX £	OPEN 1-12	

FH | Llanbrynean Farm

Llanfrynach,
Brecon,
Powys LD3 7BQ
Tel: (0874) 86222

L

Traditional Victorian farmhouse with large garden and wonderful pastoral views. Informal, friendly atmosphere. Situated on edge of quiet village, Brecon 3 miles. Ideally located for Beacons, Canal, River Usk, Llangorse Lake, pony trekking and good pub food. 2 double bedrooms (one en-suite) and one twin bedroom. Tea/coffee facilities. Sitting room, TV. Working family farm.

		SINGLE PER PERSON B&B		DOUBLE FOR 2 PERSONS B&B			3
							-
		MIN £ 13.00	MAX £ 14.00	MIN £ 26.00	MAX £ 30.00	OPEN 2-12	

FH | Lodge Farm

Talgarth,
Brecon,
Powys LD3 0DP
Tel: (0874) 711244

COMMENDED

Welcome to our working farm in the eastern section of the Brecon Beacons National Park. 1½ miles from Talgarth off A479. 18th century house offers tastefully furnished en-suite rooms with tea making facilities. Freshly prepared menus, using our own produce including vegetarian. Good base for walking, touring, Hay-on-Wye, Brecon 8 miles, Llangorse Lake 4 miles. Children welcome. Brochure Marion Meredith.

		SINGLE PER PERSON B&B		DOUBLE FOR 2 PERSONS B&B			3
							3
		MIN £ 18.00	MAX £	MIN £ 32.00	MAX £	OPEN 1-12	

FH | Maeswalter

Heol Senni,
nr. Brecon,
Powys LD3 8SU
Tel: (0874) 636629

 COMMENDED

Warm and friendly welcome. 17th Century farmhouse, log fires. Situated in picturesque countryside of the Brecon Beacons. Tastefully decorated bedrooms with TV, tea/coffee, H&C, Vanity units and en-suite. All rooms have magnificent views of the Senni Valley. Ample parking space. Near to Ystradfellte falls, Pen-y-fan, Caves, Talybont reservoirs, coast 28 miles.

		SINGLE PER PERSON B&B		DOUBLE FOR 2 PERSONS B&B			3
							2
		MIN £ 16.00	MAX £ 18.00	MIN £ 29.00	MAX £ 33.00	OPEN 1-12	

FH | Scethrog Tower

Scethrog, Brecon,
Powys LD3 7YE
Tel: (081) 969 0059/(0874) 87672
Fax: (081) 960 8246

COMMENDED

Romantic, mediaeval house surrounded by fields, mountains and river. Two spacious oak beamed bed sitting rooms, each with own en-suite toilet and wash basin, colour TV, tea and coffee. Guest fridge. Picnic in large garden overlooking kingfisher pond or in front of log fire in spring/autumn. Relaxed atmosphere. Late breakfast. Steep stone steps. Private trout fishing.

		SINGLE PER PERSON B&B		DOUBLE FOR 2 PERSONS B&B			2
							-
		MIN £ 15.00	MAX £ 18.00	MIN £ 28.00	MAX £ 32.00	OPEN 2-??	

GH | The Firs

Tretower,
Crickhowell,
Powys NP8 1RF
Tel: (0874) 730780

 HIGHLY COMMENDED

Charming country house with cottage style characteristics. Set in a secluded position surrounded by farmland. Just off A40, close to the small town of Crickhowell, good views of surrounding area, medieval Tretower Court and Castle nearby. Personal services and good food is of prime importance. Hairdryers and tea coffee trays in bedrooms. AA/RAC award.

		SINGLE PER PERSON B&B		DOUBLE FOR 2 PERSONS B&B			4
C							2
		MIN £ -	MAX £ -	MIN £ 36.00	MAX £ 38.00	OPEN 1-12	

FH | Maes-y-Coed Farm

Llandefalle,
Brecon,
Powys LD3 0ND
Tel: (0874) 754211

A comfortable 17th Century farmhouse offers a warm friendly welcome. Ideal centre for walking and touring, 8 miles from Brecon Beacons, 14 miles from the world famous town of books at Hay-on-Wye. Accommodation is in 2 double en-suite and 1 twin room with washbasin. Log fires in the winter. Evening meal by arrangement.

		SINGLE PER PERSON B&B		DOUBLE FOR 2 PERSONS B&B			3
							2
		MIN £ 15.00	MAX £ 17.00	MIN £ 30.00	MAX £ 34.00	OPEN 1-12	

FH | Trehenry Farm

Felinfach,
Brecon,
Powys LD3 0JN
Tel: (0874) 754312

 AWARD | DE LUXE

A 200 acre mixed working farm situated east of Brecon 1 mile off A470. The impressive 18th century farmhouse with breathtaking views, inglenook fireplaces and exposed beams offer select accommodation, good food, cosy rooms, TV lounge, separate tables. Central heating. Tea coffee facilities. All rooms with private bathroom. Open all year. Self catering farmhouse also available. Brochure on request.

		SINGLE PER PERSON B&B		DOUBLE FOR 2 PERSONS B&B			3
							3
		MIN £ 17.00	MAX £ 18.00	MIN £ 34.00	MAX £ 36.00	OPEN 1-12	

FH | Clog Fawr Farm

Dyffryn Crawnon,
Llangynidr, Crickhowell,
Powys NP8 1NU
Tel: (0874) 730841

Relax in the informal family atmosphere of a working farm. Enjoy the peace of this secluded valley on the edge of the Brecon Beacons. Situated in a superb walking area close to the Cambrian Way and Taff trail. Horse riding available from the farm. Other activities also arranged. Light snacks and barbecue facilities available.

		SINGLE PER PERSON B&B		DOUBLE FOR 2 PERSONS B&B			2
							-
		MIN £ -	MAX £ -	MIN £ 29.00	MAX £ 29.00	OPEN 1-12	

FH | Pwllacca Farm

Soar, Llanfihangel-Nant-Bran,
Brecon,
Powys LD3 9LY
Tel: (0874) 636255

A peaceful, homely stay on this traditional hill farm set in midst of beautiful rural countryside within easy reach of the Brecon Beacons and Black Mountain. Large beamed character farmhouse with family, double/twin and single bedrooms. Two en-suite, one bathroom. Log fire. Good home cooking. Evening meal on request. Riding pony available.

		SINGLE PER PERSON B&B		DOUBLE FOR 2 PERSONS B&B			3
							2
		MIN £ 12.00	MAX £ 15.00	MIN £ 25.00	MAX £ 30.00	OPEN 2-11	

H | Dragon House Hotel

High Street, Crickhowell,
Powys NP8 1BE
Tel: (0873) 810362
Fax: (0873) 811868

 COMMENDED

Enjoy our charming 18th Century family run hotel in a picturesque market town amidst glorious scenery within the Brecon Beacons National Park. Ideal business or pleasure. Rooms have telephones, tea/coffee facilities. Colour TV and hairdryers in en-suite rooms. Some non-smoking rooms. Our cosy bar and restaurant with real log fires serves freshly prepared meals. Residents lounge. Car park. Activities organised.

		SINGLE PER PERSON B&B		DOUBLE FOR 2 PERSONS B&B			16
							11
		MIN £ -	MAX £ -	MIN £ -	MAX £ 38.00	OPEN 1-12	

GH | The Forge

Glasbury,
nr. Hay-on-Wye,
Powys HR3 5LN
Tel: (0874) 730780

Comfortable 17th Century Welsh longhouse. Interesting, civilised accommodation. Quality early/later breakfasts. Assistance excursions, pony trekking, canoeing other activities. Remote satellite TV, beverage trays in bedrooms. H&C. Electric blankets. Central village, 3½ miles Hay-on-Wye, 12 miles east of Brecon. Superior restaurants nearby. Overwhelming natural beauty surrounds area. Exotic birds. Ideal tranquil break.

		SINGLE PER PERSON B&B		DOUBLE FOR 2 PERSONS B&B			3
							1
		MIN £ 16.00	MAX £ 18.00	MIN £ 32.00	MAX £ 34.00	OPEN 4-10	

GH | The Old Post Office

Llanigon,
Hay-on-Wye,
via Hereford HR3 5QA
Tel: (0497) 820008

COMMENDED

17th Century character house in a quiet rural position only two miles to the famous second hand book town of Hay-on-Wye and set in the lovely Brecon Beacons National Park. Close to the Black Mountains and Offa's Dyke path. Special vegetarian breakfast served including fresh orange juice, grapefruit and a wide choice of main courses.

		SINGLE PER PERSON B&B		DOUBLE FOR 2 PERSONS B&B			3
		MIN £	MAX £	MIN £	MAX £	OPEN	3
		–	–	30.00	34.00	4-12	

FH | Trephilip Farm

Sennybridge,
Brecon,
Powys LD3 8SA
Tel: (0874) 636610

HIGHLY COMMENDED

Georgian farmhouse situated in the Brecon Beacons National Park, ¾ mile off A40, ½ mile off A4067. Guests enjoy en-suite facilities, private lounge with colour TV, tea/coffee facilities, private fishing. Short riverside walk to village with excellent restaurant and public house. A warm welcome awaits you at our family farm.

		SINGLE PER PERSON B&B		DOUBLE FOR 2 PERSONS B&B			2
		MIN £	MAX £	MIN £	MAX £	OPEN	1
		–	–	30.00	32.00	1-12	

FH | Ffordd Fawr Farm Guest House

Glasbury-on-Wye,
nr. Hereford,
Powys HR3 5PT
Tel: (0497) 847332

 AWARD   HIGHLY COMMENDED

Receive a friendly welcome and feel at home, in this late 17th Century farmhouse. Close to Hay-on-Wye, a book lovers paradise. Set in the Wye Valley with beautiful unspoilt countryside. Ideal for all country pursuits. Some rooms en-suite. Tea/coffee making facilities, lounge, TV in all bedrooms. Full central heating. Large car park. Delightful gardens. Telephone Barbara for brochure.

		SINGLE PER PERSON B&B		DOUBLE FOR 2 PERSONS B&B			3
		MIN £	MAX £	MIN £	MAX £	OPEN	1
		16.00	18.00	28.00	36.00	3-11	

H | Castle Inn

Pengenffordd,
nr. Talgarth,
Powys LD3 0EP
Tel: (0874) 711353

L
COMMENDED

The Castle Inn lies at the top of an unspoilt valley in a peaceful part of Southern Powys. Grass covered mountains ascend on all sides. The Inn has its own spring water drinking supply. All rooms are in a pine and white theme with colour television, central heating. New for 1994 double/twin rooms available en-suite.

		SINGLE PER PERSON B&B		DOUBLE FOR 2 PERSONS B&B			5
		MIN £	MAX £	MIN £	MAX £	OPEN	2
		18.00	18.00	38.00	38.00	1-12	

Brecon Beacons

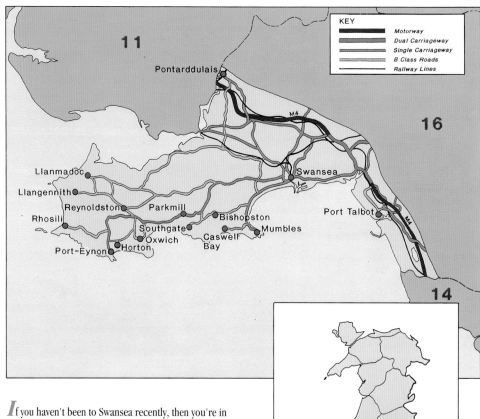

If you haven't been to Swansea recently, then you're in for a treat. The city is rightly proud of its dazzling Maritime Quarter, which has brought new life to the old waterfront. The Quarter's marina is the centrepiece of an award-winning development which includes a Leisure Centre and Maritime and Industrial Museum. Swansea successfully mixes traditional and modern influences. One of its most celebrated features is its fresh foods market – one of the best in Wales – where you can buy everything from Welshcakes to laverbread.

Swansea's setting is another of its strong points. The city is located on the grand sweep of Swansea Bay, close to the unspoilt Gower Peninsula. Mumbles, a pretty little resort and sailing centre, stands at Gower's gateway.

From here, Gower's stubby peninsula points westwards, ending in spectacular fashion at Rhosili's dizzy headland.

The peninsula was Britain's first 'Area of Outstanding Natural Beauty'. Most of its little seaside centres – they are too small to be called resorts – are located along the sandy, south-facing coast. But also visit the atmospheric saltings and cockle beds of North Gower.

Margam Country Park

BISHOPSTON
Map Ref: Ke5

Village at the gateway to Gower that almost merges with Newton and Mumbles. Only 1½ miles from sands of Caswell and Pwll-du bays.

LLANMADOC
Map Ref: Kd5

Village on north-west coast of Gower Peninsula with easy access to superb beaches along Rhosili Bay and Broughton Bay. Weobley Castle nearby.

MUMBLES
Map Ref: La4

Small resort on Swansea Bay with attractive waterfront and headland pier; centre for watersports and sailing. On fringe of Gower Peninsula, a designated 'Area of Outstanding Natural Beauty'. Oystermouth Castle and Clyne Valley Country Park and Gardens nearby.

OXWICH
Map Ref: Kd5

Popular Gower Peninsula beach with 3 miles of glorious sand and extensive dunes; easily accessible. Nature trail and visitor centre.

PARKMILL
Map Ref: Ke5

Gower Peninsula village with easy access to beaches and Swansea. Three Cliffs Bay - one of finest stretches of Gower - and historic sites nearby.

PORT TALBOT
Map Ref: Lb4

Extensive sands at Aberavon beach - bathing and surfing. Afan Lido sports centre. Margam Country Park has a deer herd, sculpture park, organgery, maze and children's fairytale village. The fascinating Welsh Miners' Museum is in the wooded Afan Argoed Country Park. ⇌

REYNOLDSTON
Map Ref: Kd5

Gower Peninsula village near sandy beaches of Oxwich, Port-Eynon and Rhosili.

Paragliding, Worm's Head

95

RHOSILI
Map Ref: Kc5

Gower's 'Lands End', a village set on headland above stunning 3 miles of sandy beach. Good surfing, hang gliding, coastal walking. A strange formation known as Worm's Head juts into sea. National Trust Visitor Centre.

SOUTHGATE
Map Ref: Ke5

Gower Peninsula village; fine beaches at Three Cliffs Bay and Oxwich, and popular Caswell and Langland bays just to the east. Close to Swansea, with its leisure centre, Maritime Quarter, museums and shopping.

SWANSEA
Map Ref: La4

Wales's second city and gateway to the Gower Peninsula, Britain's first designated 'Area of Outstanding Natural Beauty'. Superb new marina complex and Maritime Quarter - excellent leisure centre, with Maritime and Industrial Museum nearby. Art gallery, Superbowl, dry ski slope and marvellous 'Plantasia' exotic plants attraction. Good shopping. Covered market with distinctively Welsh atmosphere: try the cockles, laverbread and Gower potatoes. Swansea Festival and 'Fringe' Festival in October. Theatres and cinemas, parks and gardens, restaurants and wine bars. ⇌

Three Cliffs Bay, Gower

GH | Jezreel Guest House

168 Bishopston Road,
Bishopston, Swansea
West Glamorgan SA3 3EX
Tel: (0792) 232744

Situated at the gateway to Gower Peninsula, an Area of Outstanding Natural Beauty, near secluded bays. Wash hand basins and shaver points in bedrooms, also tea making facilities. Good home cooking with plenty of choice on the menu. Spacious lounge with TV, separate dining room, ample parking space with extra wide entrance. Friendly welcoming hosts.

		SINGLE PER PERSON B&B		DOUBLE FOR 2 PERSONS B&B			3
		MIN £	MAX £	MIN £	MAX £	OPEN	–
		14.00	15.00	28.00	30.00	3-11	

GH | Little Haven Guest House

Oxwich, Gower
Swansea,
West Glamorgan SA3 1LS
Tel: (0792) 390940

Family run guest house situated in Oxwich Village, located near beach which is ideal for most water sports. All bedrooms have hot and cold and tea making facilities. Guests can use our secluded garden to relax after enjoying the beach and the many walks. Reduced rates for children under twelve. Sorry no pets allowed.

		SINGLE PER PERSON B&B		DOUBLE FOR 2 PERSONS B&B			3
		MIN £	MAX £	MIN £	MAX £	OPEN	–
		17.00	17.00	30.00	30.00	1-12	

GH | Ty'n-y-Caeau

Margam,
Port Talbot,
West Glamorgan SA13 2NW
Tel: (0639) 883897

COMMENDED

Ty'n-y-Caeau was a 17th Century vicarage with walled garden. En-suite large bedrooms with mountain and garden views. Close to Margam Abbey and Park. Set back in fields off the A48 dual carriageway with private driveway on left, leading to large white house. Fresh home grown produce and always a warm Welsh welcome. Brochure from Mrs. R. Gaen.

		SINGLE PER PERSON B&B		DOUBLE FOR 2 PERSONS B&B			7
		MIN £	MAX £	MIN £	MAX £	OPEN	6
		18.00	–	32.00	–	2-11	

GH | Tallizmand

Llanmadoc,
Gower, Swansea,
West Glamorgan SA3 1DE
Tel: (0792) 386373

Tastefully furnished double en-suite bedrooms. Family and single room all with tea/coffee making facilities. Home cooking, vegetarians catered for. Large breakfast. Packed lunches and evening meals available. TV lounge, ample parking. Ideally situated for beaches, scenic walks, bird watching, swimming, surfing and hang gliding.

		SINGLE PER PERSON B&B		DOUBLE FOR 2 PERSONS B&B			3
		MIN £	MAX £	MIN £	MAX £	OPEN	2
		16.00	16.00	32.00	32.00	1-11	

GH | Parc Le Breos House

Parkmill,
Gower,
West Glamorgan SA3 2HA
Tel: (0792) 371636

APPROVED

Spacious 18th Century farmhouse in the heart of beautiful Gower Peninsula. Ideal base for a wide range of holiday activities around Gower. Riding holidays and day rides available, paddock rides for children. TV lounge, games room, safe lawn play area. Home grown cooked food, warm welcome. BHS approved. AA listed. SAE for colour brochure.

		SINGLE PER PERSON B&B		DOUBLE FOR 2 PERSONS B&B			10
		MIN £	MAX £	MIN £	MAX £	OPEN	9
		16.00	19.00	32.00	38.00	1-12	

FH | Greenways

Hills Farm
Reynoldston, Swansea,
West Glamorgan SA3 1AE
Tel: (0792) 390125

L

This 120 acre working farm is situated in the beautiful village of Reynoldston, adjacent to Cefn Bryn a walkers paradise. Central to all Gower bays. Own produce used when possible. Full central heating. H&C in all rooms. Separate tables, TV lounge. Pets by arrangement. Car Park. Enquiries to Mrs D. W. John.

		SINGLE PER PERSON B&B		DOUBLE FOR 2 PERSONS B&B			3
		MIN £	MAX £	MIN £	MAX £	OPEN	
		14.00	16.00	28.00	32.00	2-11	

GH | Rock Villa Guest House

1 George Bank,
Southend, Swansea ,
West Glamorgan SA3 4EQ
Tel: (0792) 366794

COMMENDED

Family run guest house. Ideal for bowling green, tennis courts, shops, water skiing, surfing, sailing. Full English breakfast. Comfortable lounge with TV. Television all rooms. Tea/coffee all rooms, shaver points. Full Fire Certificate, en-suite double also en-suite twin.

		SINGLE PER PERSON B&B		DOUBLE FOR 2 PERSONS B&B			5
		MIN £	MAX £	MIN £	MAX £	OPEN	2
		16.00	19.00	28.00	33.00	1-12	

FH | Lunnon Farm

Parkmill,
Swansea,
West Glamorgan SA3 2EJ
Tel: (0792) 371205

L

Warm Welsh welcome to our 15th Century farmhouse situated within short distance of Three Cliffs Bay and beautiful village of Parkmill. Excellent walks, easy reach of Swansea, Mumbles, all other beaches of lovely Gower Peninsula. TV lounge. Separate dining room. Shower, Central heating. All amenities in lovely Parkmill Village.

		SINGLE PER PERSON B&B		DOUBLE FOR 2 PERSONS B&B			2
		MIN £	MAX £	MIN £	MAX £	OPEN	2
		–	–	28.00	30.00	3-11	

GH | Broad Park Guest House

Rhosili, South Gower,
Swansea,
West Glamorgan SA3 1PL
Tel: (0792) 390515

L

Family run guest house with panoramic views. Ideally suited for coastal and inland walks, surfing, hang gliding and magnificent beaches for swimming. Home cooking, separate tables when available. TV lounge. Full Fire Certificate. No smoking in dining room. Large car park. Open all year.

		SINGLE PER PERSON B&B		DOUBLE FOR 2 PERSONS B&B			7
		MIN £	MAX £	MIN £	MAX £	OPEN	
		14.00	16.00	28.00	32.00	1-12	

GH | Sunnyside

Rhosili, Gower,
nr. Swansea,
West Glamorgan SA3 1PL
Tel: (0792) 390596

Small guest house with outstanding sea views and close to sandy beaches. Hand basins and tea/coffee making facilities in bedrooms. TV on request. Separate dining tables, TV lounge, special diets by arrangement. Local activities include pony trekking, hang gliding, surfing, beautiful coastal walks.

		SINGLE PER PERSON B&B		DOUBLE FOR 2 PERSONS B&B		🛏	3
						🛁	–
		MIN £ 16.00	MAX £ 16.00	MIN £ 30.00	MAX £ 30.00	OPEN 4-9	

GH | Belmont Guest House

2 Mirador Crescent,
Uplands, Swansea,
West Glamorgan SA2 0QX
Tel: (0792) 466812

Warm Welsh welcome awaits you at our quietly situated friendly guest house with own private car park. Convenient for city centre and Gower Peninsula. All bedrooms centrally heated, welcome tray, colour TV, H&C, shaver points, clock radio. Small groups welcome, basic food, Hygiene Certificate, Fire Certificate. Proprietors Mair and Tony Aston.

		SINGLE PER PERSON B&B		DOUBLE FOR 2 PERSONS B&B		🛏	7
						🛁	–
		MIN £ 16.00	MAX £ 18.00	MIN £ 30.00	MAX £ 32.00	OPEN 1-12	

GH | Cwmdulais House

Cwmdulais,
Pontarddulais, Swansea,
West Glamorgan SA4 1NP
Tel: (0792) 885008 HIGHLY COMMENDED

"Arrive as a stranger, leave as a friend". Exceptional welcome, relaxing homely atmosphere. Superb home cooking. Set amongst picturesque mountains, enjoying the tranquillity of the countryside together with convenience of location. Three miles off junction 47 M4, Swansea City 9 miles, Carmarthen 20 miles and glorious Gower on the doorstep. Golf, fishing nearby. Brochure available.

		SINGLE PER PERSON B&B		DOUBLE FOR 2 PERSONS B&B		🛏	5
						🛁	2
		MIN £ 16.00	MAX £ 18.00	MIN £ 32.00	MAX £ 36.00	OPEN 1-12	

GH | Heatherlands

1 Hael Lane,
Southgate, Gower,
West Glamorgan SA3 2AP
Tel: (0792) 233256 HIGHLY COMMENDED

Delightfully situated, Heatherlands is a modern and immaculate residence, secluded garden, near cliffs. Walking distance to the popular Three Cliffs and Pebbles Bay. Three comfortable bedrooms with H&C, shaver points, tea making facilities. One bedroom with private bath. Showers available, TV lounge, separate tables in dining room. Short car ride to Gower beaches. Car parking.

		SINGLE PER PERSON B&B		DOUBLE FOR 2 PERSONS B&B		🛏	3
						🛁	1
		MIN £ 16.00	MAX £ 17.00	MIN £ 30.00	MAX £ 32.00	OPEN 3-9	

L | Pavilion Lodge

Swansea Pavilion Services,
J47 M4 Motorway, Penllegaer,
Swansea, West Glamorgan SA4 1GT
Tel: (0792) 894894 Fax: (0792) 898806
Reservations: freephone (0800) 515836
HIGHLY COMMENDED

50 bedroomed modern lodge, situated in a rural setting just off the M4. All bedrooms have private bathroom, remote control television, hairdryer, trouser press, hospitality tray. Ideal for a stopover break or for touring the coastal area of South West Wales. Easy travelling to both Swansea and Fishguard ports.

		SINGLE PER PERSON B&B		DOUBLE FOR 2 PERSONS B&B		🛏	50
						🛁	50
		MIN £ –	MAX £ –	MIN £ 38.00	MAX £ 38.00	OPEN 1-12	

Plantasia, Swansea

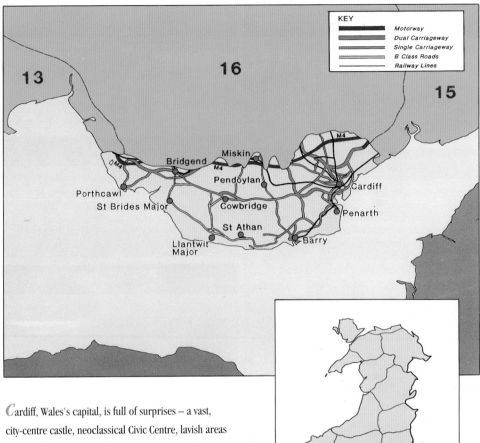

Cardiff, Wales's capital, is full of surprises – a vast, city-centre castle, neoclassical Civic Centre, lavish areas of parkland, Victorian arcades and covered market, stylish shopping centres, new Cardiff Bay waterfront development, theatres and world-class museums. More and more visitors are now discovering Cardiff, thanks also to its excellent road and rail communications – it's less than two hours by train from London.

The city stands on a coastline where you'll find everything from towering cliffs to candy floss. Barry Island and Porthcawl are two popular family seaside resorts which offer great beaches and all the fun of the fair. In between is the untouched Glamorgan Heritage Coast, a beautiful area of cliffs, tiny bays and huge sand

dunes. And on Cardiff's doorstep is Penarth, a delightful little Victorian resort complete with pier and modern marina.

Cardiff is also located on the doorstep of the Vale of Glamorgan, a pastoral area dotted with historic sites, pretty villages and handsome towns such as Cowbridge. Take time to explore the Vale's country lanes – and call in at the open-air Welsh Folk Museum, St Fagans.

BRIDGEND
Map Ref: Ld5

Bustling industrial and market town on edge of rural Vale of Glamorgan. Lively resort of Porthcawl and unspoilt Heritage Coast with cliffs and dunes nearby. Beautiful Bryngarw Country Park and ancient Ewenny Priory on doorstep. Three ruined Norman castles in the area - Coity, Newcastle and Ogmore. ≊

CARDIFF
Map Ref: Mb5

Capital of Wales, business, trade and entertainment centre. Splendid Civic Centre, lovely parkland, modern pedestrianised shopping centre, new waterfront development, good restaurants, theatres, cinemas, clubs and sports facilities, including ice-rink and Superbowl. Visit St David's Hall for top-class entertainment. Ornate city-centre castle. National Museum of Wales has a fine collection of Impressionist paintings. Industrial and Maritime Museum and Techniquest Science Centre in docklands. National Stadium is home of Welsh rugby. Wide range of accommodation at all prices. Llandaff Cathedral close by and fascinating collection of old farmhouses and other buildings at Welsh Folk Museum, St Fagans. ≊

COWBRIDGE
Map Ref: Le6

Picturesque town with wide main street and pretty houses - the centre of the Vale of Glamorgan farming community. Fine old inns, shops selling high-class clothes and country wares. 14th-century town walls. Good touring centre for South Wales. Visit nearby Beaupre Castle.

PENARTH
Map Ref: Mb6

Small resort near Cardiff offering boating, yachting, fishing, water-skiing and cliff walks. Victorian pier and promenade. New marina. Turner House Art Gallery. Cosmeston Country Park and Medieval Village nearby. ≊

PENDOYLAN
Map Ref: Le5

Vale of Glamorgan village surrounded by pleasant countryside, yet convenient for Cardiff and the South Wales coast. Llanerch Vineyard open to the public - visitor centre, vineyard trail, wine tasting. Welsh Folk Museum, St Fagans nearby.

PORTHCAWL
Map Ref: Lc6

Traditional seaside resort - beaches, funfair, promenade. Attractive harbour and quieter coast along Rest Bay. Summer entertainment at the Grand Pavilion. Sailing and windsurfing. Famous golf course. Kenfig Pool and Dunes. Convenient for visiting the unspoilt Ogwr countryside, Bryngarw Country Park and Vale of Glamorgan with its attractive villages set amid leafy lanes.

ST BRIDES MAJOR
Map Ref: Ld6

Small picturesque village in the Vale of Glamorgan, spectacular Heritage Coast to the south. Close to Bridgend and ideal for visiting Ogmore Castle and Ewenny Priory. Golf at Southerndown.

GH | April Wood

Blackmill,
Bridgend,
Mid Glamorgan CF35 6DW
Tel: (0656) 841208

You are assured of a warm and friendly welcome at April Wood. Rural location but less than five minutes from Junction 36 of the M4. An excellent base for touring South Wales or just a stopover. Free use of tennis court. Ideal for country walks.

P		SINGLE PER PERSON B&B		DOUBLE FOR 2 PERSONS B&B		🛏 2 🛁 2	
		MIN £	MAX £	MIN £	MAX £	OPEN 1-12	
		15.00	19.00	25.00	29.00		

H | Grays Hotel

Culverhouse Cross,
Cardiff,
South Glamorgan CF5 5TF
Tel/Fax: (0222) 591050

L

Excellently situated Cardiff West, close to: M4 road, Vale of Glamorgan. Coastal resorts, airport. Athletic Stadium, Ninian Park, HTV studios, Valegate Business Park, Welsh Folk Museum conveniently situated. Cardiff Arms Park, city centre 10 minutes drive. Some en-suite rooms, all rooms with TV, coffee/tea, licensed, large car park. Evening meals on request. Lounge/bar.

P		SINGLE PER PERSON B&B		DOUBLE FOR 2 PERSONS B&B		🛏 9 🛁 2	
		MIN £	MAX £	MIN £	MAX £	OPEN 1-12	
		17.50	18.50	25.00	27.00		

L | Pavilion Lodge

Cardiff West Pavilion, (M4 Exit 33),
nr. Pontyclun, Cardiff,
Mid Glamorgan CF7 8SB
Tel: (0222) 892255; Fax: (0222) 892497
Reservations: Freephone: (0800) 515836

HIGHLY COMMENDED

50 bedroomed modern lodge situated in a rural setting just off the M4. All bedrooms have private bathroom, remote control colour television with sky, radio, alarm clock, trouser press, hairdryer, hospitality tray. Ideal for stop over or centre for touring South Wales coast and Welsh Valleys. 7 miles from Cardiff City centre, 8 miles from Cardiff International Airport.

P C		SINGLE PER PERSON B&B		DOUBLE FOR 2 PERSONS B&B		🛏 50 🛁 50	
		MIN £	MAX £	MIN £	MAX £	OPEN 1-12	
		–	–	38.00	38.00		

GH | St Andrews Guest House

21 West Farm Road,
Ogmore-by-Sea, nr. Bridgend,
Mid Glamorgan, CF2 1AJ
Tel: (0656) 880183

L
APPROVED

Overlooking the sea. Quiet and secluded location. Easy reach of most sports facilities, including golf course 1½ miles. Vanity units, tea and coffee all bedrooms, full central heating. Family, double and single bedrooms. Lounge colour TV, comfortable and decorative surroundings. Proven record of good food and hospitality. 7 miles off Junction 35, M4 motorway.

P C		SINGLE PER PERSON B&B		DOUBLE FOR 2 PERSONS B&B		🛏 3	
		MIN £	MAX £	MIN £	MAX £	OPEN 1-12	
		16.00	16.00	30.00	30.00		

H | Olympos Hotel

104 Penylan Hill,
Penylan, Cardiff,
South Glamorgan CF2 5HY
Tel: (0222) 485727

A family run hotel situated by Roath Park Lake. Close to Heath Hospital and University, Wellfield Road and Albany Road. Adjacent to A48 and M4. Secure car park.

P		SINGLE PER PERSON B&B		DOUBLE FOR 2 PERSONS B&B		🛏 17 🛁 4	
		MIN £	MAX £	MIN £	MAX £	OPEN 1-12	
		19.00	–	32.00	35.00		

GH | Acorn Lodge Guest House

182 Cathedral Road,
Cardiff,
South Glamorgan CF1 9JE
Tel: (0222) 221373

L

A fine Victorian house of character and charm. Ideally situated within a few minutes walk of city centre and central to all attractions. All rooms are to high standard and have wash basins, colour televisions, tea and coffee. Full choice of breakfast menu. Car park, on main bus route, family run. Friendly personal service.

P		SINGLE PER PERSON B&B		DOUBLE FOR 2 PERSONS B&B		🛏 9	
		MIN £	MAX £	MIN £	MAX £	OPEN 1-12	
		16.00	18.00	28.00	32.00		

H | Bronte Hotel

158-164 Newport Road,
Cardiff,
South Glamorgan CF2 1DL
Tel: (0222) 499167
Fax: (0222) 473592

APPROVED

32 Bedrooms with colour TV, tea/coffee, telephone, 12 en-suite rooms. Large secure car park, comfortable bar and lounge, games room. Close to city centre and Cardiff Castle. Nearby amenities include bowling rink and ice skating rink, Roath Park and boating lake.

P C		SINGLE PER PERSON B&B		DOUBLE FOR 2 PERSONS B&B		🛏 32 🛁 12	
		MIN £	MAX £	MIN £	MAX £	OPEN 1-12	
		17.50	19.00	30.00	35.00		

H | Wynford Hotel

Clare Street, Cardiff,
South Glamorgan CF1 8SD
Tel: (0222) 371983
Fax: (0222) 340477

Very close to the city centre, train and bus stations, the Wynford, privately owned and personally supervised, offers a comfortable lounge, two cosy bars, occasional music and dancing, bistro and restaurant. All rooms have colour and satellite TV and telephone. Many have private bathroom. French, Spanish, German spoken. Night porter, video linked security car park.

P		SINGLE PER PERSON B&B		DOUBLE FOR 2 PERSONS B&B		🛏 29 🛁 20	
		MIN £	MAX £	MIN £	MAX £	OPEN 1-12	
		–	–	36.00	–		

GH | Bon Maison Guest House

39 Plasturton Gardens,
Pontcanna, Cardiff,
South Glamorgan CF1 9HG
Tel: (0222) 383660

Bon Maison is situated in a beautiful Victorian garden area. Only 1 mile from the city, castle, museums, shops and theatres. All rooms have H&C, hospitality tray, heating and colour TV. En-suite rooms also available. Non-smoking breakfast room, special diets. Children and pets catered for. Your hosts Maureen and Trevor will ensure your stay will be enjoyable.

P		SINGLE PER PERSON B&B		DOUBLE FOR 2 PERSONS B&B		🛏 3 🛁 2	
		MIN £	MAX £	MIN £	MAX £	OPEN 1-12	
		16.00	–	29.00	34.00		

GH Glan-y-Dwr

157 Lake Road West,
Roath Park, Cardiff,
South Glamorgan CF2 5PL
Tel: (0222) 758126

Glan-y-Dwr means Water's Edge. Our huge guest room in this Edwardian family house overlooks Roath Park Lake with its boats and waterfowl. The room has gas fire, wash basin, tea/coffee facilities, fruit, biscuits. Special rates for families (room can sleep five). Guests have exclusive use of TV lounge, bathroom and separate toilet. Full British breakfast. Convenient bus.

P		SINGLE PER PERSON B&B		DOUBLE FOR 2 PERSONS B&B			1
							–
		MIN £	MAX £	MIN £	MAX £	OPEN 1-12	
		18.00	18.00	30.00	30.00		

FH Cefn Llys Farm

Miskin,
Pontyclun,
Mid Glamorgan CF7 8JU
Tel: (0443) 226488

HIGHLY COMMENDED

Conveniently situated in the Vale of Glamorgan, two miles from M4 Junction 34, in peaceful surroundings with excellent views. The coast, Cardiff and the Brecon Beacons are all easily accessible. Accommodation is self contained, ground floor, twin bedded room, bathroom, lounge/dining room. Central heating, open fire, colour TV, telephone. Facilities available to prepare evening meals.

P		SINGLE PER PERSON B&B		DOUBLE FOR 2 PERSONS B&B			1
							1
		MIN £	MAX £	MIN £	MAX £	OPEN 1-12	
		16.50	17.50	33.00	33.00		

FH Llanerch Vineyard

Hensol, Pendoylan,
South Glamorgan CF7 8JU
Tel: (0443) 225877
Fax: (0443) 225546

HIGHLY COMMENDED

Traditional Welsh farmhouse, overlooking largest vineyard in Wales. All bedrooms with private bathroom. Extensive grounds with ten acres of woodlands and lakes. Children's play area. Sign posted from Junction 34 of M4. Fifteen minutes from Cardiff. Convenient for coast and Brecon Beacons. Ideal centre for touring South Wales. One of "Wales great little places".

P		SINGLE PER PERSON B&B		DOUBLE FOR 2 PERSONS B&B			3
							3
		MIN £	MAX £	MIN £	MAX £	OPEN 1-12	
		–	–	36.00	36.00		

GH Llwyncelyn House

Cwrt Llwyncelyn, Pantmawr Road,
Whitchurch, Cardiff,
South Glamorgan CF4 6XB
Tel: (0222) 692685

Llwyncelyn House is a private family house. We have one large double/family room with a luxury en-suite shower room. There are tea and coffee making facilities in the room and also a TV in the room. There is ample car parking facilities and easy access to the city centre, with a feel of the country.

P		SINGLE PER PERSON B&B		DOUBLE FOR 2 PERSONS B&B			1
							1
		MIN £	MAX £	MIN £	MAX £	OPEN 1-12	
		19.00	19.00	30.00	30.00		

FH Cartreglas Farm

Welsh St Donats,
Cowbridge,
South Glamorgan CF7 7SX
Tel: (0446) 772368
Fax: (0446) 775553

HIGHLY COMMENDED

A warm welcome awaits you at Cartreglas, where we grow flowers for drying and run workshops in the lovely Vale of Glamorgan. Conveniently situated for touring Cardiff, coast, mountains. 3 miles from M4 and 4 miles from Cowbridge. Fully equipped kitchen available for guests to make own evening meal. Children and pets welcome.

P		SINGLE PER PERSON B&B		DOUBLE FOR 2 PERSONS B&B			3
							2
		MIN £	MAX £	MIN £	MAX £	OPEN 1-12	
		16.00	18.00	32.00	36.00		

H Minerva Hotel

Esplanade Avenue,
Porthcawl,
Mid Glamorgan CF36 3YU
Tel: (0656) 782428

Comfortable Edwardian licensed hotel, AA listed and run personally by the owners Rosemarie and Tony Giblett. Occupying a central position close to promenade and shops. Rooms are centrally heated, have tea and coffee facilities and colour television. Some have bathrooms en-suite. Reduced rates for weekly bookings. Children under 12 charged half price. Evening meal menu.

		SINGLE PER PERSON B&B		DOUBLE FOR 2 PERSONS B&B			8
							4
		MIN £	MAX £	MIN £	MAX £	OPEN 1-12	
		14.00	14.00	28.00	28.00		

GH Plas-y-Bryn

93 Fairwater Road,
Llandaff, Cardiff,
South Glamorgan CF5 2LG
Tel: (0222) 561717

COMMENDED

Comfortable house outskirts of Cardiff. Short walk from pretty village of Llandaff and Cathedral. Two minutes walk from train halt (Fairwater), near bus routes. All home comforts, central heating, television lounge. Tea/coffee facilities also hand basins in all bedrooms which are quiet rooms. Good service. A48, M4 very close, also Folk Museum.

		SINGLE PER PERSON B&B		DOUBLE FOR 2 PERSONS B&B			3
							–
		MIN £	MAX £	MIN £	MAX £	OPEN 1-12	
		15.00	17.00	30.00	35.00		

GH Ardwyn

53 Cog Road, Sully,
Penarth,
South Glamorgan CF64 5TE
Tel: (0222) 530103

We have five guest rooms, all of which have welcome trays, remote control colour TV, heating and hair dryers. Three with wash hand basins, two with en-suite facilities. Visitors lounge with colour TV and video. We are within easy reach of Cardiff and the beautiful Vale of Glamorgan. Off road parking. We hope to welcome you.

P		SINGLE PER PERSON B&B		DOUBLE FOR 2 PERSONS B&B			5
							2
		MIN £	MAX £	MIN £	MAX £	OPEN 1-12	
		16.00	18.00	32.00	36.00		

H Penoyre Private Hotel

29 Mary Street,
Porthcawl,
Mid Glamorgan CF36 3YN
Tel: (0656) 784550

Penoyre is a family run licensed hotel 100 yards from beach and shopping centre. All rooms have colour TV, tea and coffee making facilities. En-suite available. There is a small friendly bar and TV lounge for guests enjoyment. Children and pets welcome. Penoyre offers excellent home cooking. Vegetarian and special diets on request. RAC listed.

		SINGLE PER PERSON B&B		DOUBLE FOR 2 PERSONS B&B			6
							1
		MIN £	MAX £	MIN £	MAX £	OPEN 1-12	
		13.00	17.00	26.00	34.00		

GH	Rockybank Guest House

15 De Breos Drive,
Porthcawl,
Mid Glamorgan CF36 3JP
Tel: (0656) 785823

A warm welcome awaits you at the first guest house off Junction 37 (M4). Situated between two excellent golf courses, quiet spot, ample parking, near village Inns, walking distance to beaches, funfair and town centre. Large family room with balcony. Children welcome half price. All rooms en-suite, hostess tray and TV. Proprietors Jean and John Lewis.

	SINGLE PER PERSON B&B		DOUBLE FOR 2 PERSONS B&B			3
						3
	MIN £	MAX £	MIN £	MAX £	OPEN	
	–	–	32.00	38.00	1-12	

GH	Villa Guest House

27 Mary Street,
Porthcawl,
Mid Glamorgan CF36 3YN
Tel: (0656) 785074

Friendly and comfortable, family run guest house. Centrally situated between Cardiff and Swansea. Ideal base to explore surrounding area. All rooms have colour TV with satellite channel and tea/coffee facilities, shower en-suite rooms available on request.

	SINGLE PER PERSON B&B		DOUBLE FOR 2 PERSONS B&B			6
						3
	MIN £	MAX £	MIN £	MAX £	OPEN	
	14.00	19.00	24.00	34.00	1-12	

FH	Penuchadre Farm

St Brides Major,
Bridgend,
Mid Glamorgan CF32 0TE
Tel: (0656) 880313

15th Century historic farmhouse. High quality accommodation comprising one double and one family bedroom. M4 motorway 5 miles (farmhouse easily found). Real farm atmosphere, wonderful for children. Heritage coast, Southerndown Bay within walking distance. 18 hold championship golf course nearby. Evening meals available in local public houses. Idyllic countryside surroundings. A warm welcome awaits you at Penuchadre Farm.

	SINGLE PER PERSON B&B		DOUBLE FOR 2 PERSONS B&B			2
						–
	MIN £	MAX £	MIN £	MAX £	OPEN	
	17.00	17.00	34.00	34.00	1-12	

City Hall, Cardiff

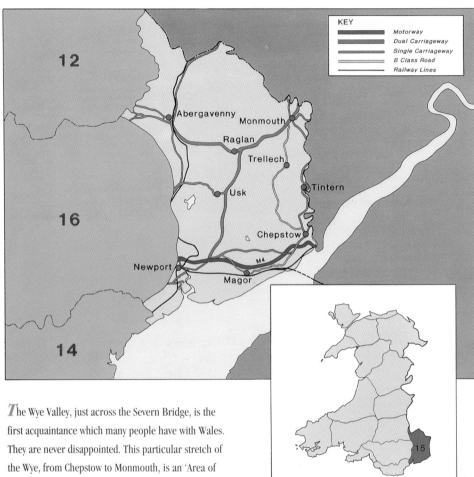

The Wye Valley, just across the Severn Bridge, is the first acquaintance which many people have with Wales. They are never disappointed. This particular stretch of the Wye, from Chepstow to Monmouth, is an 'Area of Outstanding Natural Beauty' by virtue of the way in which the stately river meanders through a thickly wooded vale. Along the way, it passes the serene ruins of Tintern Abbey, describes lazy loops beneath a curtain of cliffs, and flows alongside Chepstow Castle, Britain's first stone-built fortress.

Chepstow is rich in history. So too is the other gateway town of Monmouth, with its fortified bridge, Henry V associations and wealth of period buildings. Historic sites are plentiful in these parts. Visit the outstanding late-medieval castle at Raglan and Caerleon's Roman remains, which include an amphitheatre, barracks and bath-house.

The Usk – like the Wye a celebrated fishing river – flows in a lovely valley past Abergavenny and the eponymous little town of Usk to meet the sea at Newport. On Newport's outskirts there's yet more history – the splendid 17th-century Tredegar House, set in its own country park.

ABERGAVENNY
Map Ref: Mc1

Flourishing market town with backdrop of mountains at south-eastern gateway to Brecon Beacons National Park. Pony trekking in nearby Black Mountains. Castle, Museum of Childhood, leisure centre. Monmouthshire and Brecon Canal runs just to the west of the town. Excellent touring base for the lovely Vale of Usk and Brecon Beacons. ⇌

MONMOUTH
Map Ref: Me1

Historic market town in picturesque Wye Valley - birth place of Henry V and Charles Rolls (of Rolls-Royce). Interesting local history museum with collection of Nelson memorabilia. Rare fortified gateway still spans the River Monnow. Ruined castle close to town centre. Good touring base.

NEWPORT
Map Ref: Mc4

Busy industrial, commercial and shopping centre. Interesting murals in main hall of Civic Centre. Newport Museum and Art Gallery in John Frost Square (named after Chartist leader) and leisure centre with wave machine. On the outskirts, magnificently restored Tredegar House with extensive country park, and 14 Locks Canal Visitor Centre. St Woolos Cathedral on hill overlooking town centre. Ruined castle on riverside near shops and attractive Victorian market hall. ⇌

RAGLAN
Map Ref: Md2

Historic village dominated by Raglan Castle, noted for its impressive Great Tower of Gwent. Convenient for touring the Usk and Wye valleys and eastern Brecon Beacons.

TINTERN
Map Ref: Me2

Riverside village in particularly lovely stretch of Wye Valley. Impressive ruins of Tintern Abbey not to be missed. The former railway station has a visitors' interpretive centre and a picnic site with refreshments. Excellent walks and good fishing.

USK
Map Ref: Md3

Ancient borough on River Usk; excellent salmon fishing and inns. Good walks. Rural Life Museum, grass skiing. Great castle of Raglan 5 miles north. Sailing and other watersports on nearby Llandegfedd Reservoir. Good central location for sightseeing.

Raglan Castle

ABERGAVENNY

H | Rock & Fountain Hotel

Main Road, Clydach,
Abergavenny,
Gwent NP7 0LL
Tel: (0873) 830393

16th Century family run hotel. Beautiful setting with spectacular views over the breathtaking Clydach Gorge. Charming restaurant with home cooked meals using local produce. All rooms are en-suite with colour television and tea/coffee facilities. The route of a lovely walk used by many ramblers passes the door. Pony trekking, fishing and golf is nearby.

P		SINGLE PER PERSON B&B		DOUBLE FOR 2 PERSONS B&B			3
C							3
		MIN £	MAX £	MIN £	MAX £	OPEN 1-12	
		19.00	19.00	35.00	38.00		

GH | Park Guest House

36 Hereford Road,
Abergavenny,
Gwent NP7 5RA
Tel: (0873) 853715

COMMENDED

Attractive detached Georgian guest house, close town centre. All rooms with hand basins, beverage trays, TV's and radios. Two bathrooms, TV lounge, dining room with separate tables. High quality four course evening meals available by arrangement. Fully licensed. Free private parking. Convenient for Brecon Beacons, "Big Pit", Castles and Museums. Detailed brochure available on request.

P		SINGLE PER PERSON B&B		DOUBLE FOR 2 PERSONS B&B			6
							–
		MIN £	MAX £	MIN £	MAX £	OPEN 1-12	
		19.00	19.00	32.00	36.00		

FH | The Gaer Farm

Cwmyoy,
Abergavenny,
Gwent NP7 7NE
Tel: (0873) 890345

Relax high in the Black Mountains. Period farmhouse offers peace and wonderful views. Direct access to Hill. Superb walking and bird watching. Close pony trekking. Good selection of pubs and restaurants. TV. Guests private entrance. See our rare breed cattle.

P		SINGLE PER PERSON B&B		DOUBLE FOR 2 PERSONS B&B			1
							–
		MIN £	MAX £	MIN £	MAX £	OPEN 1-12	
		16.00	18.00	32.00	36.00		

GH | Hafod Swn-y-Dwr

Dardy, Crickhowell,
Powys NP8 1PU
Tel: (0873) 810821
Fax: (0873) 810821

HIGHLY COMMENDED

Stone built property circa 1833, fronts directly onto Monmouth and Brecon Canal, situated within Brecon Beacons National Park, with superb views over Usk Valley, Crickhowell and Black Mountains. Unique lounge - exposed beams, baby grand piano. All bedrooms en-suite, with colour TV and beverage tray, traditional/vegetarian breakfast and welcome. Many places to visit.

P		SINGLE PER PERSON B&B		DOUBLE FOR 2 PERSONS B&B			3
C							3
		MIN £	MAX £	MIN £	MAX £	OPEN 4-12	
		17.00	19.00	32.00	36.00		

GH | Pentre House

Brecon Road, Abergavenny,
Gwent NP7 7EW
Tel: (0873) 853435
Fax: (0873) 853435

HIGHLY COMMENDED

Small period Country House situated at the turning for Sugar Loaf Mountain. Set in 1 acre of award winning gardens. Guest bathroom and separate shower room, sitting room, television, wood burning stove. Very comfortably furnished. Tea making facilities, wonderful views. Plenty of parking. Pony trekking, lovely walks, River Usk just down the lane. Brochure on request.

P		SINGLE PER PERSON B&B		DOUBLE FOR 2 PERSONS B&B			3
							–
		MIN £	MAX £	MIN £	MAX £	OPEN 1-12	
		17.00	19.00	30.00	36.00		

FH | Great Tre-Rhew Farm

Llanvetherine,
Abergavenny,
Gwent NP8 8RA
Tel: (0873) 821268

Warm welcome on a family working farm, sheep and beef cattle. Good home cooking in a 15th Century farmhouse. Quiet situation near Offa's Dyke and White Castle. Fishing in farm stream and River Trothy. Ideal for touring Wye Valley, Black Mountains, Brecon Beacons and Medieval border Castles. Lovely walks and pony trekking. TV lounge and games room.

P		SINGLE PER PERSON B&B		DOUBLE FOR 2 PERSONS B&B			2
							–
		MIN £	MAX £	MIN £	MAX £	OPEN 1-12	
		13.00	18.00	26.00	34.00		

GH | Heathfield

Nant-y-Derry,
Abergavenny,
Gwent NP7 9DP
Tel: (0873) 880675

HIGHLY COMMENDED

Attractive country house, surrounded by mature gardens in the Usk Valley. A friendly warm welcome and relaxing stay is assured. Spacious rooms all with H&C, central heating, tea/coffee facilities, TV lounge. Quality cooking, evening meals available. Scenic walks, excellent golf courses in the local area. Fishing in the River Usk. National gardens to visit.

P		SINGLE PER PERSON B&B		DOUBLE FOR 2 PERSONS B&B			3
							1
		MIN £	MAX £	MIN £	MAX £	OPEN 4-11	
		–	–	25.00	34.00		

GH | White Gables

Abergavenny Road, Gilwern,
Abergavenny,
Gwent NP7 0AB
Tel: (0873) 831745

Situated on outskirts of Gilwern village in the beautiful Brecon Beacons National Park, with panoramic views towards the Sugar Loaf Mountain. Lovely garden. Five minutes walking distance to the Monmouthshire Brecon Canal. Ample parking. Excellent location for a variety of day excursions. Large residents lounge, colour TV, special/vegetarian diets catered for. Welcome Host Certificate.

P		SINGLE PER PERSON B&B		DOUBLE FOR 2 PERSONS B&B			2
C							–
		MIN £	MAX £	MIN £	MAX £	OPEN 3-10	
		19.00	19.00	30.00	30.00		

FH | Penyclawdd Farm

Llanfihangel Crucorney,
Abergavenny,
Gwent NP7 7LB
Tel: (0873) 890591

COMMENDED

Penyclawdd is situated at the foothills of the Black Mountains within easy reach of pony trekking, walking in the mountains, golf, canal, hang gliding. It is a family run mixed farm, sheep, store cattle, dairy cows. We are 20 miles Hereford and 3 miles Abergavenny. Shower available and good home cooked breakfast. Centrally heated. Enjoy the peacefulness of our farm.

P		SINGLE PER PERSON B&B		DOUBLE FOR 2 PERSONS B&B			2
							–
		MIN £	MAX £	MIN £	MAX £	OPEN 1-12	
		14.00	14.00	28.00	28.00		

FH | Wern Goch Lyn Farm

Llantilio Pertholey,
Abergavenny,
Gwent NP7 8UB
Tel: (0873) 857357

2 en-suite bedrooms one family room in 12th Century farmhouse. 2½ miles from the market town of Abergavenny under Skirrid Mountain. Many friendly farm animals, ducks, geese, horses, sheep, goats, chickens. Also indoor swimming pool and games room. Good walks from farm. Shop 1½ miles. Colour television and coffee/tea making facilities in bedrooms.

	SINGLE PER PERSON B&B		DOUBLE FOR 2 PERSONS B&B		2
					2
	MIN £ 15.00	MAX £ 18.00	MIN £ 30.00	MAX £ 36.00	OPEN 1-12

GH | Pendine Guest House

6 Bridge Street,
Chepstow,
Gwent NP6 5EY
Tel: (0291) 623308

This small family guest house is located close to Chepstow's historic Castle and famous racecourse and only a few minutes drive from the spectacular Wye Valley and all its attractions. All the rooms are beautifully decorated and offer a drinks tray and colour TV's, en-suite facilities are available. Guests lounge with Sky TV. Evening meals and special diets catered for.

	SINGLE PER PERSON B&B		DOUBLE FOR 2 PERSONS B&B		3
					1
	MIN £ –	MAX £ –	MIN £ 30.00	MAX £ 34.00	OPEN 1-12

GH | Cadogan House

12 Monk Street,
Monmouth,
Gwent NP5 3NZ
Tel: (0600) 716186

Georgian Grade II listed building within easy walking distance of the town centre. Access to Wye Valley, Forest of Dean and the Black Mountains. Local golf and canoeing. No objection to muddy walking boots, bicycles or children. Packed lunches and evening meals available on request. For pre-season forward booking please telephone (09818) 443.

	SINGLE PER PERSON B&B		DOUBLE FOR 2 PERSONS B&B		4
					–
	MIN £ 15.00	MAX £ 15.00	MIN £ 30.00	MAX £ 30.00	OPEN 4-10

H | Castle View Hotel

16 Bridge Street,
Chepstow,
Gwent NP6 5EZ
Tel: (0291) 620349
Fax: (0291) 627397

HIGHLY COMMENDED

Enjoy comfort, good food and personal attention in surroundings retaining 18th Century charm. All bedrooms have bathrooms, colour TV, movies, telephone, tea tray, hairdryer, mini bar. Award wining restaurant with Egon Ronay and Johansen commended food, making imaginative use of fresh local produce. Vegetarian menu also available. Real ale. Large family rooms including cottage suite.

	SINGLE PER PERSON B&B		DOUBLE FOR 2 PERSONS B&B		13
					13
	MIN £ –	MAX £ –	MIN £ 38.00	MAX £ 38.00	OPEN 1-12

FH | Cribau

The Cwm, Llanvair Discoed,
nr. Chepstow,
Gwent NP6 6RD
Tel: (0291) 641528

16th Century farmhouse at the end of no through road. TV, tea/coffee making, 1 twin bedded room, 1 double bedded room, both have shower room en-suite. Good pub food. Golf, walking, scenic drive close by, six miles from Severn Bridge. Take A48 Caerwent right turn Llanvair Discoed, right Cwm, Cribau sign at T junction.

	SINGLE PER PERSON B&B		DOUBLE FOR 2 PERSONS B&B		3
					2
	MIN £ 14.00	MAX £ 18.00	MIN £ 32.00	MAX £ 32.00	OPEN 1-12

GH | Church Farm Guest House

Mitchel Troy,
Monmouth,
Gwent NP5 4HZ
Tel: (0600) 712176

A spacious and homely 16th Century former farmhouse with oak beams and inglenook fire places. Set in large attractive garden with stream. Easy access to A40 and only 2 miles from historic Monmouth. Excellent base for Wye Valley, Forest of Dean and Black Mountains. Large car park, terrace, barbecue, colour TV, central heating, tea/coffee making facilities.

	SINGLE PER PERSON B&B		DOUBLE FOR 2 PERSONS B&B		6
					4
	MIN £ 16.00	MAX £ 18.50	MIN £ 32.00	MAX £ 37.00	OPEN 1-12

GH | Bridge House

Pwllmeyric,
Chepstow,
Gwent NP6 6LF
Tel: (0291) 622567

A friendly home situated 1½ miles from Chepstow on main A48 Newport Road. Ideal for touring Wye Valley. Near St. Pierre Golf Club. Break your journey travelling to and from Wales. Family room and double room. Hot and cold in both rooms. Sharing bathroom. Own TV lounge. Excellent food available within walking distance. Enquiries to Mrs B Gleed.

	SINGLE PER PERSON B&B		DOUBLE FOR 2 PERSONS B&B		2
					–
	MIN £ 16.00	MAX £ 16.00	MIN £ 32.00	MAX £ 32.00	OPEN 1-12

FH | Great Llanmelyn Farm

Llanvair Discoed,
nr. Chepstow,
Gwent NP6 6LU
Tel: (0291) 641210

Welcome to our large historical farmhouse on working dairy farm. Spacious bedrooms, hospitality trays, centrally heated. Family room, en-suite. TV lounge. Pub food nearby. Peaceful setting in beautiful countryside. Many repeat bookings. Central tourist area for Castles, Wye Valley, St. Pierre Golf Club, ½ hour Cardiff, Bristol. 6 miles Severn Bridge, Heathrow 2 hours. Convenient Channel ports. 1 mile A48.

	SINGLE PER PERSON B&B		DOUBLE FOR 2 PERSONS B&B		2
					–
	MIN £ 16.00	MAX £ 16.00	MIN £ 32.00	MAX £ 32.00	OPEN 3-10

FH | Mill House Farm

Llanvihangel-Ystern-Llewern,
Monmouth,
Gwent NP5 4HN
Tel: (0600) 85468

A comfortable 17th Century farmhouse between Monmouth and Abergavenny. Excellent base for visiting the Wye Valley, Offa's Dyke, The Forest of Dean and the Black Mountains. Activities in the area include golf, fishing, walking and pony trekking. All rooms have tea/coffee making facilities. Evening meals available, vegetarians welcome.

	SINGLE PER PERSON B&B		DOUBLE FOR 2 PERSONS B&B		3
					1
	MIN £ 15.00	MAX £ 15.00	MIN £ 30.00	MAX £ 34.00	OPEN 1-12

FH | Upper Llantrothy Farm

Dingestow,
Monmouth,
Gwent NP5 4EB
Tel: (0600) 83685

Situated on the Welsh/English border, ½ mile from Offa's Dyke. This peaceful and secluded 115 acre working farm has cattle, sheep and horses. The farm was originally a monastery fish farm, and the remains of the ponds are still visible. The area is rich in history and convenient for exploring the Wye Valley, Forest of Dean and the Black Mountains.

P C		SINGLE PER PERSON B&B		DOUBLE FOR 2 PERSONS B&B		3 2
		MIN £ 15.00	MAX £ 17.00	MIN £ 30.00	MAX £ 34.00	OPEN 1-12

GH | Langtree Guest House

49 Cardiff Road,
Newport,
Gwent NP5 2EN
Tel: (0633) 213832

COMMENDED

Ideally situated close to town centre, opposite hospital convenient for tourists and commercial. Friendly personal service of proprietors. Near coach station and leisure/entertainment complex. We are happy to welcome guests old and new for the seventh year. Recent alterations provide double room with private bathroom, two other rooms share newly fitted large bathroom.

C		SINGLE PER PERSON B&B		DOUBLE FOR 2 PERSONS B&B		3 1
		MIN £ 16.00	MAX £ 16.00	MIN £ 30.00	MAX £ 32.00	OPEN 1-12

FH | Pentre-Tai Farm

Rhiwderin,
Newport,
Gwent NP1 9RQ
Tel: (0633) 893284

HIGHLY COMMENDED

Situated 3 miles from J28 M4, 12 miles Cardiff. Why not make this your first stop in Wales? Peaceful sheep and horse farm. Ideal for visiting Wye Valley, Brecon Beacons, wonderful Welsh Castles, South Wales coast. Special rates for children. One family room. All rooms with colour TV. Excellent pub food nearby. French spoken.

P		SINGLE PER PERSON B&B		DOUBLE FOR 2 PERSONS B&B		2
		MIN £ 17.00	MAX £ 19.00	MIN £ 30.00	MAX £ 32.00	OPEN 2-11

H | Manor Hotel

147 Stow Hill,
Newport,
Gwent NP9 4HB
Tel: (0633) 264685

Five minutes M4. Well established small family hotel convenient for town centre and ideal base for Wye Valley, South Wales coast etc. Family, double, twin and single rooms each with colour television, separate residents television lounge and dining room. Lovely well established garden, forecourt car parking facilities. Bed and excellent breakfast. Genuine homely welcome.

P		SINGLE PER PERSON B&B		DOUBLE FOR 2 PERSONS B&B		7 –
		MIN £ 16.00	MAX £ 17.00	MIN £ 30.00	MAX £ 32.00	OPEN 1-12

GH | The Park Guest House

381 Chepstow Road,
Newport,
Gwent NP9 5DG
Tel: (0633) 280333

We are a family run guest house, three miles from the M4, near Newport. We offer nine rooms, three en-suite, all with tea/coffee making facilities. We provide a friendly and welcoming atmosphere for either business or pleasure. The guest house is centrally placed for many areas of outstanding beauty and for sites of interest.

P		SINGLE PER PERSON B&B		DOUBLE FOR 2 PERSONS B&B		9 3
		MIN £ 15.00	MAX £ –	MIN £ 25.00	MAX £ 30.00	OPEN 1-12

FH | Lower Pen-y-Clawdd Farm

Dingestow,
nr. Monmouth,
Gwent NP5 4BG
Tel: (060083) 223/677

This tastefully converted cider mill nestles next to a 17th Century farmhouse, set in attractive gardens situated between Raglan and Monmouth A40. Ideal base for touring Wye Valley, Brecon Beacons and Forest of Dean. A warm welcome awaits you on this family run beef and sheep farm.

P		SINGLE PER PERSON B&B		DOUBLE FOR 2 PERSONS B&B		3
		MIN £ 15.00	MAX £ 16.00	MIN £ 28.00	MAX £ 30.00	OPEN 1-12

GH | Chapel Guest House

Church Road, St Brides,
Wentloog,
Gwent NP1 9SN
Tel: (0633) 681018

COMMENDED

Comfortable accommodation in a converted chapel in centre of charming country village between Newport and Cardiff. Pleasant walks, fishing, golf, horse-riding nearby. Guest TV lounge with pool table. Tea/coffee and TV in all rooms. Children welcome, special rates. Leave M4 junction 28, take A48 Newport, at roundabout take 3rd exit B4239 St. Brides.

P C		SINGLE PER PERSON B&B		DOUBLE FOR 2 PERSONS B&B		2
		MIN £ 16.00	MAX £ 19.00	MIN £ 28.00	MAX £ 34.00	OPEN 1-12

GH | Westwood Villa Guest House

59 Risca Road,
Cross Keys,
Gwent NP1 7BT
Tel: (0495) 270336/273001

HIGHLY COMMENDED

Six miles Junction 28 M4, Westwood Villa originally built as a manse. Beautiful bedrooms with colour TV, washbasins, tea coffee facilities, radio alarms, two bathrooms. Close to Newport, Cardiff, Sirhowy and Wye Valleys, Brecon Beacons. Entertainment and leisure centres, restaurants, good English home cooking. Beautiful scenery part of Cambrian Way. Warm welcome awaits from Bob and Maureen.

P		SINGLE PER PERSON B&B		DOUBLE FOR 2 PERSONS B&B		7 –
		MIN £ 18.00	MAX £ 18.00	MIN £ 30.00	MAX £ 30.00	OPEN 1-12

GH | The Old Rectory

Tintern,
Chepstow,
Gwent NP6 6SG
Tel: (0291) 689519

A free and easy welcome awaits at this imposing 18/19th Century house with its own spring water. Most bedrooms have beautiful views, H&C, tea/coffee facilities. Central heating, log fires and dining room serving good food, own bread and produce in season. Central for fishing, walking, golf, horse riding. Tintern Abbey ½ mile. Ideal for touring the border country.

P		SINGLE PER PERSON B&B		DOUBLE FOR 2 PERSONS B&B		4
		MIN £ 13.50	MAX £ 14.50	MIN £ 27.00	MAX £ 29.00	OPEN 1-12

GH	Valley House

Raglan Road,
Tintern,
Gwent NP6 6TH
Tel: (0291) 689652

18th Century house situated in picturesque Angidy Valley within one mile of Tintern Abbey. Delightful en-suite rooms with tea/coffee making facilities and colour TV's. An ideal base for sightseeing and walking with forest walks straight from our doorstep. Freshly cooked, hearty breakfasts always served. Peaceful lounge and relaxed atmosphere. Numerous places to eat nearby.

P		SINGLE PER PERSON B&B	DOUBLE FOR 2 PERSONS B&B		3
					3
	MIN £ –	MAX £ 36.00	MIN £ –	MAX £ 38.00	OPEN 2-11

FH	Rhydwern Farm

Llangwm,
Usk,
Gwent NP5 1NQ
Tel: (0291) 650306

Situated in quiet wooded valley in beautiful border country. A small farm with a big welcome to our 18th Century stone farmhouse. Convenient for Brecon Beacons, Wye and Usk Valleys and many castles. Only 30 minutes from the Severn Bridge. Log fire and home cooking with garden produce. Feed the lambs or enjoy the wildlife.

P		SINGLE PER PERSON B&B	DOUBLE FOR 2 PERSONS B&B		2
					–
	MIN £ –	MAX £ –	MIN £ 26.00	MAX £ 26.00	OPEN 1-12

FH	Ty-Gwyn Farm

Gwehelog,
Usk,
Gwent NP5 1RT
Tel: (0291) 672878

HIGHLY COMMENDED

Wake up and sit up to magnificent views of Brecon Beacons National Park, at this Award Winning farmhouse. Hearty breakfasts including homemade preserves served in spacious dining room, or conservatory overlooking secluded lawns. Tea making facilities and TV's in bedrooms. Explore castles, mountains, Monmouthshire canals, golf courses and fishing nearby. Excellent meals, vegetarians and own wine welcome. Brochure available.

P		SINGLE PER PERSON B&B	DOUBLE FOR 2 PERSONS B&B		3
					2
	MIN £ 18.00	MAX £ 19.00	MIN £ 32.00	MAX £ 34.00	OPEN 1-12

FH	Pentwyn Farm

Little Mill, Pontypool,
Gwent NP4 0HQ
Tel: (0495) 785249
Fax: (0495) 785249

HIGHLY COMMENDED

On the edge of the Brecon Beacons National Park, Pentwyn is a typical Welsh longhouse surrounded by a large garden with wonderful views and swimming pool. Our reputation for good food and hospitality is of prime importance. Three pretty bedrooms (2 en-suite) with tea making facilities. 10 acres of woodland provide a natural playground. Licensed. Enquiries Ann Bradley.

P		SINGLE PER PERSON B&B	DOUBLE FOR 2 PERSONS B&B		3
					2
	MIN £ 18.50	MAX £ –	MIN £ 27.00	MAX £ 34.00	OPEN 2-11

FH	Ty-Cooke Farm

Mamhilad,
Pontypool,
Gwent NP4 8QZ
Tel: (0873) 880382

COMMENDED

A working farm set on the edge of the Brecon Beacons National Park. ½ mile from Goitre Wharf on the Monmouthshire Brecon Canal. It is a spacious 18th Century farmhouse in a peaceful rural setting yet only 10 minutes walk from a pub serving excellent meals. Ideal base for touring South Wales.

P		SINGLE PER PERSON B&B	DOUBLE FOR 2 PERSONS B&B		3
					–
	MIN £ –	MAX £ 18.00	MIN £ –	MAX £ 32.00	OPEN 3-11

SLIDE SETS

Ask about our attractive range of 35mm colour slides showing views of Wales, available at 75p per slide.

For a complete list of subjects please contact the Photographic Librarian, Wales Tourist Board, Davis Street, Cardiff CF1 2FU.

Monmouth

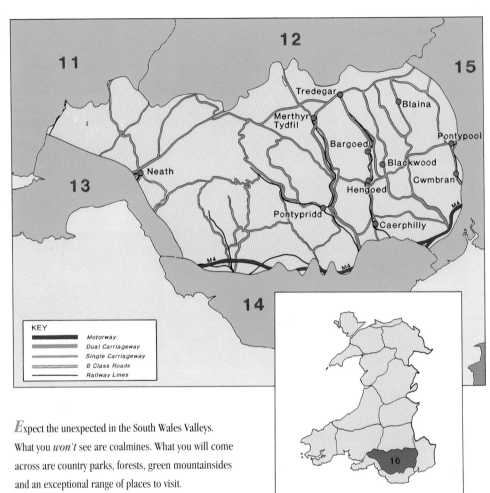

KEY
▬▬▬	Motorway
▬▬▬	Dual Carriageway
▬▬▬	Single Carriageway
▬▬▬	B Class Roads
─────	Railway Lines

*E*xpect the unexpected in the South Wales Valleys. What you *won't* see are coalmines. What you will come across are country parks, forests, green mountainsides and an exceptional range of places to visit.

The 'Valleys' have for too long been perceived – quite inaccurately – as a place despoiled by heavy industry. That picture is now changing, helped by the existence of country parks such as the Dare Valley and Sirhowy Valley, together with a host of attractions. Visit mighty Caerphilly Castle, one of Europe's greatest medieval fortresses, and the 'living history' manor house of Llancaiach Fawr. Travel along the spectacular Cwmcarn Scenic Forest Drive, or explore the 'Little Switzerland' of the wooded Afan Argoed Country Park.

Near Neath, there's a famous wildlife park. And at Merthyr Tydfil, you can ride a narrow-gauge railway into the foothills of the Brecon Beacons.

Bygone times have not been forgotten. The Valleys' rich industrial heritage is remembered at places such as the Big Pit Mining Museum, the Rhondda Heritage Park and the Cefn Coed Colliery Museum.

BARGOED
Map Ref: Ma3

Town set amid hillsides in Rhymney Valley between Newport and Merthyr Tydfil with hilltop views over to the Brecon Beacons. Bryn Bach Park a few miles to the north. Llancaiach Fawr historic house nearby. ≹

BLACKWOOD
Map Ref: Mb3

Gwent valley town now surrounded by pine-clad cwms rising to mountain tops. Visit Penyfan Pond, a country park a few miles to the north, attractive Parc Cwm Darran and the Sirhowy Valley Country Park. Tour Stuart Crystal's glass factory nearby.

CAERPHILLY
Map Ref: Ma4

A sight not to be missed - 13th-century Caerphilly Castle is one of Europe's finest surviving medieval strongholds and has a famous leaning tower. Golf course, shopping, excellent centre for exploring Valleys and visiting Cardiff. Caerphilly Mountain offers fine views and pleasant walks. Caerphilly cheese made at the Old Courthouse. ≹

CWMBRAN
Map Ref: Mc4

A "new town" and administration centre of Gwent. Good sports and leisure facilities, Llantarnam Grange Arts Centre. Shopping and sports centre with international athletics stadium. Theatre and cinemas. Good touring centre for the Vale of Usk and the South Wales Valleys. ≹

MERTHYR TYDFIL
Map Ref: Le2

Once the 'iron capital of the world', the museum in Cyfarthfa Castle, built by the Crawshay family of ironmasters and set in pleasant parkland, tells of those times. Visit the birthplace of hymn-writer Joseph Parry and the Ynysfach Engine House. The narrow-gauge Brecon Mountain Railway makes the most of the town's location on the doorstep of the Brecon Beacons National Park. Garwnant Forest Visitor Centre and scenic lakes in hills to the north. ≹

NEATH
Map Ref: Lb3

Busy town, now emerging from its industrial past. Home of the 1994 Royal National Eisteddfod, to be held in August. Museum and country park. The Vale of Neath has a wide variety of tourist attractions including an abbey, Penscynor Wildlife Park and Aberdulais Falls and Canal Basin. Superbly located for a choice of activities, surrounded by forests. ≹

PONTYPOOL
Map Ref: Mc3

Historic metal-producing town in eastern edge of South Wales Valleys. Park contains Valley Inheritance Centre and dry ski slope. Big Pit Mining Museum nearby. ≹

H | Parc Hotel

Cardiff Road, Bargoed,
Mid Glamorgan CF8 8SP
Tel: (0443) 837599/839828
Fax: (0443) 834818

COMMENDED

Welsh hospitality at its best. Enjoy the luxurious furnishings in the lounge bar and extensive selection of dishes and fine wines in the Steak House Restaurant. Family owned and run the Parc Hotel is set in the heart of the Rhymney Valley within easy access to some of the most exciting tourist attractions in South Wales. The perfect choice.

		SINGLE PER PERSON B&B		DOUBLE FOR 2 PERSONS B&B			12
		MIN £ 19.00	MAX £ 19.00	MIN £ 38.00	MAX £ 38.00	OPEN 1-12	4

GH | Lamb House

Westside,
Blaina,
Gwent NP3 3DB
Tel: (0495) 290179

Close to Heads of the Valleys, ideally situated for visiting South Wales tourist attractions, i.e. Big Pit Mining Museum, Scenic Forest Drive, etc., impressive scenery. Good mountain walks. Twin and double rooms with H&C, two double rooms full en-suite, full central heating, colour TV in lounge. Personal service in friendly family atmosphere. Proprietor John Chandler.

		SINGLE PER PERSON B&B		DOUBLE FOR 2 PERSONS B&B			3
		MIN £ 15.00	MAX £ 18.00	MIN £ 30.00	MAX £ 36.00	OPEN 1-12	2

FH | Wern Ganol Farm

Nelson,
Mid Glamorgan CF46 6PS
Tel: (0443) 450413

Sixty acre dairy farm with pleasant views over surrounding countryside towards Llancaiach Fawr Manor House. Providing homely atmosphere for guests who may wish to relax in the lounge or on patio. Easy access to Brecon Beacons and South Wales coast. Large private car park, all rooms on ground floor. 20 minutes M4 Junction 32.

		SINGLE PER PERSON B&B		DOUBLE FOR 2 PERSONS B&B			5
		MIN £ 17.00	MAX £ –	MIN £ 34.00	MAX £ 34.00	OPEN 1-12	5

GH | Wyrleod Lodge

Manmoel, Blackwood,
nr. Newport,
Gwent NP2 0RN
Tel: (0495) 371198

COMMENDED

Old farm with Victorian style home, having spacious en-suite rooms with tea/coffee making, colour televisions, one family room with adjoining room for two children, lounge, dining room with separate tables. Situated in small village with pub, church, 20 homes, beautiful views, walks. Ideal for touring Cardiff, South Wales Valleys, Brecon, Big Pit, Newport.

		SINGLE PER PERSON B&B		DOUBLE FOR 2 PERSONS B&B			3
		MIN £ 16.00	MAX £ 16.00	MIN £ 32.00	MAX £ 32.00	OPEN 1-12	3

FH | Chapel Farm

Blaina,
Gwent NP3 3DJ
Tel: (0495) 290888

COMMENDED

15th Century renovated farmhouse, farming Welsh mountain sheep. Panoramic views, good base for touring Abergavenny, Big Pit Mining Museum, Brecon Beacons all in 9 mile radius. Rooms have private showers, H&C and tea facilities. Lounge has original oak beams and inglenook fireplace, central heating, 'two rooms', large family room, double room can be used as twin. Children welcome. Evening meals.

		SINGLE PER PERSON B&B		DOUBLE FOR 2 PERSONS B&B			2
		MIN £ 16.00	MAX £ 18.00	MIN £ 32.00	MAX £ 36.00	OPEN 1-12	

GH | Springfields Guest House

371 Llantarnam Road,
Llantarnam, Cwmbran,
Gwent NP44 3BN
Tel: (0633) 482509

HIGHLY COMMENDED

Family run for 21 happy years, in a pleasant area. 1¼ miles from Cwmbran, 4 miles from M4. Central for touring Wye Valley, Caerleon, 'Big Pit', Brecon, Cardiff. My visitors have enjoyed Springfields, I have enjoyed their company. Come and see the beauty of South Wales. You will come again. Thank you old and new customers Joan Graham.

		SINGLE PER PERSON B&B		DOUBLE FOR 2 PERSONS B&B			10
		MIN £ 13.00	MAX £ 15.00	MIN £ 26.00	MAX £ 30.00	OPEN 1-12	5

H | Queen's Hotel

Abertillery Road,
Blaina,
Gwent NP33 3DW
Tel: (0495) 290491

The Queen's Hotel is near the 1992 Garden Festival site at Ebbw Vale, Big Pit Museum, Blaenafon, and situated in Blaina, Gwent making it an ideal base for touring South East Wales. Sunday lunch a speciality, à la carte restaurant, special rates for children. Golf, horse riding, canal boating, fishing nearby. Ask for Claire or Mrs. Thomas for booking information.

		SINGLE PER PERSON B&B		DOUBLE FOR 2 PERSONS B&B			4
		MIN £ –	MAX £ 19.00	MIN £ –	MAX £ 35.00	OPEN 1-12	4

GH | The Cottage Guest House

Pwll-y-Pant,
Caerphilly,
Mid Glamorgan CF8 3HW
Tel: (0222) 869160

A homely welcome awaits you at this 300 year old cottage. All bedrooms have hospitality trays and central heating, en-suite available. Television lounge and car park. Owner a registered Wales and England Tour Guide offers free touring advice. Convenient selection of restaurants in town. Perfect centre for castles, coast and mountains.

		SINGLE PER PERSON B&B		DOUBLE FOR 2 PERSONS B&B			3
		MIN £ 16.00	MAX £ 18.00	MIN £ 30.00	MAX £ 36.00	OPEN 1-12	1

H | Church Tavern

Vaynor,
nr. Merthyr Tydfil,
Mid Glamorgan CF48 2TT
Tel: (0685) 723769

The Church Tavern is positioned in an idyllic situation, bounded by Brecon Beacons National Park. Offering industrial and local history on the Taff Trail, rambling, cycling, lakes, fishing, Brecon Mountain Railway, all adjacent by road/footpaths adjoining the Tavern. Surrounded by burial grounds and churches dated 1600BC - 1750AD.

		SINGLE PER PERSON B&B		DOUBLE FOR 2 PERSONS B&B			3
		MIN £ 15.00	MAX £ 15.00	MIN £ 25.00	MAX £ 25.00	OPEN 1-12	

GH | Europa Hotel

32/34 Victoria Gardens,
Neath,
West Glamorgan SA11 3BH
Tel: (0639) 635094

COMMENDED

A family run guest house in conservation area overlooking beautiful Victoria Gardens. An ideal base for touring and visiting nearby attractions/activities close to bus/train stations with M4 and Irish Ferries short car ride away. All bedrooms a high standard, we ensure your comfort and well being. Small car park at rear.

P		SINGLE PER PERSON B&B		DOUBLE FOR 2 PERSONS B&B		🛏 12
C						-
		MIN £	MAX £	MIN £	MAX £	OPEN
		17.00	18.00	32.00	34.00	1-12

FH | Green Lantern Guest House

Hawdref Ganol Farm,
Cimla, Neath,
West Glamorgan SA12 9SL
Tel: (0639) 631884

HIGHLY COMMENDED

Family run 18th century luxury centrally heated farmhouse with beautiful scenic views over open countryside. Close to Afan Argoed and Margam Parks. Ideal for walking, cycling, horse riding from farm. Perfect base for touring South Wales Valleys and the beautiful Gower coast. Large guest room with inglenook fireplace and TV. Tea and coffee facilities all rooms. 3 nights or more 10% discount, reductions for children. Phone for colour brochure.

P		SINGLE PER PERSON B&B		DOUBLE FOR 2 PERSONS B&B		🛏 3
C						2
		MIN £	MAX £	MIN £	MAX £	OPEN
		18.00	-	36.00	-	1-12

FH | Mill Farm

Cwmavon, nr. Pontypool,
Gwent NP4 8XJ
Tel: (0495) 774588
Fax: (0495) 790309

Fifteenth Century farmhouse - inglenooks, beams, log fires, heated indoor pool. All bedrooms en-suite. 30 acres grounds, situated edge Brecon Beacon National Park. Gardens, woodlands, all set in tranquil locality close to all amenities. Home cooking, beverage tray, meals/sandwiches by arrangement. Pets welcome. Stabling for own horses - tariff on request. Adults only for carefree restful environment.

P		SINGLE PER PERSON B&B		DOUBLE FOR 2 PERSONS B&B		🛏 3
						3
		MIN £	MAX £	MIN £	MAX £	OPEN
		-	-	36.00	38.00	1-12

GH | 3 Main Road

Cadoxton, Neath,
West Glamorgan SA10 8AP
Tel: (0639) 639423

L

Three Welsh cottages converted into family run guest house. Colour TV in sitting room with tea making facilities. Convenient for Neath one mile away. Penscynor Park, Aberdulais Falls and many more attractions. Next door to Crown and Sceptre pub and restaurant.

	SINGLE PER PERSON B&B		DOUBLE FOR 2 PERSONS B&B		🛏 2
					-
	MIN £	MAX £	MIN £	MAX £	OPEN
	12.00	12.00	24.00	24.00	1-12

GH | Tree Tops Guest House

282 Neath Road,
Briton Ferry, Neath,
West Glamorgan SA11 2SL
Tel: (0639) 812419

HIGHLY COMMENDED

Why not join us at Tree Tops where a warm Welsh welcome and good home cooking awaits you. Situated on the A474, 5 minutes from Neath town centre. Ideal for exploring, with Gower Peninsula, Black Mountains, Brecon Beacons within ½ hour drive. Evening meals by arrangement. Special diets. Car parking at rear. Beautiful gardens for guest's use.

P		SINGLE PER PERSON B&B		DOUBLE FOR 2 PERSONS B&B		🛏 4
						1
		MIN £	MAX £	MIN £	MAX £	OPEN
		17.00	-	32.00	38.00	1-12

Brecon Mountain Railway

Use the Wales Tourist Board's network of TICs when you're on your travels. TICs provide information on what to see and where to go, scenic routes and local events – and they stock a comprehensive range of tourist literature. TICs also operate a free bed booking service for those looking for accommodation either locally or further afield.

NORTH WALES

OPEN ALL YEAR

Betws-y-Coed
Royal Oak Stables, Betws-y-Coed,
Gwynedd LL24 0AH
Tel (0690) 710426

Caernarfon
Oriel Pendeitsh, Castle Street,
Caernarfon, Gwynedd
LL55 2PB
Tel (0286) 672232

Colwyn Bay
40 Station Road, Colwyn Bay,
Clwyd LL29 8BU
Tel (0492) 530478

Conwy
Conwy Castle Visitor Centre,
Conwy, Gwynedd
Tel (0492) 592248

Ewloe
Autolodge Site, Gateway Services,
A55 Westbound, Northophall
Ewloe, Clwyd CH6 6HE
Tel (0244) 541597

Holyhead
Marine Square, Salt Island
Approach, Holyhead,
Gwynedd LL65 1DR
Tel (0407) 762622

Llandudno
1–2 Chapel Street, Llandudno,
Gwynedd LL30 2YU
Tel (0492) 876413

Llanfair PG
Station Site, Llanfair PG,
Gwynedd LL61 5UJ
Tel (0248) 713177

Llangollen
Town Hall, Castle Street,
Llangollen, Clwyd
LL20 5PD
Tel (0978) 860828

Porthmadog
High Street, Porthmadog,
Gwynedd LL49 9LP
Tel (0766) 512981

Rhyl
Town Hall, Wellington Road,
Rhyl, Clwyd LL18 1BB
Tel (0745) 355068/344515

Ruthin
Ruthin Craft Centre, Park Road,
Ruthin, Clwyd LL15 1BB
Tel (0824) 703992

Wrexham
Lambpit Street, Wrexham,
Clwyd LL11 1AY
Tel (0978) 292015

OPEN SUMMER ONLY

Bangor
Theatr Gwynedd, Deiniol Road,
Bangor, Gwynedd LL57 2TL
Tel (0248) 352786

Blaenau Ffestiniog
Isallt, High Street, Blaenau
Ffestiniog, Gwynedd LL41 3HD
Tel (0766) 830360

Llanberis
Amgueddfa'r Gogledd/Museum
of the North, Llanberis,
Gwynedd LL55 4UR
Tel (0286) 870765

Mold
Town Hall, Earl Street,
Mold, Clwyd CH7 1AB
Tel (0352) 759331

Prestatyn
Scala Cinema, High Street,
Prestatyn, Clwyd LL19 9LH
Tel (0745) 854365

Pwllheli
Min y Don, Station Square, Pwllehli,
Gwynedd LL53 5HG
Tel (0758) 613000

Rhos on Sea
The Promenade, Rhos on Sea,
Clwyd
Tel (0492) 548778

Towyn
Sandbank Road, Towyn, Clwyd
Tel (0745) 332025

MID WALES

OPEN ALL YEAR

Aberaeron
The Quay, Aberaeron,
Dyfed SA46 0BT
Tel (0545) 570602

Aberystwyth
Terrace Road, Aberystwyth,
Dyfed SY23 2AG
Tel (0970) 612125

Builth Wells
Groe Car Park, Builth Wells,
Powys LD2 3BT
Tel (0982) 553307 (open Friday
and Saturday only in winter)

Cardigan
Theatr Mwldan, Bath House Road,
Cardigan, Dyfed SA43 1JY
Tel (0239) 613230

Knighton
The Offa's Dyke Centre, West Street,
Knighton, Powys LD7 1EW
Tel (0547) 528753

Llanidloes
Town Hall, Great Oak Street,
Llanidloes, Powys SY18 6BN
Tel (0686) 412605

Llandrindod Wells
Old Town Hall, Memorial Gardens,
Llandrindod Wells, Powys LD1 5DL
Tel (0597) 822600

Machynlleth
Owain Glyndŵr Centre,
Machynlleth, Powys SY20 8EE
Tel (0654) 702401

Rhayader
Leisure Centre, North Street,
Rhayader, Powys
Tel (0597) 810591

Tregaron
The Square, Tregaron,
Dyfed SY25 6JN
Tel (0974) 298248

Welshpool
Flash Leisure Centre, Salop Road,
Welshpool, Powys
Tel (0938) 552043

OPEN SUMMER ONLY

Aberdovey
Wharf Gardens, Aberdovey,
Gwynedd LL35 0ED
Tel (0654) 767321

Bala
High Street, Bala, Gwynedd LL23 7NH
Tel (0678) 520367

Barmouth
Old Library, Station Road,
Barmouth, Gwynedd LL42 1LU
Tel (0341) 280787

Borth
High Street, The Promenade, Borth,
Dyfed SY24 5HY
Tel (0970) 871174

Corris
Craft Centre, Corris, Gwynedd
SY20 9SP
Tel (0654) 761244

Dolgellau
Tŷ Merion, Eldon Square, Dolgellau,
Gwynedd LL40 1PU
Tel (0341) 422888

Elan Valley
Elan Valley Visitor Centre, Elan
Valley, Rhayader, Powys LD6 5HP
Tel (0597) 810898

Harlech
Gwyddfor House, High Street,
Harlech, Gwynedd LL46 2YA
Tel (0766) 780658

Lake Vyrnwy
Unit 2, Vyrnwy Craft Workshops,
Lake Vyrnwy, Powys
Tel (0691) 73346

Llanwrtyd Wells
Old School Workshops, Llanwrtyd
Wells, Powys
Tel (05913) 666

New Quay
Church Street, New Quay, Dyfed
SA45 9NZ
Tel (0545) 560865

Newtown
Central Car Park, Newtown,
Powys SY16 2PW
Tel (0686) 625580

Presteigne
The Old Market Hall, Broad Street,
Presteigne, Powys LD8 2AW
Tel (0544) 260193

Tywyn
High Street, Tywyn, Gwynedd
LL36 9AD
Tel (0654) 710070

SOUTH WALES
OPEN ALL YEAR

Brecon
Cattle Market Car Park, Brecon,
Powys LD3 9DA
Tel (0874) 622485

Caerleon
Ffwrrwm Art and Craft Centre, High
Street, Caerleon, Gwent NP6 1AG
Tel (0633) 430777

Cardiff
Central Station, Central Square
Cardiff, South Glamorgan CF1 1QY
Tel (0222) 227281

Carmarthen
Lammas Street, Carmarthen,
Dyfed SA31 3AQ
Tel (0267) 231557

Cwmcarn
Visitor Centre, Cwmcarn Forest
Drive, nr Cross Keys,
Gwent NP1 5AL
Tel (0495) 272001

Fishguard
4 Hamilton Street, Fishguard,
Pembrokeshire, Dyfed SA65 9HL
Tel (0348) 873484

Haverfordwest
Old Bridge, Haverfordwest,
Pembrokeshire, Dyfed SA61 2EZ
Tel (0437) 763110

Llanelli
Public Library, Vaughan Street,
Llanelli, Dyfed SA15 3AS
Tel (0554) 772020

Magor
Granada Services West, Junction 23
M4, Magor, Gwent
Tel (0633) 881122

Merthyr Tydfil
14a Glebeland Street, Merthyr Tydfil,
Mid Glamorgan CF47 8AU
Tel (0685) 379884

Narberth
Town Hall, Narberth,
Pembrokeshire, Dyfed
Tel (0834) 860061

Newport
Newport Museum and Art Gallery,
John Frost Square, Newport,
Gwent NP9 1HZ
Tel (0633) 842962

Pembroke
Pembroke Visitor Centre, Commons
Road, Pembroke, Pembrokeshire,
Dyfed
Tel (0646) 622388

Pont Abraham
Pont Abraham Services, Junction 49
M4, Llanedi, Dyfed SA4 1FP
Tel (0792) 883838

Pont Nedd Fechan
nr Glyn Neath, West Glamorgan
SA11 5NR
Tel (0639) 721795 (open weekends
only October–March)

Pontypridd
Pontypridd Historical and Cultural
Centre, The Old Bridge, Pontypridd,
Mid Glamorgan CF37 3PE
Tel (0443) 402077

Porthcawl
Old Police Station, John Street,
Porthcawl, Mid Glamorgan CF36 3DT
Tel (0656) 786639

Sarn
Sarn Services, Junction 36 M4,
nr Bridgend, Mid Glamorgan CF32 9SY
Tel (0656) 654906

Swansea
PO Box 59, Singleton Street,
Swansea, West Glamorgan SA1 3QN
Tel (0792) 468321

Tenby
The Croft, Tenby, Pembrokeshire,
Dyfed SA70 8AP
Tel (0834) 842402

OPEN SUMMER ONLY

Aberdulais
Aberdulais Basin, Aberdulais,
West Glamorgan SA10 8ED
Tel (0639) 633531

Abergavenny
Swan Meadow, Cross Street,
Abergavenny, Gwent NP7 5HH
Tel (0873) 857588

Barry
The Triangle, Paget Road, Barry
Island, South Glamorgan CF6 8TJ
Tel (0446) 747171

Caerphilly
Old Police Station, Park Lane,
Caerphilly, Mid Glamorgan CF8 1AA
Tel (0222) 851378

Chepstow
Castle Car Park, Bridge Street,
Chepstow, Gwent
Tel (0291) 623772

Crickhowell
Beaufort Chambers, Beaufort Street,
Crickhowell, Powys
Tel (0873) 812105

Kilgetty
Kingsmoor Common, Kilgetty,
Pembrokeshire, Dyfed SA68 0YA
Tel (0834) 813672

Llandovery
Central Car Park, Broad Street,
Llandovery, Dyfed SA20 0AR
Tel (0550) 20693

Milford Haven
94 Charles Street, Milford Haven,
Dyfed SA73 2HL
Tel (0646) 690866

Monmouth
Shire Hall, Agincourt Square,
Monmouth, Gwent NP5 3DY
Tel (0600) 713899

Newcastle Emlyn
Market Hall, Newcastle Emlyn,
Dyfed SA38 9AE
Tel (0239) 711333

Penarth
Penarth Pier, The Esplanade,
Penarth, South Glamorgan
Tel (0222) 708849

WALES IN LONDON'S WEST END
If you're in London, be sure to call
in at the Wales Information Bureau,
British Travel Centre, 12 Lower
Regent Street, Piccadilly Circus,
London SW1Y 4PQ. Tel (071) 409
0969. Staff there will give you all the
information you need to plan a
visit to Wales.

FURTHER INFORMATION
Holiday and travel information is
available from the following address,
together with a free leaflet explaining
our 'Quest for Quality' inspection
schemes.

Wales Tourist Board
Dept WTS 3
Davis Street
Cardiff
South Glamorgan CF1 2FU
Tel (0222) 475226

*Y*our enquiries will be welcome at the offices of the British Tourist Authority in the following countries:

Australia
British Tourist Authority, 8th Floor, The University Centre, 210 Clarence Street, Sydney, NSW 2000
Tel (02) 267 4555
Fax (02) 267 4442

Belgium
British Tourist Authority, Avenue Louise 306, 1050 Brussels
Tel (02) 646 3510
Fax (02) 642 3986

Brazil
British Tourist Authority, Avenida Nilo Pecanha 50 - Conj. 2213, 20040-900 Rio de Janiero - RJ
Tel (021) 220 1187/7260
Telex 21-30694 EINGBR
Fax (021) 240 8779

Canada
British Tourist Authority, 111 Avenue Road, Suite 450, Toronto, Ontario, M5R 3J8
Tel (416) 925 6326
Fax (416) 961 2175

Denmark
British Tourist Authority, Montergade 3, 1116 Copenhagen K
Tel 33 339188
Fax 33 140136

France
British Tourist Authority, La Maison de la Grande-Bretagne, 19 Rue des Mathurins (entre Auber et Tronchet), 75009 Paris
Tel (1) 44 51 56 20
Fax (1) 44 51 56 21
MINTEL 3615 BRITISH

Germany
British Tourist Authority, Taunusstrasse 52-60, 60329 Frankfurt 1
Tel 069-2380711
Fax 069-2380717

Ireland
British Tourist Authority, 123 Lower Baggot Street, Dublin 2
Tel (01) 6614188
Fax (01) 6785280

Italy
British Tourist Authority, Corso Vittorio Emanuele 337, 00186 Rome
Tel 06/68806464 or 68806821

Japan
British Tourist Authority, Tokyo Club Bldg, 3-2-6 Kasumigaseki, Chiyoda-ku, Tokyo 100
Tel (03) 3581 3603
Fax (03) 3581 5797

Netherlands
British Tourist Authority, Stadhouderskade 2 (5e), 1054 ES Amsterdam
Tel 020-685 50 51

New Zealand
British Tourist Authority, Suite 305, 3rd Floor, Dilworth Building, corner Queen and Customs Streets, Auckland 1
Tel (09) 3031 446
Fax (09) 3776 965

Norway
British Tourist Authority, Postboks 1554 Vika, 0117 Oslo 1
Tel (02) 41 18 49

Singapore
British Tourist Authority, 24 Raffles Place, 20-21 Clifford Centre, Singapore 0104
Tel 5352966
Fax 5344703

South Africa
British Tourist Authority, Lancaster Gate, Hyde Lane, Hyde Park, Johannesburg 2196 (*for personal callers only*)
Tel 325 0343
Postal address: PO Box 41896, Craighall 2024

Spain
British Tourist Authority, Torre de Madrid 6/7, Pza. de Espana, 28008, Madrid
Tel (91) 541 1396
Fax (91) 542 8149

Sweden
British Tourist Authority, Klara Norra, Kyrkogata 29, S-10135 Stockholm (*visitors only*); Box 745, S-10135 Stockholm (*postal address*)
Tel 08-21 24 44
Fax 08-21 31 29

Switzerland
British Tourist Authority, Limmatquai 78, CH-8001 Zurich
Tel 01-261 42 77
Fax 01-251 44 56

USA
Atlanta - British Tourist Authority, 2580 Cumberland Parkway, Suite 470, Atlanta GA 30339-3909
Tel (404) 432 9635
Fax (404) 432 9641

Chicago - British Tourist Authority, 625 N Michigan Avenue, Suite 1510, Chicago IL 60611
Tel (312) 787 0490
Fax (312) 787 7746

Los Angeles - British Tourist Authority, 350 South Figueroa Street, Suite 450, Los Angeles, CA 90071
Tel (213) 628 3525
Fax (213) 687 6621

New York - British Tourist Authority, 551 Fifth Avenue, New York, NY 10176
Tel (212) 986 2200
Fax (212) 986 1188

Three Cliffs Bay, Gower Peninsula

Holidays WALES

PROVIDING A FREE RESERVATION SERVICE
ON BEHALF OF THE WALES TOURIST BOARD

FOR SHORT BREAK
OR LONGER STAY

CALL

☎ **(0792) 645555**

7 days each week
Dec, Jan, Feb, Mon-Fri 8.30am-7pm
Sat & Sun 9am-5pm
February onwards 9am-7pm
9pm on Fridays
*(Remember, it's cheaper to call evenings
or weekends)*

• *Arranging your visit couldn't be simpler. Talk to our Holiday Advisors and with their help and guidance you'll find that booking your accommodation is easy.*

• *Many of the Hotels, Guest Houses and Farmhouses contained in this guide can be booked through this service. Our computer also holds details of hundreds of establishments throughout Wales which are not featured in this brochure.*

• *Whatever your requirements in Wales – we can help.*

• *We can also arrange Holiday Insurance, coach and rail tickets or a hire car.*

HOLIDAYS WALES LTD, 149 ST HELENS ROAD,
SWANSEA SA1 4DF

BOOKING CONDITIONS

1. Payment – A deposit of £25 per person per week is required on bookings. If required, your premium for holiday cancellation insurance will be added to the sum required as a deposit. The balance is payable to Holidays Wales 42 days prior to departure. If the booking is made within 42 days of departure full payment is required at that time.

2. Cancellation by you – Cancellation of your holiday may be made at any time by the person who signed the booking form and must be submitted in writing. There will be cancellation charges in accordance with the following scale.

MORE THAN 42 DAYS (6 WEEKS)	DEPOSIT
29-42 DAYS	30%
15-28 DAYS	45%
1-14 DAYS	60%
DEPARTURE DATE OR AFTER	100%

3. Alteration or cancellation by us – Circumstances may arise where we have no alternative but to cancel your accommodation. If such an exceptional situation should occur, we will make a complete refund to you or offer suitable alternative accommodation.

In the event that we have to cancel your holiday at any time, we will be liable only for any money paid to us at the time of cancellation. Holidays Wales Limited accepts no further liability whatsoever.

4. VAT – is included in all prices at the current rate of 17.5%, where applicable. In the event of any changes in the VAT regulations, these will be passed on to the client (only applicable if VAT has been included in the price).

5. Outside Agencies – All bookings for accommodation and other facilities are made by us as agents for the establishment concerned upon the understanding that we shall not accept any liability whatsoever for any injury, loss, damage, accident or delay caused by or in any way connected with the acts or defaults of any Company or person engaged in carrying out the bookings or of any proprietor or servant, or any liability whatsoever arising in any way directly or indirectly in connection with the making of the booking.

6. Holidays Wales Limited cannot accept liability for losses, additional expenses or any claim whatsoever due to changes in accommodation establishment, sickness, weather, strikes or any other cause. All such losses, additional expenses or claims will be borne by the client.

7. Any shortcomings – You are asked to notify any shortcomings or complaints to the hotel or owner immediately, so that they can be remedied for you. No claim can be considered for shortcomings not so notified. If you write to us on this subject please always quote your booking reference number.

Complaints received by us later than 14 days of the completion of your holiday cannot be considered.

*I*f you want more information or are still undecided on a place to stay, then look no further. You'll find everything you need in this extensive range of publications.

To order any of the publications featured here, please write enclosing the appropriate remittance in the form of a cheque or postal/money order in £ sterling to: Wales Tourist Board, Dept WTS 3, Davis Street, Cardiff CF1 2FU.

'Where to Stay' Guides

Wales – Bed and Breakfast is one of a series of three official accommodation guides. All places listed have been checked out by the Wales Tourist Board.

Wales – Hotels, Guest Houses and Farmhouses 1994 £2.95

A wide cross-section of accommodation, with a great choice of places to stay throughout Wales. Something for all tastes and pockets.

Wales – Self-Catering 1994 £2.95

Thousands of self-catering properties, including cottages, flats, chalets and caravan holiday home parks. Also huge range of sites for touring caravans, motorhomes and tents.

Wales Tourist Map £2

 A best-seller – and now better than ever. Detailed 5 miles/inch scale, fully revised. Also includes suggested car tours, town plans, information centres.

Visitor's Guides to North, Mid and South Wales £3.55 each

These three information-packed books give you the complete picture of Wales's holiday regions. In full colour, and fully updated in new editions for 1994. Don't think of visiting Wales without them!

* Descriptions of resorts, towns and villages
* Where to go and what to see
* Hundreds of attractions and places to visit
* Scenic drives, castles, crafts, what to do on a rainy day
* Detailed maps and town plans.

A Journey Through Wales £4.80

A magnificent production – 64 big-format pages of the best images in Wales, with descriptive text by Roger Thomas. The 90 photographs take the reader on a tour of Wales's mighty castles, spectacular mountains and coastline, country towns and colourful attractions. An ideal memento or gift.

Wales – Castles and Historic Places £7

Describes more than 140 sites, including castles,

 abbeys, country houses, prehistoric and Roman remains. A historic introduction sets the scene, and detailed maps help visitors plan their routes. In full colour, and a joint production between the Wales Tourist Board and Cadw: Welsh Historic Monuments.

Wales – Touring Guide to Crafts £6.80

Specially devised tours take you to galleries,

woodcarvers, potters, jewellers and woollen mills. Nearly 100 craft workshops are listed, together with other places to visit. Full colour and imaginatively designed with fold-out tours and comprehensive details on each establishment.

'By Car' Guides:-
The Pembrokeshire Coast £2.30
Brecon Beacons £2.30

Two of the 32-page White Horse series.

Attractive routes, maps and photographs – the ideal car touring guide to this beautiful part of Wales.

Ordnance Survey Pathfinder Guides:-
Snowdonia Walks (Anglesey/Llŷn Peninsula) £7.45
Pembroke and Gower Walks £7.45
Brecon Beacons and Glamorgan Walks £7.45

80-page guides, with detailed maps, colour illustrations and descriptions which guide you safely along attractive walking routes.

Videos
The Wonder of Wales (VHS) £10.50

The breathtaking beauty and myriad attractions of Wales encapsulated in 24 memorable minutes. Narrated by Siân Phillips. Also available in NTSC format at £12.50

Heritage of a Nation (VHS) £10

Narrated by Richard Burton, this 25-minute video presents the heritage of Wales from prehistoric to present times.

All prices include postage and packing

❑ Wales – Hotels, Guest Houses & Farmhouses 1994	£2.95	
❑ Wales – Self-Catering 1994	£2.95	
❑ Wales Tourist Map	£2	
❑ A Visitor's Guide to North Wales	£3.55	
❑ A Visitor's Guide to Mid Wales	£3.55	
❑ A Visitor's Guide to South Wales	£3.55	
❑ A Journey Through Wales	£4.80	
❑ Wales – Castles and Historic Places	£7	
❑ Wales – A Touring Guide to Crafts	£6.80	
❑ 'By Car' – Pembrokeshire Coast	£2.30	
❑ 'By Car' – Brecon Beacons	£2.30	
❑ Snowdonia Walks	£7.45	
❑ Pembroke and Gower Walks	£7.45	
❑ Brecon Beacons and Glamorgan Walks	£7.45	
❑ Wonder of Wales Video (VHS)	£10.50	
❑ Wonder of Wales Video (NTSC)	£12.50	
❑ Heritage of a Nation Video (VHS)	£10	

Posters:
❑ North Wales scenes £1.30
❑ Mid Wales scenes £1.30
❑ South Wales scenes £1.30
❑ Llangrannog Beach £1.20

To: *Wales Tourist Board, Dept WTS 3, Davis Street, Cardiff CF1 2FU*

Total remittance enclosed: £......................

Cheque/PO or Money Order No. ....

Name (Please Print) ....

Address: ....

....

....

.... Post Code ....

*T*he maps which follow divide Wales into 12 sections, each with a slight overlap. The grid overlaying each map will help you find the town or village of your choice, for against the entry of each of them in this book is a reference number indicating the section of map and grid square. Simply turn to the appropriate map sheet, look for the grid square quoted in the code and pick out the place itself in that square. The maps are at 5 miles or 8 kilometres to the inch .

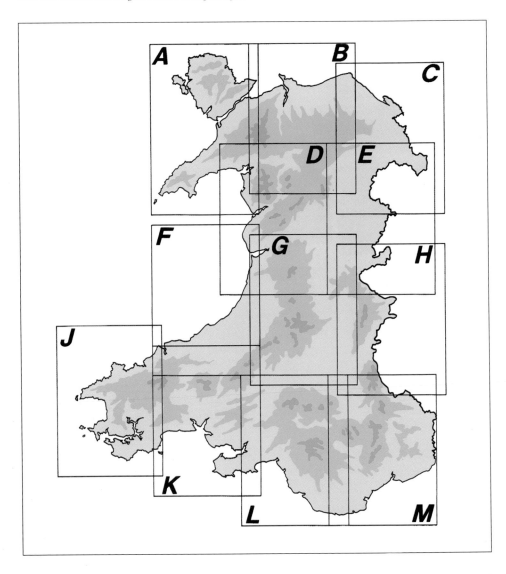

N

Miles 0 1 2 3 4 5
Kilometres 0 1 2 3 4 5 6 7 8

a   b   c   d   e

The Skerries

N
Holyhead Mount
S. Stack
720ft.

Carmel Hd.

Hen Borth

Cemlyn Bay

Neuadd   Bull Bay

Porth-wen

Porth-yr-ysgaw

Porth-yr-yche

Point Lynas

Cemaes Bay

Tregele

Amlwch

Llaneilian

Ynys Dulas

1

Llanfair -ynghornwy

Bodewryd

Penysarn
Nebo

Llanwenllwyfo

Parys Mountain

Traeth-yr-ora

Dulas Bay

Llanfechell

Rhosgoch

Rhydwen

Llanrhuddlad

Rhos -y-bol

Penrhos Lligwy

A5025

Traeth Lligwy

♦ **Moelfre**

Church Bay

Llanfaethlu

Llanbabo

Llandyfrydog

Llanallgo

Traeth Bychan

Porth Trefadog

A5025

Llanddeusant

Llanerchymedd

Llanfihangel Tre'r-Beirdd

Benllech

Puffin Is

2

Porth Tywyn-mawr

Llanfwrog

Porth Pen-rhyn- mawr

A N G L E S E Y

Bryngwran

Llanfachraeth

Bodedern

Trefor

Llangwyllog

Red Wharf Bay

Traeth Coch

Mynydd Llwydiarth

Penmon ♦

haire & Dublin

HOLYHEAD BAY

N.Stack

Mynytho
Holyhead Mount
S. Stack
720ft.

CAERGYBI HOLYHEAD

Llanfwrog

Traeth-y-gribin

Llyn Llywenan

Afon Beg

B5111

B5109

B5110

B5109

Llanbedr- goch

Llanddona

Llangoed

Llanfaes

Pe

y Island

A5

Valley

Caer-geiliog

Llanfaes

Bodffordd

Rhos- meirich

Talwrn

Pentraeth

A545   BEAUMARIS

Porthdafarch
Porth-y-post

Four Mile Br.

R.A.F.

AIRFIELD

Heneglwys

LLANGEFNI

Llansadwrn

B5109

PENRHOS CASTLE

3

Trearddur Bay

Rhoscolyn

Cymyran Bay

A4080

Gwalchmai

Cerrigceinwen

Llanfairpwllgwyngyll

Menai Bridge

Garth

A5122

Pentre'r- beirw

A5

Gaerwen

Llandegfan

Traeth Lafan

Porth Nobla

Rhosneigr

Llanfaelog

Ty-Croes

Groeslon

Bodorgan

B4422

B4419

Cefni

Llanddaniel Fab

Llangaffo

☙ ANGLESEY SEA ZOO

★ BANGOR

Y'-bont

Llanllechid

Rachub

Beth

Gerla

Porth Trecastell

Llyn Coron

Llangadwaladr

Glasinfryn

B4356

A5

4

Aberffraw

Hermon

Malltraeth

A4080

Brynsiencyn

Port Dinorwic

Pentir

Rhiwlas

Penisarwaun

Newborough

Dwyran

B4366

Seion

Bethel

Deiniolen

Cwm-y-glo

LLANBERIS LAKE RAILWAY

Y Garn
3104ft.

Newborough Forest

B4366

BRYN BRAS

CAERNARFON

Aber Menai Pt.

Bontnewydd

Llanrug

Llanddwyn I.

Caeathro

A4086

DOLBADARN CASTLE

Nant Peris

326

3279ft
Glyder Fawr

LLANBERIS

Moel Eilio
2382ft.

SNOWDON MOUNTAIN RAILWAY

LLANBERIS PASS

5

Ty-hen
Porth-oer

Llandygwynning

Mynydd Rhiw
999ft.

Llangian

Mynytho

Llanfaglan

Rhostryfan

A4085

Bets Garmon

Rhyd-ddu

Y Garn
3560ft.
Wyddfa

SNOWDON
3560ft.
Yr Aran

Llyd

Methlem

Rhosirwaun

PLAS YN RHIW

Rhiw

Abersoch

AIRFIELD

Llanwnda

Mynydd Mawr

2290ft.

Llyn Cwellyn

Mynydd Anelog
628ft.

B4413

Llanfaelrhys

Llanengan

Porth Neigwl
(Hell's Mouth)

Dinas Dinlle

Llandwrog

Y Groeslon

Carmel
Nantlle

2381ft.

Aberdaron

Pen-y-cil

Bardsey Sd.

Porth Ce

Porth Neigwl

Trwyn Cilan

Penygroes

Glyn ifon

Talysarn

Rhyd-ddu

245ft.
Yr Aran

SNOWDON

Llyw

6

Pontllyfni

Llanllyfni

Nebo

Nazareth

Garnedd goch
2301ft.

Y Garn
2080ft.

1984ft.

Beddgelert Forest

Llyn Dinas

Beddgelert

Aberdesach

Clynnog Fawr

A487

1996ft.

Pant-glas

2566ft.
Moel Hebog

ABERGLASLYN PASS

Nantmor

Cnicht
2265ft.
M Las

Bwlch Mawr
1670ft.

Mynydd Cennin
859ft.

Bryncir

Moel Ddu
1811ft.

A498

Pen-lan

Tanyb

1712ft.
Gyrn Ddu

Garndolbenmaen

A4085

Trefor

Yr Eifl
1850ft.

Nant Gwrtheyrn

Llanaelhaearn

A499

Dolbenmaen

Penmorfa

Garre

WELSH HIGHLAND RLY.

Tremadog

Minffordd

Penrhyn

B441

Porthdinllaen

FFYNNON-GYBI

B4411

Dwyryd

Pentrefelin

A498

PORTHMADOG

B4354

Nefyn

Garn
Boduan
918ft.

Llangybi

A487

Criccieth

Toll

Minffordd

Portmeirion

Edern

Morfa Nefyn

PEN FFor

B4354

Llanystumdwy

Morfa Bychan

Talsarn

Porth Ysgaden

B4417

PENINSULA

Chwilog

PENNARTH FAWR

Abererch

Black Rock Sands

Traeth Bach

Llanfihangel -y-traethau

Eisingrug

Morfa Harlech

7

Porth Ychen

Traeth Penllech

Tudweiliog

Dinas
Garn Fadryn
1217ft.

A497

Llannor

Efailnewydd

Penychain

A496

Harlech

Penllech

B4415

Rhyd-y-clafdy

☙ **PWLLHELI**

Porth Colmon

Llaniestyn

Penrhos

A499

South Beach

TREMADOG

Langwnnadl

B4413

Bryncroes

Sarn Mellteyrn

Llanbedrog

PLAS GLYN-Y-WEDDW

BAY

Ty-hen

Botwnnog

Mynytho

121

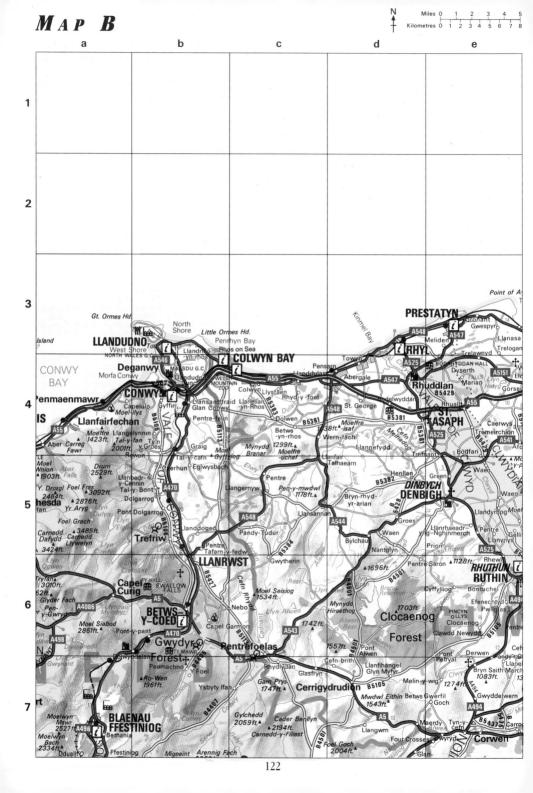

MAP B

MAP C

N

Miles 0 1 2 3 4 5
Kilometres 0 1 2 3 4 5 6 7 8

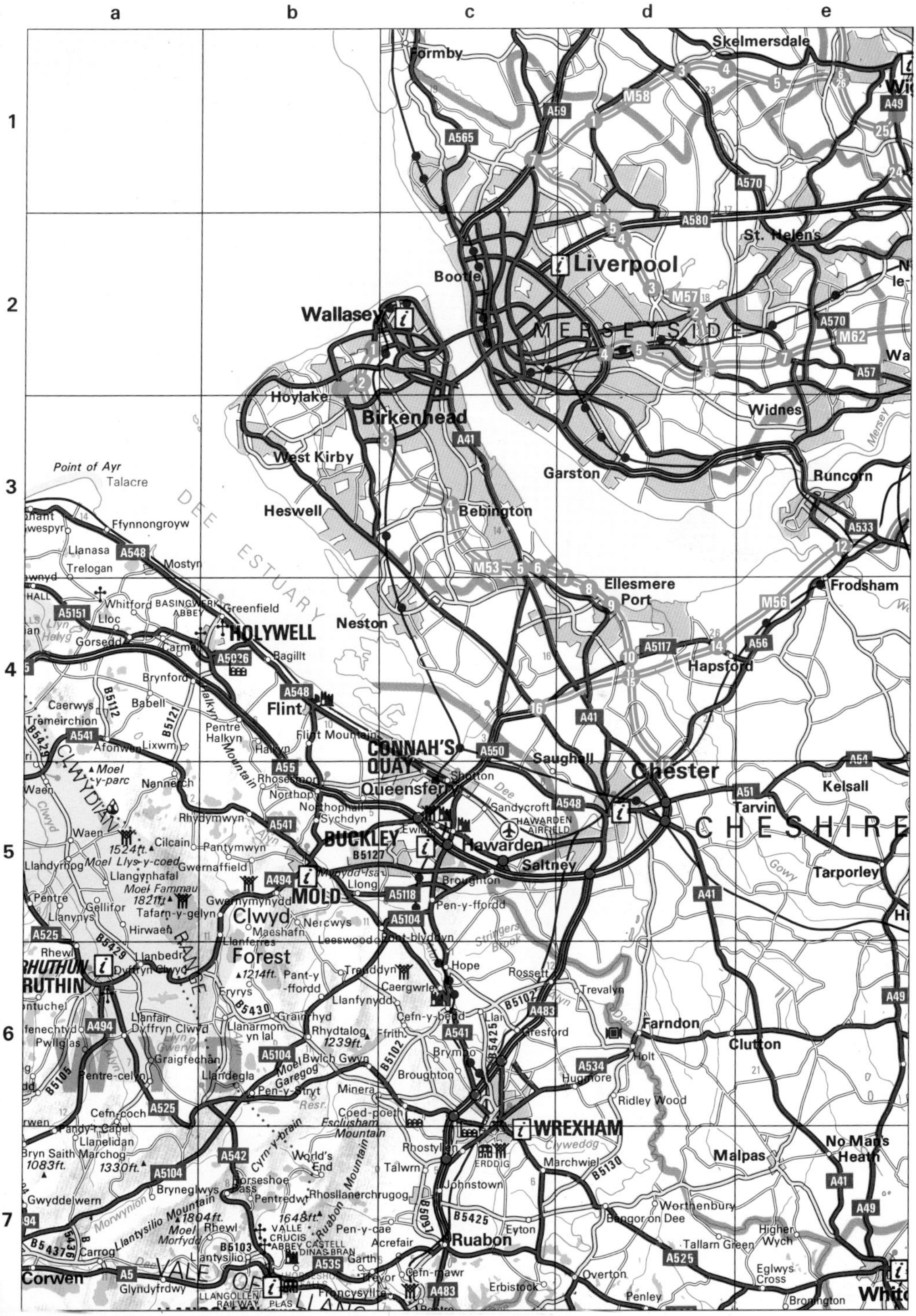

a　　b　　c　　d　　e

1
2
3
4
5
6
7

Formby
Skelmersdale
M58
A59
A565
A570
A580
Liverpool
St. Helen's
Bootle
Wallasey
MERSEYSIDE
M57
A570
M62
Hoylake
Birkenhead
A57
Widnes
West Kirby
A41
Garston
Heswell
Bebington
Runcorn
A533
Point of Ayr
Talacre
M53
Frodsham
DEE ESTUARY
Ellesmere Port
M56
Ffynnongroyw
A548
Llanasa
Mostyn
Neston
A5117
A56
Hapsford
Trelogan
Whitford BASINGWERK ABBEY
Greenfield
HOLYWELL
A5151
Lloc
Gorsedd
Bagillt
Chester
Caerwys
A5026
Tarvin
Kelsall
Brynford
Babell
Flint
A548
CHESHIRE
Tremeirchion
Lixwm
Flint Mountain
Saughall
Caerwys
Afonwen
Pentre Halkyn
Halkyn
CONNAH'S QUAY
A550
A51
Moel-y-parc
A55
Queensferry
A548
Tarporley
Nannerch
Rhosesmor
Northop
Sandycroft
HAWARDEN AIRFIELD
A41
Rhydymwyn
A541
Northophall
Sychdyn
BUCKLEY
Hawarden
Moel Llys-y-coed
Gwernaffield
B5127
Saltney
Llandyrnog
Moel Fammau
1824ft.
Llangynhafal
Tafarn-y-gelyn
MOLD
A494
Llong
A5118
Broughton
Pen-y-ffordd
Clwyd
Maeshafn
A5104
A525
Llanferres
Leeswood
Pen-t-blydlyn
RUTHIN
Forest
1214ft.
Pant-y-ffordd
Treuddyn
Hope
Rossett
Llanfynydd
Caergwrle
A494
Fryrys
Grainrhyd
Cefn-y-bedd
Trevalyn
Llanarmon yn Ial
Rhydtalog
1239ft.
Frith
A483
Farndon
Graigfechan
B5430
Llandegla
Bwlch Gwyn
Brymbo
A541
Clutton
Cefn-coch
A525
Moel
Pen-y-Stryt
Minera
A534
Holt
Ridley Wood
Cynwyd
Coed-poeth
Esclusham Mountain
WREXHAM
No Mans Heath
Bryn Saith Marchog
1083ft.
A542
World's End
Rhostyllen
ERDDIG
Marchwiel
B5130
Malpas
A41
1330ft.
A5104
Bryneglwys Mountain
Talwrn
Worthenbury
A49
Gwyddelwern
HORSESHOE PASS
Pentredwr
Rhoslanerchrugog
Johnstown
Bangor on Dee
Higher Wych
Moel Morfydd
1804ft.
Rhewl
VALLE CRUCIS ABBEY
CASTELL DINAS BRAN
1648ft.
Pen-y-cae
Acrefair
Eyton
Tallarn Green
Corwen
A5
Carrog
Llantysilio
B5103
Garth
Ruabon
A525
Eglwys Cross
Glyndyfrdwy
LLANGOLLEN RAILWAY
PLAS
Trevor
Cefn-mawr
A483
Erbistock
Penley
Bromfield
Whit
VALE OF
Llandysilio
Froncysyllt

123

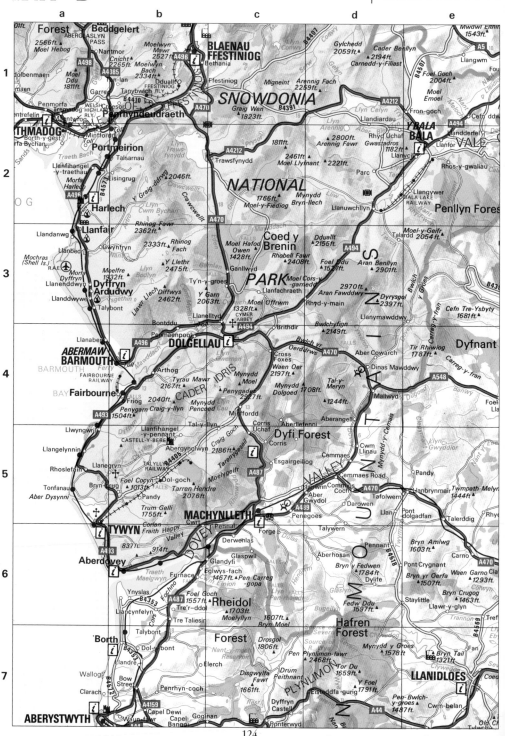

N

Miles 0 1 2 3 4 5
Kilometres 0 1 2 3 4 5 6 7 8

a   b   c   d   e

1

Betws Gwerfil Goch
A494
Maerdy Tyn-y-cefn
B4376
Four Crosses Dwyryd
Glan-yr-afon
Corwen
A5
Carrog
Glyndyfrdwy
Llantysilio Mountain 1804ft.
Moel Rhewl
Morwynion
Moel Fferna
B5103
VALE CRUCIS ABBEY CASTELL
DINAS BRAN
LLANGOLLEN
i
PLAS NEWYDD
1648ft. Ruabon
B5425 Eyton
Pen-y-cae
Acrefair
Cefn-mawr
A483
Pentre
Overton
A525
Penley
A539

LLANGOLLEN
2071ft. Moel Fferna
Cynwyd
Foel 1713ft.
MOUNTAINS OF LLANGOLLEN
Chirk
Erbistock
Knolton
Han

ddwysarn
Mynyllod
Llandrillo
Cefn-coch
Ceiriog Forest
Pen-plaenau 1775ft.
Glynceiriog
Pontfadog
CEIRIOG
Pandy
Dolywern
Llwynmawr
B4500
Teirw

2

BERWYN
Cadair Bronwen 2572ft.
Clochnant
Nant-cwm-llawenog
Llanarmon D.C.
Cadair Berwyn 2713ft.
Moel Sych
Mynydd Tarw 2230ft.
Garneddwen 1628ft.
Blaen Glaswen
Milltir Cerrig
PISTYLL RHAEADR FALLS
Y Clogydd 1954ft.
Tregeiriog
Moelfre
Llansilin
VALE
B4579
B4580
A495
A528
Oswestry i
A5
Whittington
Ellesmere
B4580

3

rest
B4391
Pennant Melangell
Llangynog
Penybontfawr
Hirnant
B4396
Pen-y-garnedd
Llanrhaeadr ym Mochnant
Pentre'r felin
Llangedwyn
Pen-y-bont
Llanerch Emrys
Bwlch-y-ddar
Llansantffraid ym Mechain
B4393
B4396
A5
Baschurch
Walford
Harn
Llanymynech
Lake Vyrnwy
A4393
Llanwyddyn
Abertridwr
Llanfechain
Llanfyllin i

4

nt Forest
B4395
Pont Llogel
Pont Robert
Dolanog
Foel Llangadfan
A548
Llanerfyl
A4392
Meifod
A495
Bwlch-y-Cibau
Four Crosses
Llandrinio
Crew Green
Allt-y-main 1168ft.
Sarnau
Geuffordd
Pool Quay
Middletown
Trewern
Cefn-y-castell 1523ft.
Breidden Hill 1202ft.
Crigdion
Cardeston
A458
Broniarth Hill
Guilsfield
Groes-lwyd
Maes-mawr
Westbury
S
A488

5

Llyn Hir
Einion
Melin-y-ddol
A548
Llanfair Caereinion
B4385
Banw
Sylfaen
WELSHPOOL AND
LLANFAIR RAILWAY
TRALLWNG
WELSHPOOL
POWIS CASTLE
Castle Caereinion
i
A548
B4388
Leighton
LONG MOUNTAIN
Buttington
Minsterley
Pontesbury

6

Melyn
Mynydd y Gribin
Cefn Coch
Llanllugan
Manafon
A4389
Berriew
MID WALES AIRPORT
Forden
Kingswood
Chirbury
Garthmyl
Adfa
Llanwyddelan
New Mills
Rhiw
Rhyd
Y Glonc 1513ft.
Tregynon
B4390
Betws Cedewain
Gregynog Hall
Bwlch-y-ffridd
Highgate
A483
Aberhafesp
Llandysul
Cefn y Coed
Abermule
DOLFORWYN
B4385
Montgomery
Corndon Hill 1683ft.
Church Stoke
A488
Hyssington
Snead
Lydham
LONG MYND

Clatter
6ft.
Llawnog
A489
Caersws
Trefeglwys
B4568
DRENEWYDD
NEWTOWN
i
Mule
Sarn
A489
B4385
LONG MYND

7

Llyn Ebyr
A470
Mochdre
Llandinam
Dolfor
Ceri Forest
Kerry
Bishop's Castle
Lydbury North
Wist
Trefeglwys
Berth-ddu
Pentre
Source of Ithon
Anchor
Clun Forest
A489
Source of R. Teme
Aston
Cray
Coed-y-gaer 1183ft.
Y Foel 1423ft.
Rhydd Hywel 1920ft.
Llyn-dwr Hill
Black Mountain 1469ft.
B4368
Felindre
Clun
A488
1398ft.
Chapel Hill
A483
Bryn Gydfa 1573ft.
Beguildy
B4355

125

Miles 0 1 2 3 4 5
Kilometres 0 1 2 3 4 5 6 7 8

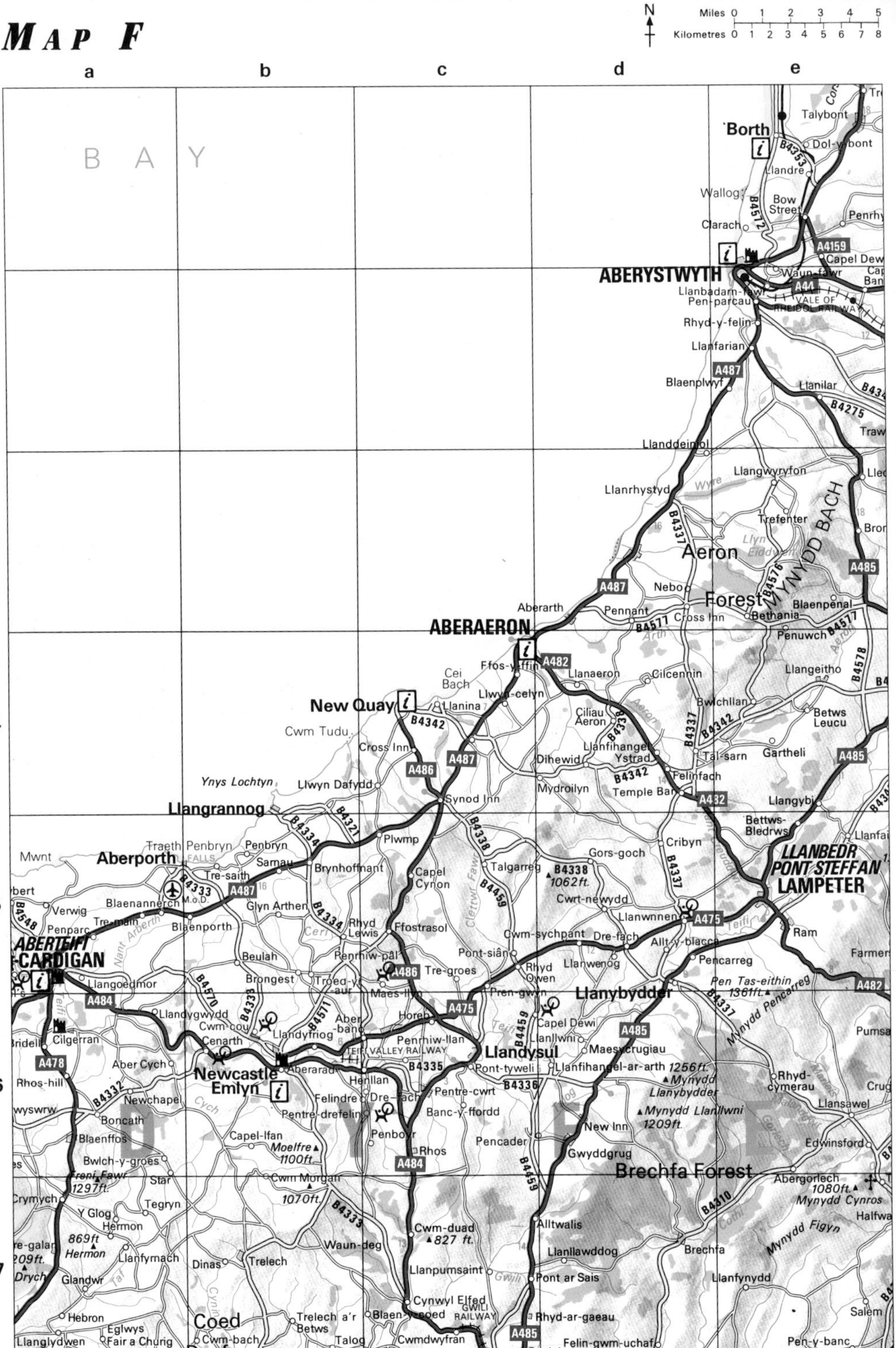

N

a b c d e

B A Y

Borth
Talybont
B4353
Dol-y-bont
Landre
Wallog
Bow Street
Clarach
Penrhy
Waun-fawr
Capel Dew
ABERYSTWYTH
A44
Llanbadarn
Pen-parcau
VALE OF
RHEIDOL RAILWAY
Rhyd-y-felin
Llanfarian
A487
Blaenplwyf
Llanilar
B4275
Llanddeiniol
Traw

1

2

Llanrhystyd
Wyre
Llangwyryfon
Llanwnnen
Trefenter
Bron
Llyn
Eiddwen
Aeron
A485
A487
Nebo
Forest
Blaenpenal
Aberarth
Pennant
Cross Inn
Bethania
B4577
ABERAERON
Penuwch
B4578
Cei
Bach
Ffos-y-ffin
A482
Llanaeron
Cilcennin
Llangeitho
New Quay
Llwyn-celyn
Ciliau
Aeron
Bwlchllan
Betws
Leucu
Llanina
Gartheli
Cwm Tudu
B4342
Cross Inn
Llanfihangel
Ystrad
Tal-sarn
A485
A486
A487
Dihewid
Felinfach
Llwyn Dafydd
Synod Inn
Mydroilyn
Temple Bar
A432
Llangybi
Ynys Lochtyn
B4338
Llangrannog
B4321
Cribyn
Bettws-
Bledrws
Traeth Penbryn
Penbryn
Plwmp
Gors-goch
LLANBEDR
PONT STEFFAN
LAMPETER
Mwnt
FALLS
Talgarreg
B4338
Aberporth
Sarnau
Brynhoffnant
Capel
Cynon
1062 ft.
Cwrt-newydd
A487
Glyn Arther
Cefn
B4334
Rhyd
Lewis
Clettwr Fawr
B4459
Cwm-sychpant
Dre-fach
A475
Ram
Verwig
Tre-main
Blaenporth
Beulah
Ffostrasol
Pont-siân
Allt-y-blacca
Pencarreg
A482
Pen Tas-eithin
1361 ft.
A484
Tre-groes
A486
Llanwenog
ABERTEIFI
CARDIGAN
Llangoedmor
Brongest
Troed-y-aur
Maes-llyn
Pren-gwyn
Rhyd
Owen
Llanybydder
B4571
Horeb
A475
B4570
Llandygwydd
Aber
cowin
Llandyfriog
Capel Dewi
A485
Mynydd Pencarreg
B4332
Cenarth
Penrhiw-llan
Llanllwni
Maes-y-crugiau
Rhyd-
cymerau
A478
Aber Cych
Aberarad
Penrhiw-pal
Llandysul
B4335
Llanfihangel-ar-arth
1256 ft.
Llansawel
Rhos-hill
Newchapel
Pont-tyweli
Pentre-cwrt
Mynydd
Llanybydder
Newcastle
Emlyn
Felindre
Dre-fach
Banc-y-ffordd
Edwinsford
Boncath
Pentre-drefelin
Penboyr
Pencader
New Inn
Mynydd Llanllwni
1209 ft.
Capel-Ifan
Moelfre
1100 ft.
Rhos
A484
Gwyddgrug
Brechfa Forest
Abergorlech
Mynydd Cynros
Blaenffos
Bwlch-y-groes
Cwm Morgan
B4459
1080 ft.
Star
1070 ft.
Mynydd Figyn
Y Glog
869 ft
Hermon
Tegryn
Waun-deg
Alltwalis
Brechfa
B4310
Halfw
Llanfynach
Dinas
Trelech
827 ft.
Llanllawddog
Llanfynydd
Glandwr
Hebron
Eglwys
Fair a Churig
Trelech a'r
Betws
Llanpumsaint
Pont ar Sais
Gwili
Salem
Llanglydwen
Coed
Deufor
Cwm-bach
Talog
Cynwyl Elfed
GWILI
RAILWAY
Blaen
coed
Cwmdwyfran
A485
Rhyd-ar-gaeau
Felin-gwm-uchaf
Peniel
Pen-y-banc

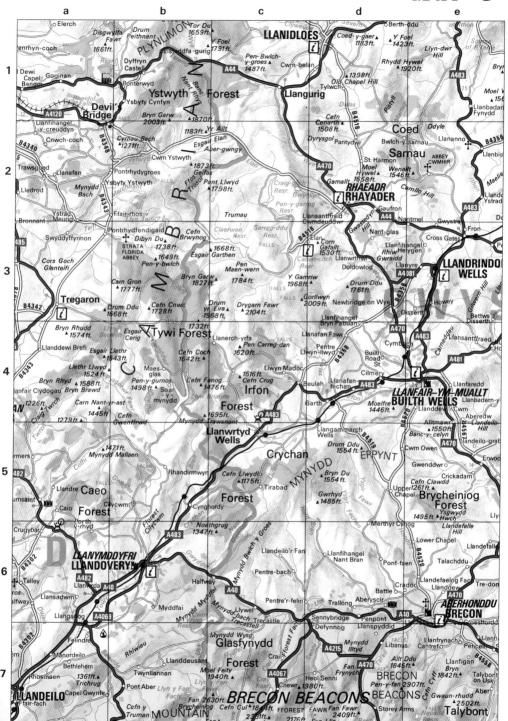

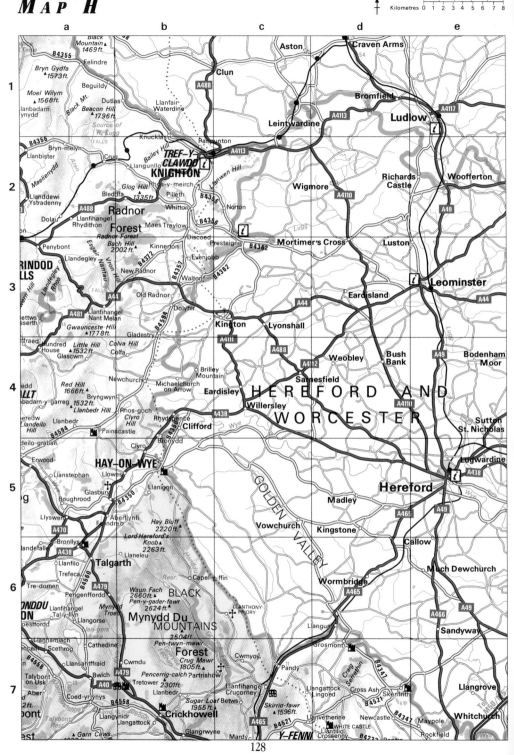

MAP H

a   b   c   d   e

1

Black Mountain 1469ft.
Bryn Gydfa 1573ft.
B4355
Felindre
Aston
Craven Arms
Clun
Moel Wilym 1568ft.
Beguildy
Black Mt.
Dutlas
Llanfair Waterdine
A488
Bromfield
Ludlow
A4117
llanbadarn ynydd
Beacon Hill 1796ft.
Source of R. Lugg
FALLS
A4113
Leintwardine

2

B4356
Bryn-melyn
Llanbister
Maelienydd
Bailey Hill
Knighton
Llangunllo
TREF-Y-CLAWDD
KNIGHTON
Rhos-y-meirch
Pilleth
Wigmore
A4110
Richards Castle
Woofferton
A49
Llanfair Waterdine
Knucklas
Rampunton
A4113
Janwen Hill
B4355
Llandewi Ystradenny
Glog Hill 1335ft.
Bleddfa
Whitton
Norton
B4356

Dolau
A488
Radnor Forest
Radnor Forest
Bach Hill 2002ft.
Maes Treylow
Kinnerton
Discoed
Presteigne
B4362
Mortimer's Cross
Luston
Penybont
Llandegley
Esgair Nantau
Vron Hill
Evenjobb
B4357
B4362
BRINDOD LLS
Llandegley Rhos
New Radnor
Walton
Lugg

3

FALLS
A44
Old Radnor
Dolyhir
A44
Eardisland
Leominster
A44
ettws esserth
A481
Llanfihangel Nant Melan
Gwaunceste Hill 1778ft.
Gladestry
Kington
Lyonshall
Red Hill 1666ft.
Bryngwyn 1532ft.
Llanbedr Hill
Rhos-goch
Clyro Hill
Little Hill 1532ft.
Colva Hill
Colfa
Brilley Mountain
A4111
Weobley
A488
A412
Bush Bank
Bodenham Moor
Hundred House
Glascwm
Newchurch
Michaelchurch on Arrow
Eardisley
Sarnesfield

4

LLT
badarn-y-garreg
Llanbedr
B4594
Llandeilo Hill
eilo-graban
Painscastle
Rhydspence
Clifford
Bronydd
Clyro
Wye
Willersley
HEREFORD AND WORCESTER
A411U
Sutton St. Nicholas

5

Erwood
Llanstephan
Boughrood
B4350
Llowes
HAY-ON-WYE
Glasbury
Llanigon
Hay Bluff 2220ft.
GOLDEN
Madley
Hereford
A438
Lugwardine
A465
A49
Llyswen
A470
Bronllys
Aberllynfi Felindre
Lord Hereford's Knob 2263ft.
Llaneleu
VALLEY
Vowchurch
Kingstone
Callow

6

landefalle
A438
Llanfilo
Trefecca
Talgarth
B4560
Capel-y-ffin
Resr.
BLACK
Waun Fach 2660ft.
Pen-y-gader-fawr 2624ft.
LLANTHONY PRIORY
Wormbridge
A465
Much Dewchurch
A466
A49
Tre-domen
A479
Pengenffordd
Mynydd Troed
Mynydd Du
MOUNTAINS
2504ft.
Pen-twyn-mawr
Llangua
Grosmont
Sandyway

7

ONDDU ON
Llanhamlach
Scethrog
Cathedine
Llansantffraid
B4558
Llangorse
an-gors Lake
Cwmdu
Forest
Crug Mawr 1805ft.
Partrishow
Cwmyoy
Pandy
Craig Serrethin
B4347
Llangrove
Talybont on Usk
Aber
A40
Coed-yr-ynys
B4479
Tretower
Llanbedr
Pencerrig-calch 230ft.
Llanfihangel Crucorney
Llangattock Lingoed
Cross Ash
Skenfrith
B4521
Whitchurch
Bwlch
B4558
Llangynidr
Llangattock
Sugar Loaf Betws 1955ft.
Crickhowell
Skirrid-fawr 1596ft.
Llanvetherine
Newcastle
B4347
Maypole
Garn Caws
Glangrwyne
Mardy
Y-FENNI
A465
B4521
WHITE CASTLE
Llantilio Crossenny
Rockfield

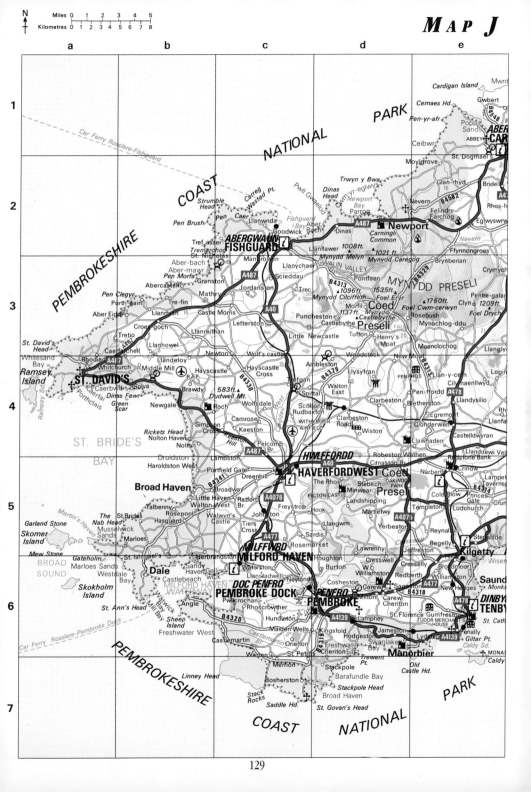

N

Miles 0 1 2 3 4 5
Kilometres 0 1 2 3 4 5 6 7 8

a   b   c   d   e

1

2

3

4

5

6

7

Cardigan Island
Mwnt
Cemaes Hd.
Gwbert
Pen-yr-afr
Poppit
Sands
ABBEY
CAR
Moylgrove
St. Dogmael's
Car Ferry Rosslare-Fishguard
COAST
NATIONAL
PARK
Aber

Trwyn y Bwa
Glan-rhyd
Bridel
Dinas
Head
Pwll Gwaelod
Trefasser
Strumble
Head
Carreg Wastad Pt.
Newport
Bay
Parrog
Nevern
Felindre
Farchog
Rhos-n
Eglwyswrw
Pen Brush
Pen Caer
Llanwnda
Fishguard
I Bay
Aber-
bach
Dinas
Newport
Carningli
Common
Crymych
Pen
Goodwick
ABERGWAUN
FISHGUARD
Llanllawer
1008ft.
1021 ft.
Ffynnongroes
Tref asser
Tremarchog
St. Nicholas
Manorowen
Llanychaer
GWAUN VALLEY
Mynydd Melyn
Mynydd Caregog
Brynberian
Aber-mawr
Aber-bach
Pen Morfa
Granston
Scleddau
Llanychaer
MYNYDD PRESELI
Abercastell
A487
Trec
Pontfaen
1535ft.
Pentre-galar
Clyn
1209ft.
Abercastell
Jordanston
1096ft.
Foel Eryr
Foel Cwm-cerwyn
Mathry
Castle Morris
Morfil
Mynydd
1137 ft.
Castlebythe
1760ft.
Rosebush
Foel Drych
Porth-gain
Tre-fin
Letterston
Little Newcastle
Castlebythe
Tufton
Mynachlog-ddu
Coed
Preseli
Aber Eidy
Llanrhian
16
Puncheston
Henry's
Moat
St. David's
Head
Croes-goch
Castle Morris
Llanreithan
Wolf's Castle
Woodstock
New Moat
Maenclochog
Llangly
Whitesand
Bay
Tretio
Caerfarchell
Llanhowel
Newton
Ambleston
Login
Ramsey
Island
Rhodiad
Whitchurch
Llandeloy
Middle Mill
Hayscastle
Cross
Trefgarn
Spittal
Llysyfran
PENROS
Llan-y-cefn
Llandysilio
Llanfa
Rh
ST. DAVID'S
Caerbwdi
Solva
Brawdy
583ft.
Dudwell Mt.
Hayscastle
R.A.F.
Treffgarne
Walton
East
Clarbeston
Pen-ffordd
Bletherston
Cilymaenllwyd
Dinas Fawr
Green
Scar
Newgale
Roch
Wolfsdale
Scolton
Rudbaxton
Clarbeston
Road
Egremont
Castellwyran
Llanddewi
Porthclais
Simpson
Cross
Camrose
WITHYBUSH
AIRFIELD
Wiston
Llawhaden
ST. BRIDE'S
BAY
Rickets Head
Nolton Haven
Nolton
Pelcomb
Br.
Keeston
Robeston Wathen
Crinow
Druidston
Haroldston West
Lambston
Portfield Gate
HWLFFORDD
Canaston Br.
Redstone Bank
Narberth
Lampet
Broad Haven
Dreenhill
HAVERFORDWEST
Coed
Princes
Gate
Broadway
The Rhos
Minwear
OAKWOOD
PARK
Preseli
Cold Blow
Crun
Little Haven
Walton West
Ratford
Br.
PICTON CASTLE
Slebech
Landshipping
Templeton
Ludchurch
Talbenny
Rosepool
Johnston
Martletwy
A4075
Reynalton
St
The
Nab Head
St Brides
Hasguard
Walwyn's
Castle
Tiers
Cross
Hook
Llangwm
Yerbeston
Begelly
Kilgetty
Garland Stone
Musselwick
Sands
Marloes
Sardis
Lawrenny
Jeffreston
Broadmoor
New Hedges
Wisen
Skomer
Island
Rosemarket
Cresswell
W.
Williamston
Saund
Mew Stone
MILFFWRD
Houghton
Burton
Redberth
BROAD
SOUND
Gateholm
Marloes Sands
Westdale
St. Ishmael's
Herbrandston
MILFORD HAVEN
Neyland
Cosheston
Williamston
DINBY
TENBY
Skokholm
Island
Sandy
Haven
Gelliswick
Waterston
Llanstadwell
Carew
St. Florence
Gumfreston
St. Cath
Dale
MILFORD HAVEN
WATERWAY
DOC PENFRO
PEMBROKE DOCK
Milton
Carew
Cheriton
TUDOR MERCHANT'S
HOUSE
Monks
St. Ann's Head
Westwick
Angle
Pwllcrochan
PEMBROKE
PENFRO
Lamphey
Gumfreston
Lyd
Giltar Pt.
MONAS
Freshwater West
Rhoscrowther
Hundleton
B4139
Jameston
A4139
Caldy Sd.
Castlemartin
Maiden Wells
Kingsfold
Freshwater
Cheriton
Swanlake
Manorbier
Caldy
Linney Head
Warren
St Petrox
Orielton
Merrion
Trewent
Pt.
Old
Castle Hd.
Stack
Rocks
Bosherston
Stackpole
Barafundle Bay
PARK
Saddle Hd.
Saddle Hd.
St. Govan's Head
Stackpole Head
Broad Haven
Car Ferry Rosslare-Pembroke Dock
PEMBROKESHIRE
COAST
NATIONAL

129

Miles 0 1 2 3 4 5
Kilometres 0 1 2 3 4 5 6 7 8

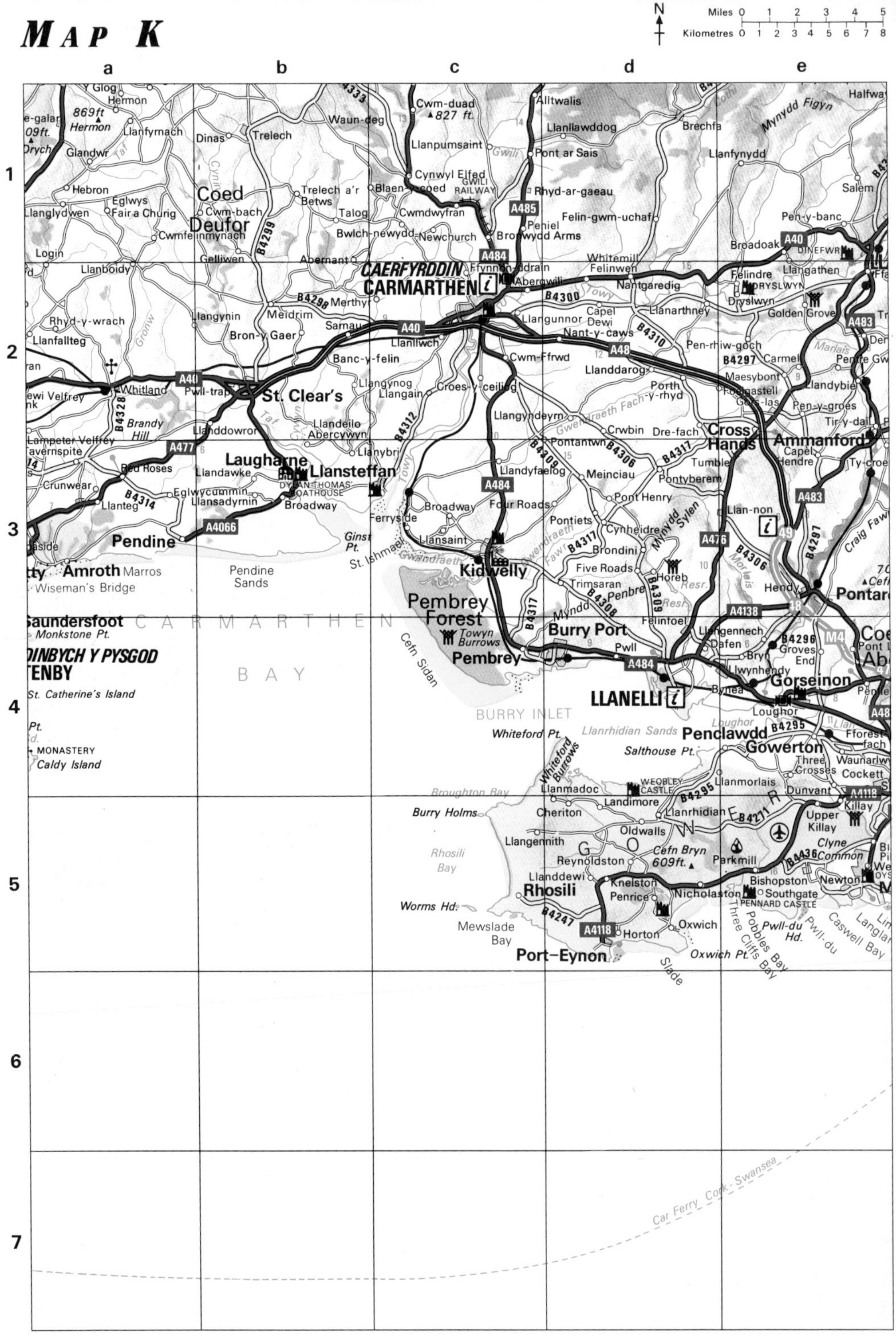

N

a b c d e

1

e-galan
869ft
Hermon
09ft.
Hermon
Llanfyrnach
Drych
Glandwr
Dinas Trelech
Waun-deg
Cwm-duad
827 ft.
Alltwalis
Brechfa
Mynydd Figyn
Halfw
Hebron
Eglwys
Fair a Churig
**Coed
Deufor**
Trelech a'r
Betws
Talog
Blaen-coed
GWILI
RAILWAY
Llanpumsaint
Llanllawddog
Pont ar Sais
Llanfynydd
Salem
Llanglydwen
Cwm-bach
Cwmfelinmynach
Gelliwen
Bwlch-newydd
Cwmdwyfran
Newchurch
Cynwyl Elfed
Peniel
Felin-gwm-uchaf
Bronwydd Arms
Pen-y-banc
Broadoak
A40
DINEFWR
Login
Llanboidy
Abernant
A485
A484
Rhyd-ar-gaeau
Whitemill
Felindre
CILDRYSLWYN
Llangathen

**CAERFYRDDIN
CARMARTHEN** i
Frynnon-ddrain
Abergwili
Felinwen
Dryslwyn
Golden Grove

2

Rhyd-y-wrach
Llanfallteg
Llangynin
Meidrim
Merthyr
Bron-y-Gaer
Sarnau
Banc-y-felin
A40
Llangunnor
Nant-y-caws
Capel
Dewi
Nantgaredig
Llanarthney
Pen-rhiw-goch
A483
A4297 Carmel
Maesybont
Fochastell
Gurs-las
Pen-y-groes
Pentre Gw
Llandybie
ewi Velfrey
nk
Whitland
B4328
Pwll-trap
St. Clear's
A40
A48
Llanddarog
Porth-y-rhyd
Lampeter Velfrey
avernspite
Brandy
Hill
Llanddowror
Llandeilo
Abercywyn
Llangynog
Llangain
Croes-y-ceiliog
Cwm-Ffrwd
Crwbin
Dre-fach
**Cross
Hands**
Ammanford
Capel
Hendre
Ty-ce
14
Crunwear
Bad Roses
A477
Laugharne
Llandawke
Llansteffan
Llanybri
B4312
Llangyndeyrn
Pontantwn
B4306
B4309
Tumble
Llan-non
A483

3

Llanteg
B4314
Eglwycummin
Llansadyrnin
DYLAN THOMAS
BOATHOUSE
Broadway
Broadway
Four Roads
Pontiets
Meinciau
Pont Henry
Cynheidre
Pontyberem
Mynydd Sylen
i
19
A476
Craig Faw
Pendine
A4066
Ginst
Pt.
St. Ishmael
Llansaint
Brondini
Five Roads
Trimsaran
Penbre
B4317
B4306
A4297
Pontar

tty
Amroth
Marros
Wiseman's Bridge
Pendine
Sands
Kidwelly
Horeb
Resr.
Pontard

Saundersfoot
Monkstone Pt.
Cefn Sidan
**Pembrey
Forest**
Town
Burrows
Felintoel
B4317
Mynydd
B4308
B4309
A4138
Henlldo
Coe
Pont I
Ab

4

DINBYCH Y PYSGOD
TENBY
Pembrey
Burry Port
Pwll
Llangennech
Dafen
Bryn
Groves
End
A4296
M4
St. Catherine's Island
Pembrey
A484
LLANELLI i
Bynea
Llwynhendy
Gorseinon
A48
Pt.
CARMARTHEN BAY
BURRY INLET
Loughor
Penclawdd
Loughor
A4295
Forest
fach
d.
MONASTERY
Caldy Island
Whiteford Pt.
Llanrhidian Sands
Salthouse Pt.
Gowerton
Three
Crosses
Waunarlw
Cockett
Llanmorlais
Dunvant
A4118
Killay
Bl
We

Burry Holms
WEOBLEY
CASTLE
Llanmadoc
Landimore
Broughton Bay
B4295
Llanrhidian
B4271
Upper
Killay
M
oxs

5

Rhosili
Bay
Cheriton
Oldwalls
Oxwich
Clyne
Common
Worms Hd.
Llangennith
Reynoldston
Cefn Bryn
609ft.
Parkmill
B4436
Bishopston
Newton
Llanddewi
Knelston
Nicholaston
Southgate
Newt
Lin
Langla
We
Mewslade
Bay
Rhosili
Penrice
PENNARD CASTLE
Caswell Bay
B4247
A4118
Horton
Oxwich
Pobbles Bay
Pwll-du
Hd.
Pwll-du
Port-Eynon
Oxwich Pt.
Three Cliffs Bay
Slade

6

7

Car Ferry Cork-Swansea

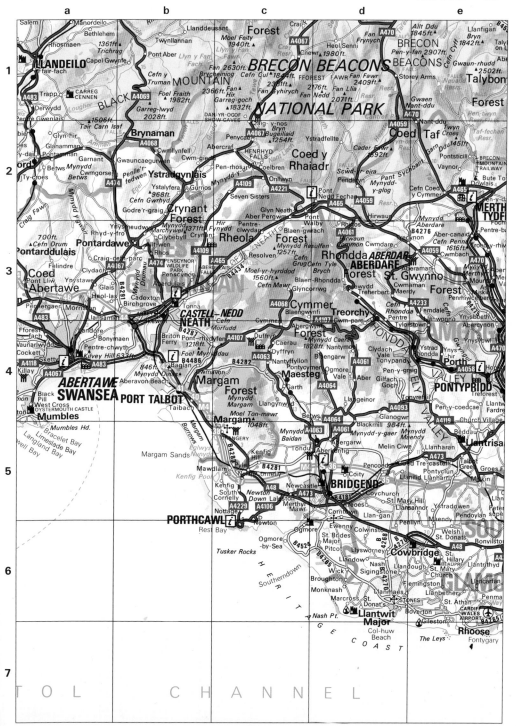

MAP L

N

Miles 0 1 2 3 4 5
Kilometres 0 1 2 3 4 5 6 7 8

a   b   c   d   e

Salem   Manordeilo
Bethlehem   Llanddeusant   Forest   Crai   A470   Allt Ddu   Llanfigan
Rhosmaen   Moel Feity   Cnewr   Heol Senni   1845ft.   Bryn   Taly
136ift   Twynllanan   1940ft.   1980ft.   BRECON   1842ft.   on L

1
LLANDEILO   Trichrug   Capel Gwynfe   Pont Aber   Llyn y Fan   Fan   BRECON   Storey Arms   Gwaun-rhudd   Talybon
Ffair-fach   Cefn y   Fach   Fan 2630ft.   Fforest   Frynych   2907ft.   2502ft.
A483   Trapp   CARREG   Truman   MOUNTAIN   Brycheiniog 1841ft.   FAWR   Fan Fawr
CENNEN   A4069   Foel Fraith   2366ft.   Cefn Cul   FFOREST   2409ft.   Forest
Derwydd   1982ft.   Fan Gyhirych   2176ft.   Resr   Gwaen
Pentre Gwenlais   1506ft.   Garreg-lwyd   1832ft.   Fan Nedd   Nant-ddu
2028ft.   DAN-YR-OGOF   2071ft.   A470
Glyn-hir   Brynaman   SHOW CAVES   Coed Taf
Glanamman   A4068   Penycae   Bryn   Ddu145ft.
Ty-croes   Pontamman   Gwauncaegurwen   Bugeiliaid   Ystradfellte   Cader Fawr   Pontsticill

2
Garnant   Abercraf   1254ft.   1592ft.
Betws   Cwmgors   Cwm-gied   HENRHYD   Coed y   Vaynor
Mynydd   Pen-rhos-y   FALLS   Rhaiadr   Cefn Coed
Ystradgynlais   Coelbren   Scwd-r-eira   y Cymmer
A474   Marchywel   Onllwyn   Pendeyrn   Mynydd   MERTHYR
Cefn Gwrhyd   Gurnos   A4109   A4221   Pont   y-glog   TYDF
968ft.   Seven Sisters   Nedd Fechan   A4059
Craig Fawr   Crynant   Hirwaun   A465   Aberdare   Aber-canaid
Cefn Drum   Mynydd   Glyn Neath   Cwmdare   B4276   Pentre-ba
Forest   Aber Pergwm   Rhigos   Mynydd   Penrhiw
700ft.   1371ft.   Pentre-   Pont   Aberdare

3
Pontardawe   Rhyd-y-fro   clwydau   Blaen-gwrach   A4061   Rhondda ABERDAR   A4059
Pontarddulais   Ynysmeudwy   Fynydd   Rheola   Forest   Cefn Penn   A470
Coed   Craig-cefn-parc   A4109   Resolven   Mynydd Resulfen   Hirwaun   Cwmbach   Mynydd
Abertawe   Felindre   A4067   PENSCYNOR   1257ft.   Common   ABERDARE   St. Gwynno   Merthyr
Ynystawe   WILDLIFE   A465   Cefn   Brych   Forest   Penrhiw
Pontarddulais   Clydach   PARK   Cefn Mawr   Grug   Tyle   Mountain
Glais   A474   ABERDULAIS   B4434   Moel-yr-hyrddod   Blaen-Rhondda   Cwmaman
Penllergaer   Morriston   Penscynor   FALLS   1560ft.   Glyncorrwg   Treherbert   Maerdy
Heol-las   Cadoxton   Gelliwydd   Cefn y   Ferndale
A483   Llansamlet   Birchgrove   Tonna   A4068   Cymmer   Rhondda   Ynysbooth
Fforest   Vaunarlwydd   Landore   CASTELL—NEDD   Cefn   Blaengwynfi   Treorchy   Pentre   Abercynon
fach   Bonymaen   NEATH   Morfudd   A4107   Cwm-parc   Tylorstown
Cockett   Pentre-chwyth   B4287   Forest   Mynydd Caerau   RHONDDA   Ystrad   A470

4
Vauarlwydd   Kilvey Hill 633ft.   Pont-rhydyfen   Duffryn   Abergwynfi   1828ft.   Clydach   rhondda   Porth
A4118   Killay   Briton   1218ft.   A4107   Caerau   Vale   Tonypandy   Ynys-hir
Ferry   Foel Mynyddau   Dyffryn   Blaengarw   A4061   Pen-y-graig   A4058   Hop
ABERTAWE   846ft.   B4486   Nantyffyllon   Pontycymer   Ogmore   Gilfach   Tonyrefail   PONTYPRIDD
A4067   Baglan   B4282   Vale   Goch   Treforest
SWANSEA   PORT TALBOT   Aberavon Beach   Cwmavon   Maesteg   Aber   A4093
Black   Mynydd Dinas   A4064   Llangeinor   Pen-y-coedcae
West Cross   Pill   Taibach   Margam   Betws   A4119
OYSTERMOUTH CASTLE   Forest   A4063   A4064   Glanogwr   Church Village
Mumbles   Margam   Llangynwyd   Bryncethin   Blackmill 984ft.   LLANTRISA
Bracelet Bay   Mynydd   MARGAM   1048ft.   Bettws   Mynydd-y-gaer   Mynydd   A473
Limeslade Bay   Margam   Moel Ton-mawr   A4063   A4061   Maendy   Talbot   Llanharan
Langland Bay   Margam Sands   Moel Ton-mawr   ORANGERY   Tondu   Melin Ciwe   Green   Groes F
Well Bay   Nydd   Kenfig   Aberkenfig   Hill   A473   Mkin

5
Mawdlam   Llwys   Pyle   B4281   M4   Pencoed   Tre'r-castell   Pontyclun
Kenfig Pool   Kenfig   Cornelly   M4   BRIDGEND   Coity   Llanilid   Llanharry   Llandow
South   Newton   36   Newcastle   Coychurch   St. Mary Hill   A4222
PORTHCAWL   Cornelly   Down   Laleston   A473   Llanharan   Ystradowen   Peter
A4229   Nottage   A48   Merthyr   B4181   Corntown   St. Mary Hill   Llansannor   Pendoylan   Llan
Rest Bay   Newton   A4106   Mawr   Ewenny   Llan-gan   Penllyn   Maendy
Ogmore   Welsh   St. Brides   Pitcot   Llysworney   A48   St. Donats   Bonvilsto

6
Tusker Rocks   by-Sea   Major   Llandow   A4265   Cowbridge   St.   Llancarfa
Broughton   Llanmaes   Wick   Nash   Llandough   St. Hilary   Llantrithyd   Penma
Monknash   Sigingstone   Flemingston   BEAUPRE   Church   Llanbethery
Marcross   St.   Llanmaes   CASTLE   St. Athan   CARDIFF   Boverton   Rhoose
Nash Pt.   Donat's   STONES   Gileston   WALES   Fontygary
Llantwit   Col-huw   AIRPORT
Major   Beach   Boverton   Rhoose
The Leys   Fontygary

7
TOL   CHANNEL

131

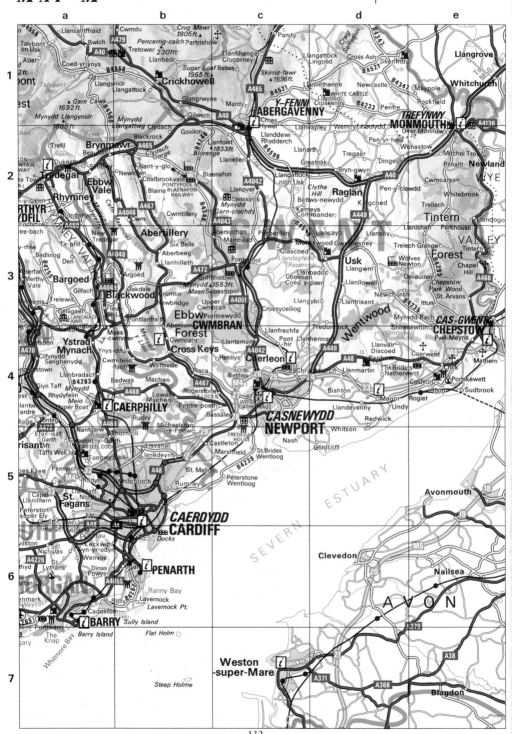

N